SEVEN SEAS ENTERTAINMENT PRESENTS

MAGICAL GIRL SPEC-OPS ASUKA VOL. 5

story **MAKOTO FUKAMI** / art **SEIGO TOKIYA** / military advisor **NAOYA TAMURA**

TRANSLATION
Christine Dashiell

ADAPTATION
Tom Speelman

LETTERING AND RETOUCH
James Adams

COVER DESIGN
Nicky Lim

PROOFREADER
Shanti Whitesides

EDITOR
J.P. Sullivan

PRODUCTION ASSISTANT
CK Russell

PRODUCTION MANAGER
Lissa Pattillo

EDITOR-IN-CHIEF
Adam Arnold

PUBLISHER
Jason DeAngelis

MAGICAL GIRL SPEC-OPS ASUKA VO...
©2017 Makoto Fukami, Seigo Tokiy...
First published in Japan in 201...
English translation rights a...
and SEVEN SEAS E... ...nc.
Translation ©201...

Seven Seas book... ...ased in bulk for promotional, educational, or
business use. Pleas... ...ct your local bookseller or the Macmillan Corporate
and Premium Sales Department at 1-800-221-7945, extension 5442, or by
e-mail at MacmillanSpecialMarkets@macmillan.com.

ISBN: 978-1-626929-72-2

Printed in Canada

First Printing: January 2019

10 9 8 7 6 5 4 3 2 1

FOLLOW US ONLINE: *www.sevenseasentertainment.com*

READING DIRECTIONS

This book reads from *right to left*, Japanese style.
If this is your first time reading manga, you start
reading from the top right panel on each page and
take it from there. If you get lost, just follow the
numbered diagram here. It may seem backwards at
first, but you'll get the hang of it! Have fun!!

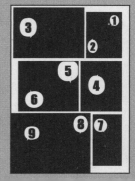

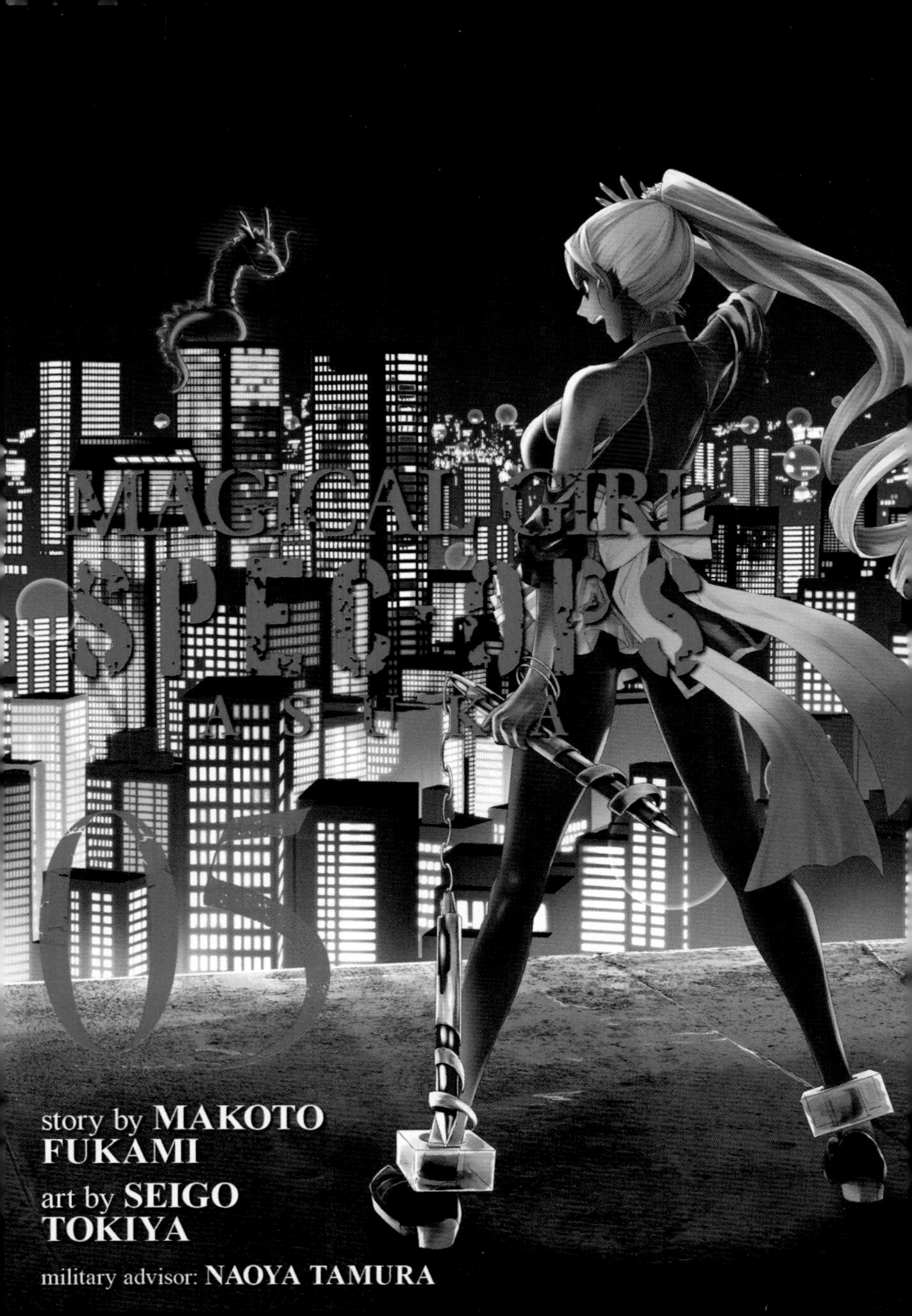
MAGICAL GIRL
SPEC-OPS
ASUKA
05
story by MAKOTO FUKAMI
art by SEIGO TOKIYA
military advisor: NAOYA TAMURA

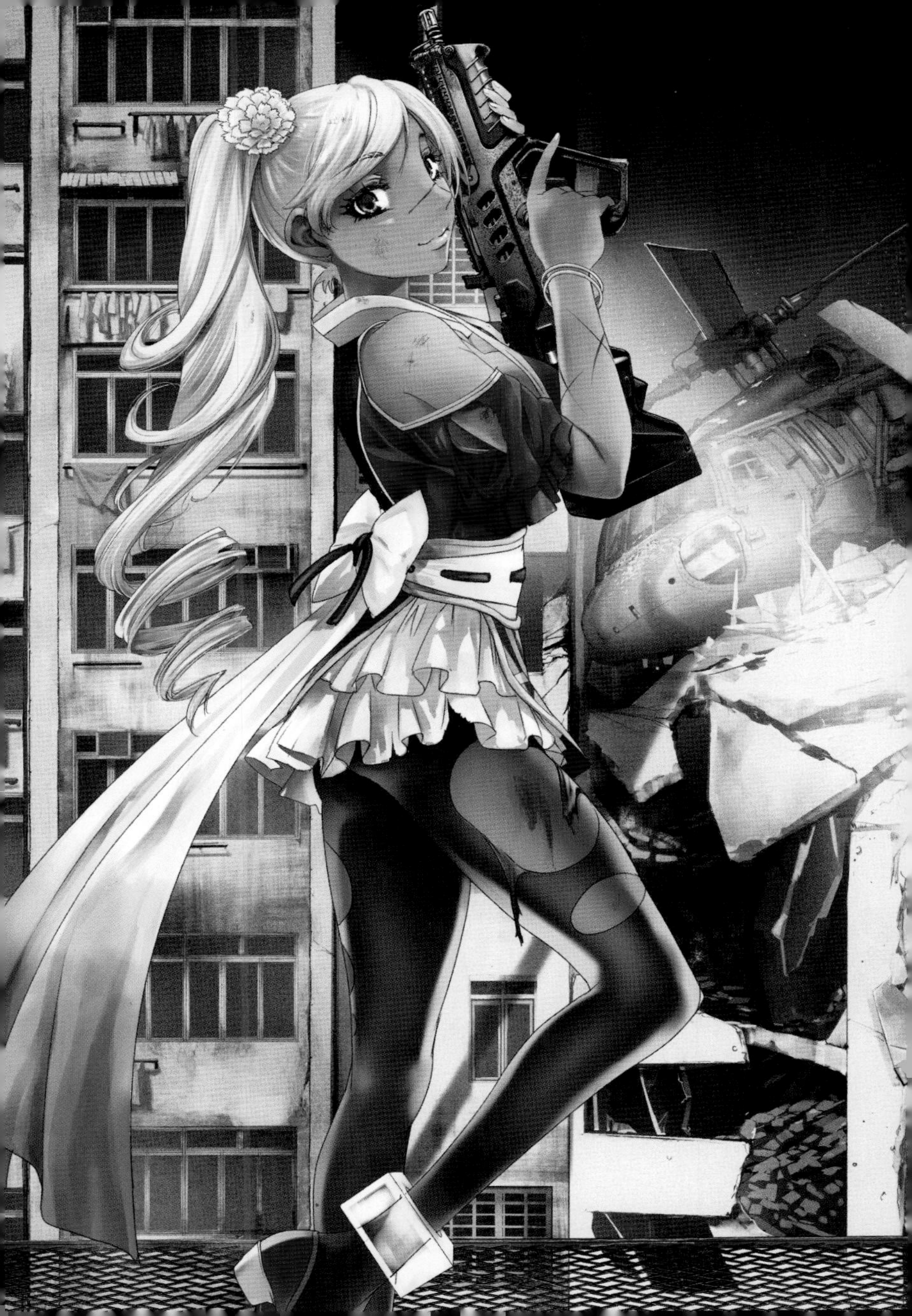

Thailand.

Patong Beach: GMT +7 Hours.

MM!

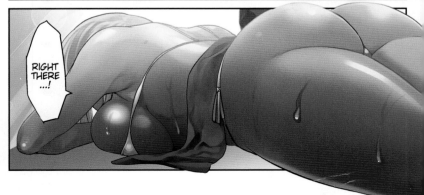

RIGHT THERE ...!

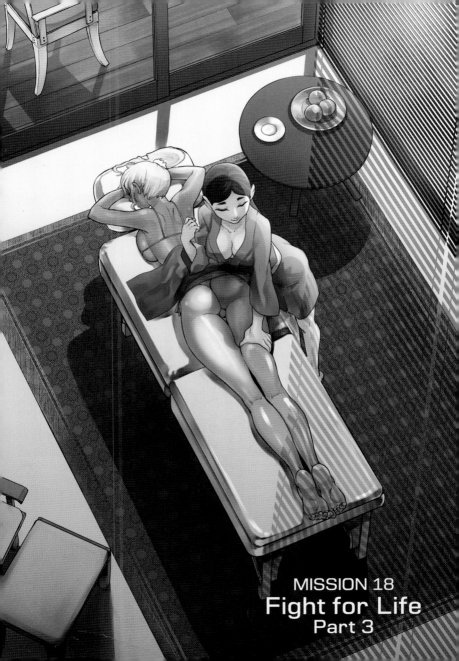

MISSION 18
Fight for Life
Part 3

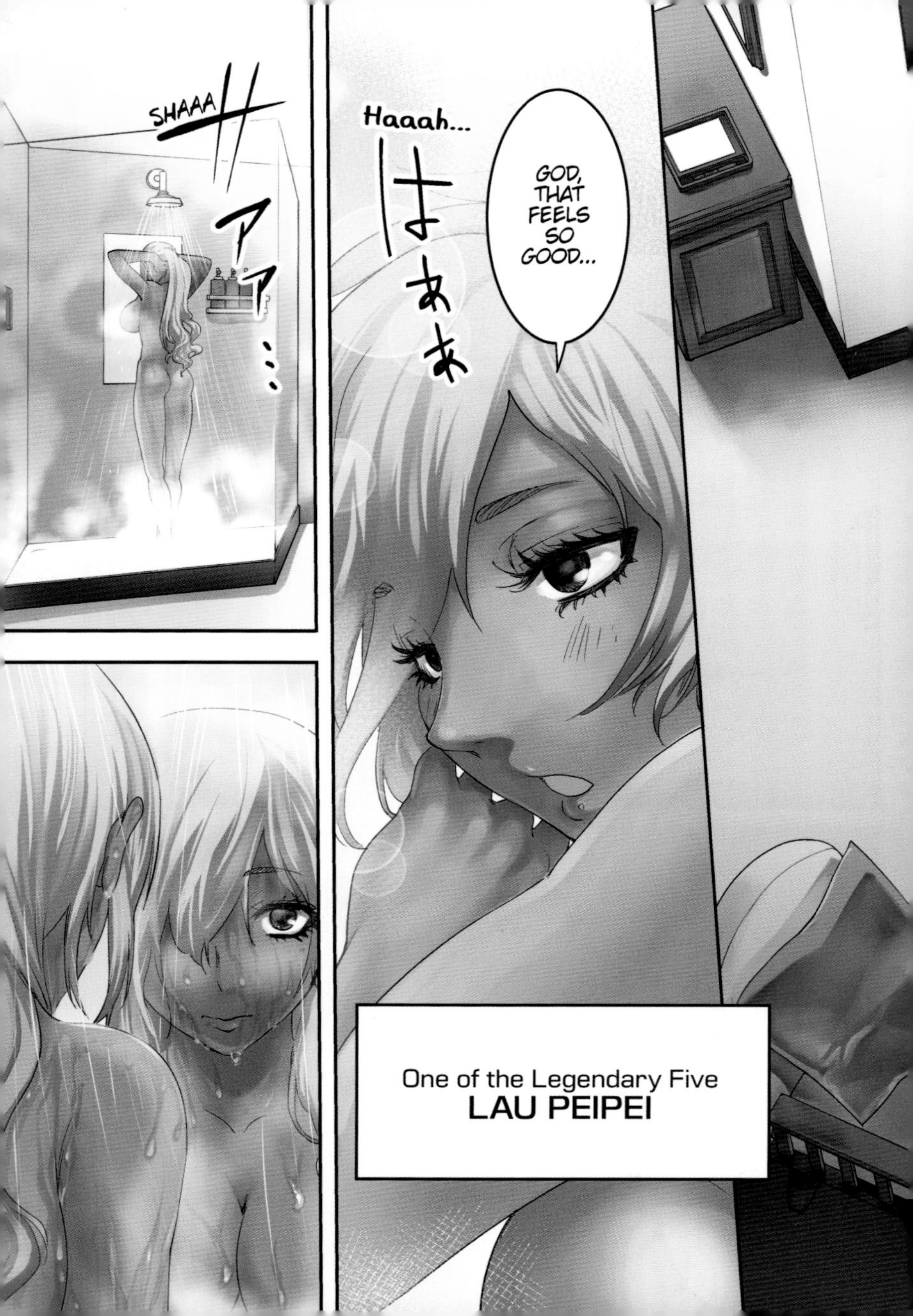
Haaah...
はぁぁ
GOD, THAT FEELS SO GOOD...
One of the Legendary Five
LAU PEIPEI
SHAAA
アア…

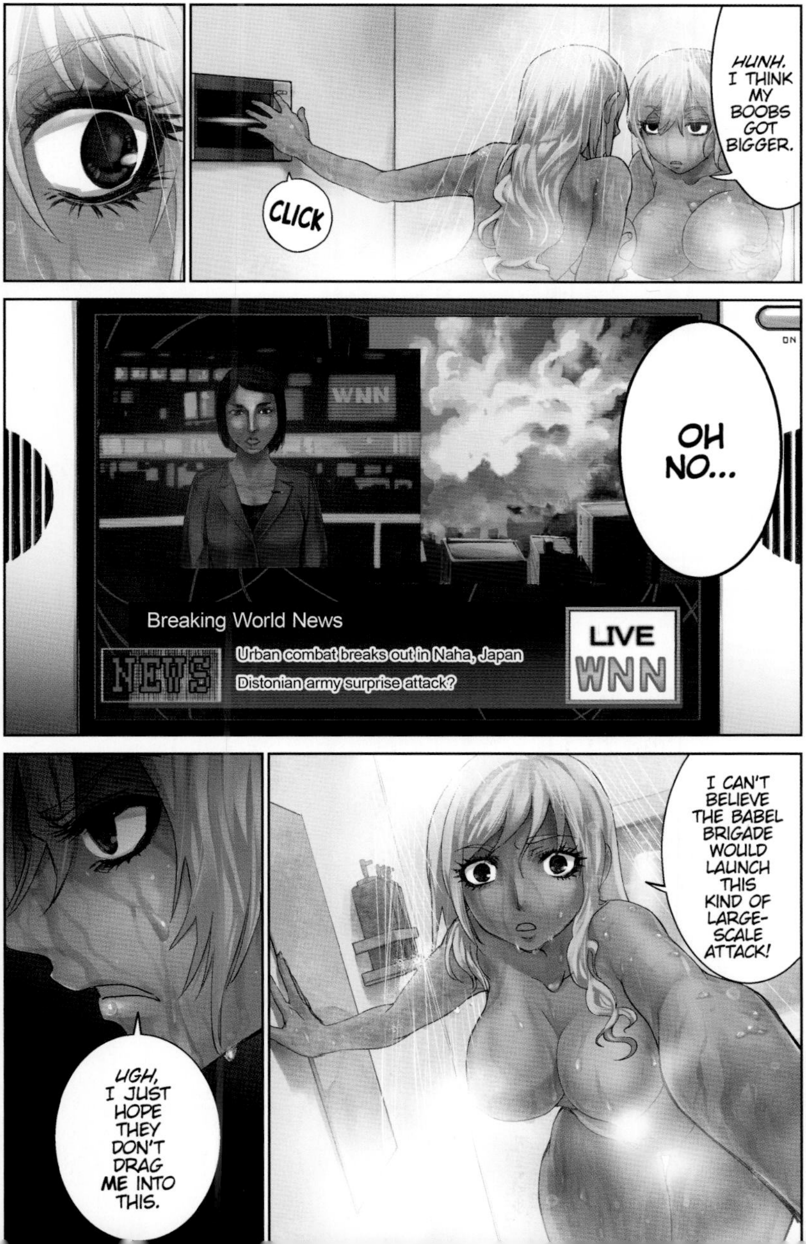
HUNH. I THINK MY BOOBS GOT BIGGER.
CLICK
ON
OH NO...
WNN
Breaking World News
LIVE WNN
NEWS
Urban combat breaks out in Naha, Japan
Distonian army surprise attack?
I CAN'T BELIEVE THE BABEL BRIGADE WOULD LAUNCH THIS KIND OF LARGE-SCALE ATTACK!
UGH, I JUST HOPE THEY DON'T DRAG ME INTO THIS.

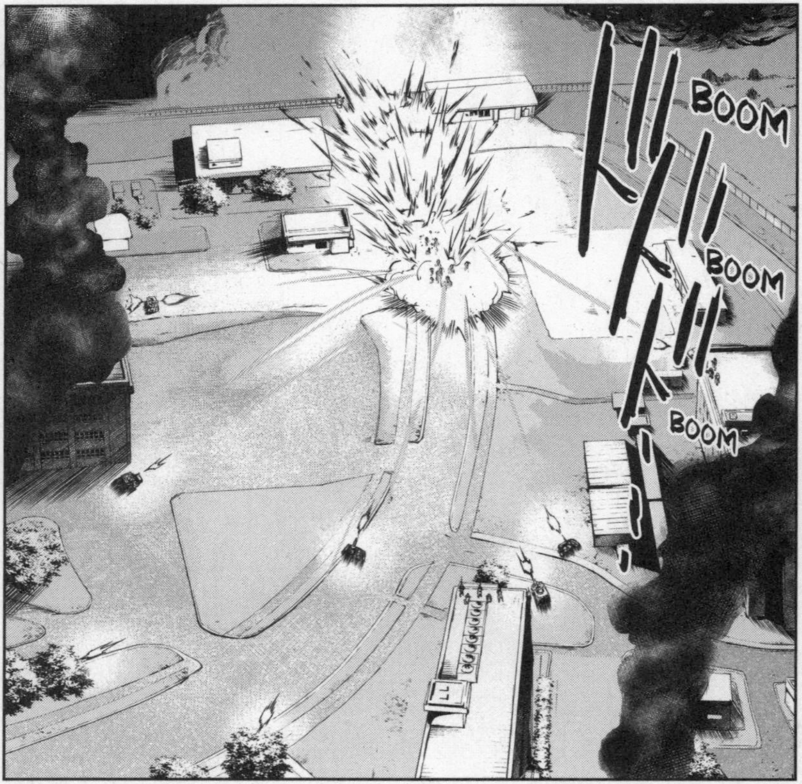
BOOM
BOOM
BOOM
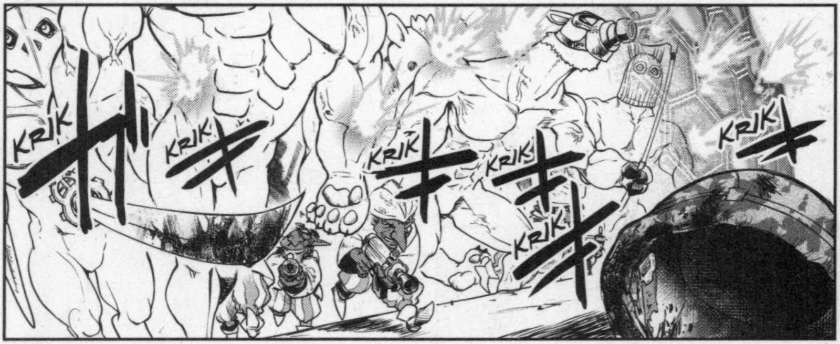
KRIK
KRIK
KRIK
KRIK
KRIK
KRIK

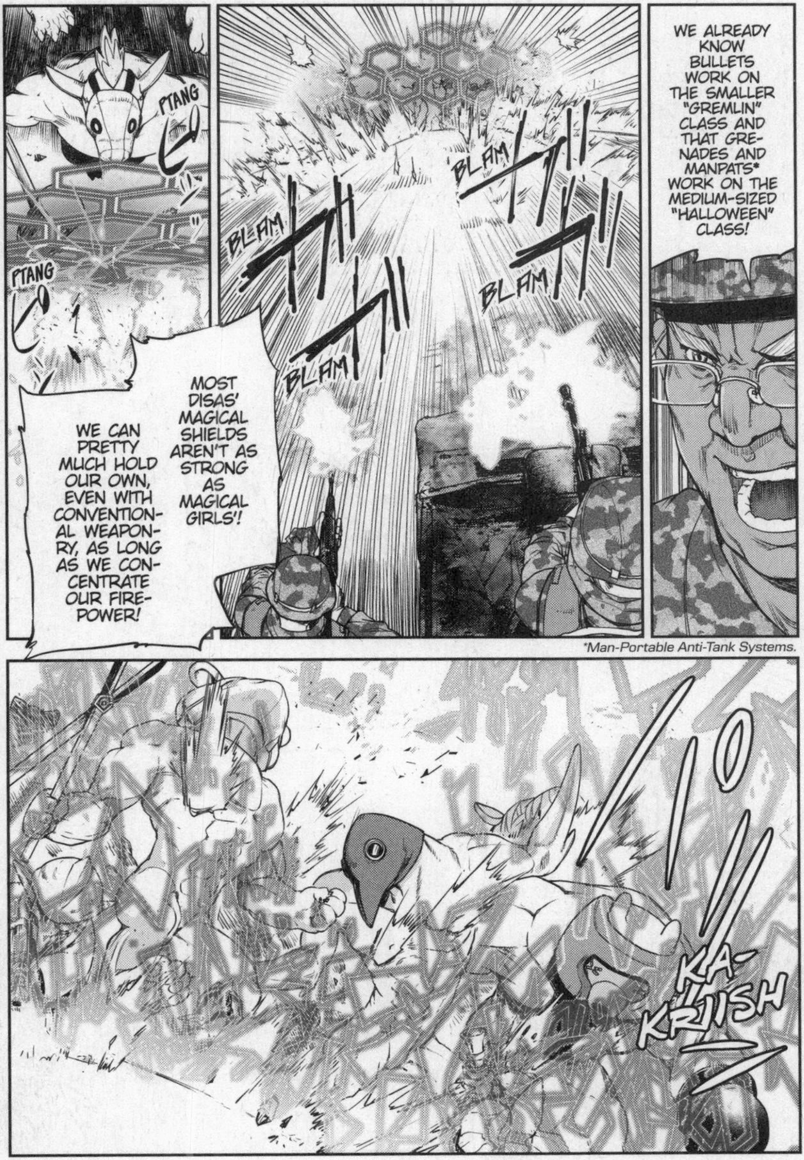
WE ALREADY KNOW BULLETS WORK ON THE SMALLER "GREMLIN" CLASS AND THAT GRENADES AND MANPATS* WORK ON THE MEDIUM-SIZED "HALLOWEEN" CLASS!
BLAM
BLAM
BLAM
BLAM
MOST DISAS' MAGICAL SHIELDS AREN'T AS STRONG AS MAGICAL GIRLS'!
WE CAN PRETTY MUCH HOLD OUR OWN, EVEN WITH CONVENTIONAL WEAPONRY, AS LONG AS WE CONCENTRATE OUR FIREPOWER!
PTANG
PTANG
KA-KRIISH
*Man-Portable Anti-Tank Systems.

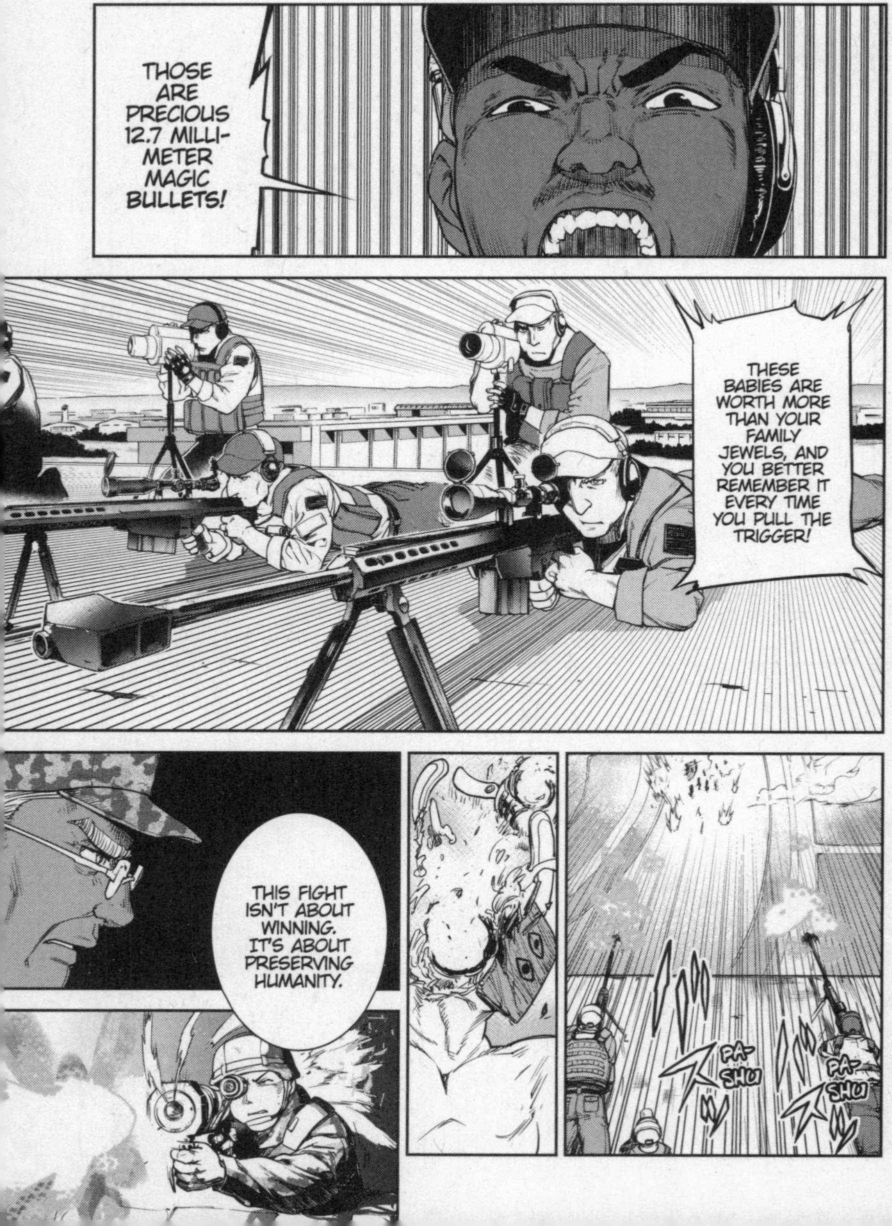
THOSE ARE PRECIOUS 12.7 MILLI-METER MAGIC BULLETS!
THESE BABIES ARE WORTH MORE THAN YOUR FAMILY JEWELS, AND YOU BETTER REMEMBER IT EVERY TIME YOU PULL THE TRIGGER!
PA-SHU
PA-SHU
THIS FIGHT ISN'T ABOUT WINNING. IT'S ABOUT PRESERVING HUMANITY.

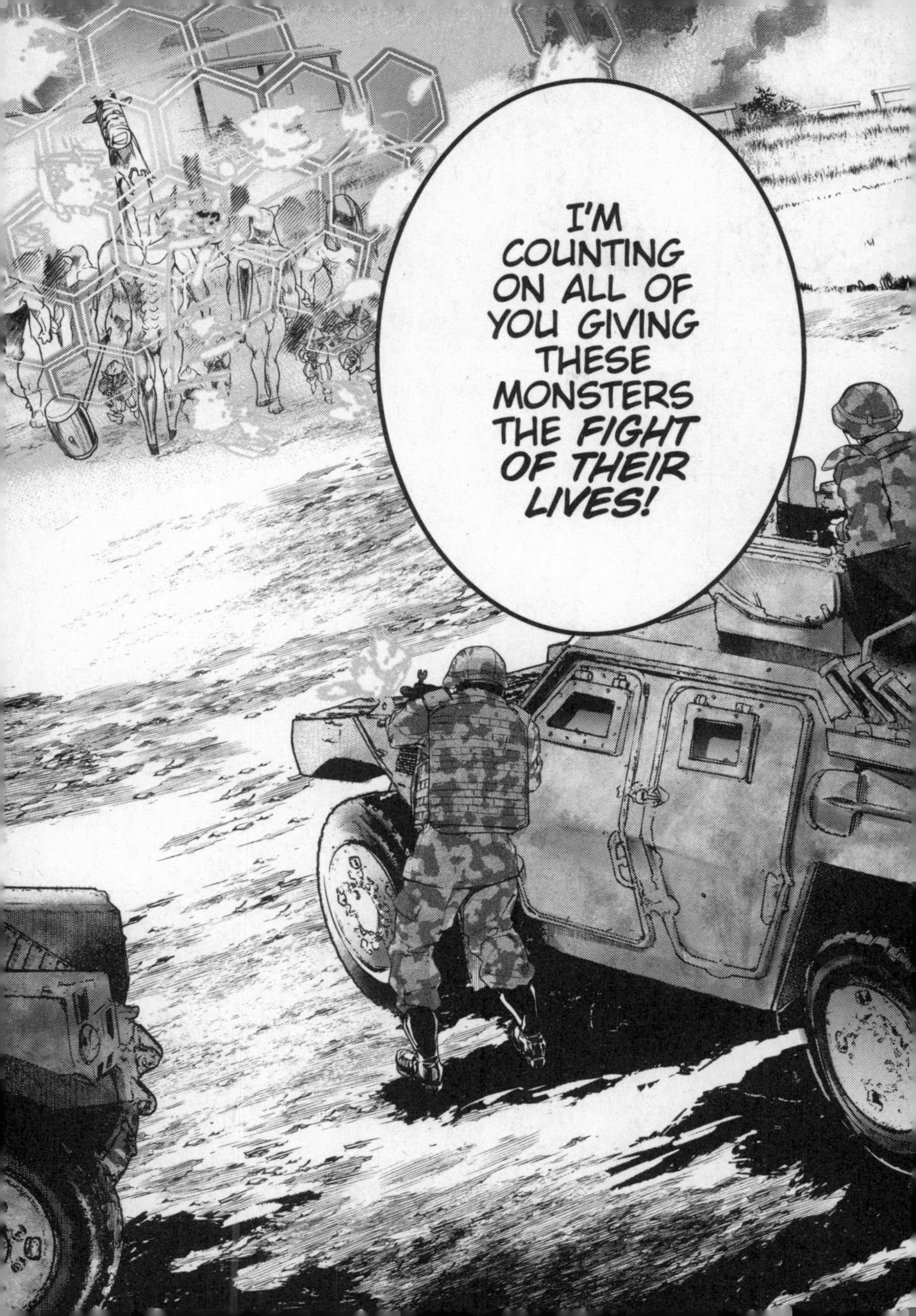
I'M COUNTING ON ALL OF YOU GIVING THESE MONSTERS THE *FIGHT OF THEIR LIVES!*

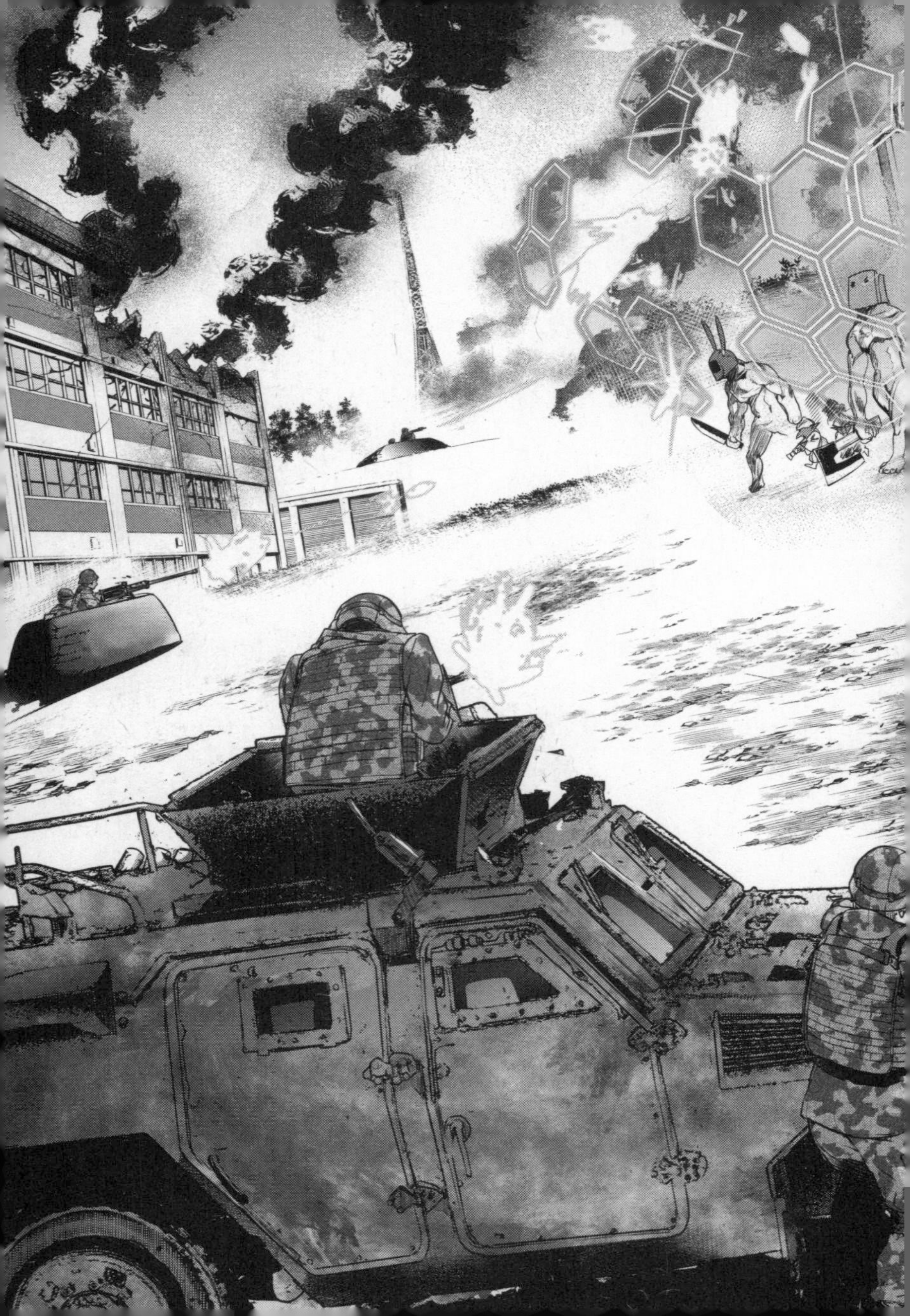

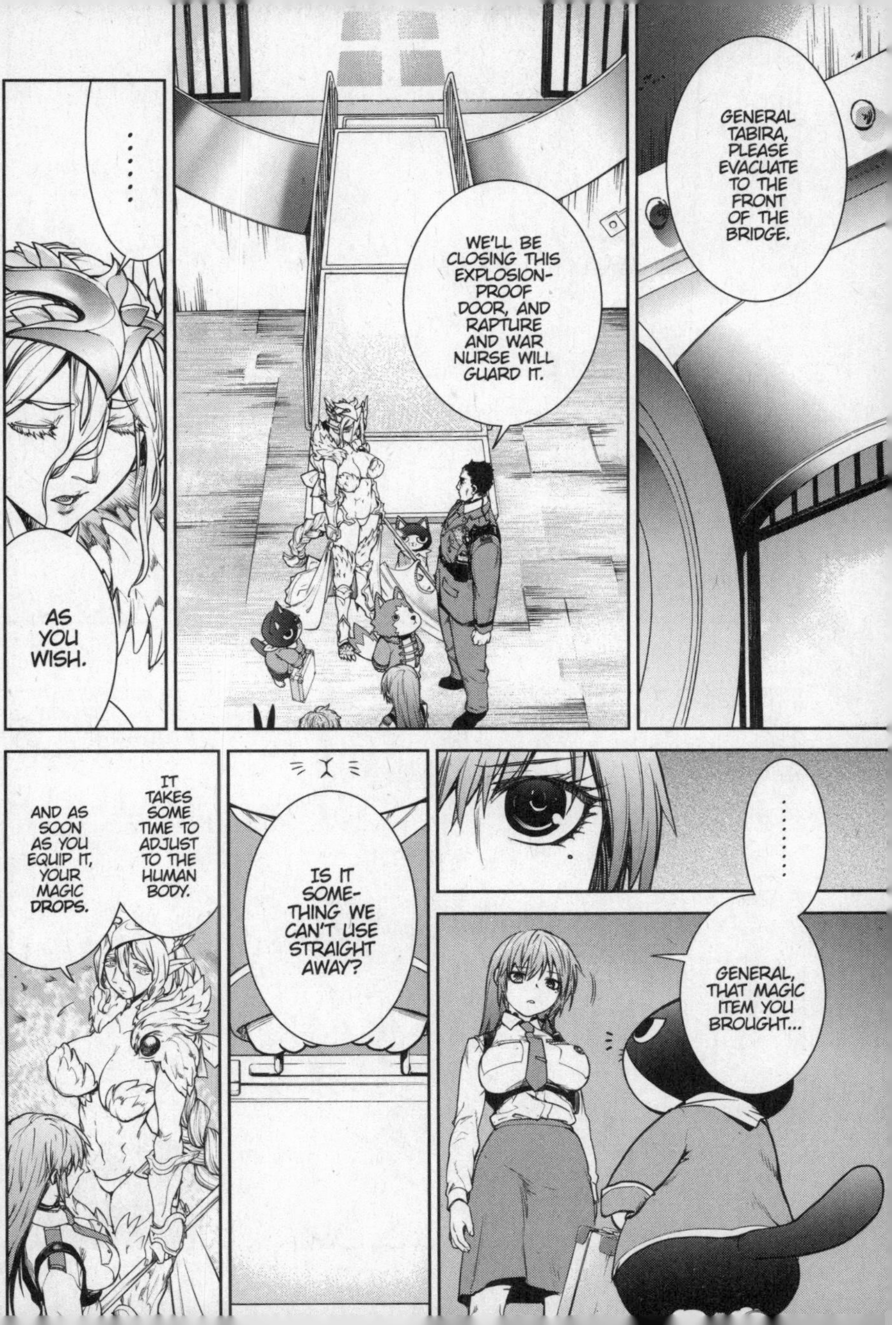
GENERAL TABIRA, PLEASE EVACUATE TO THE FRONT OF THE BRIDGE.
WE'LL BE CLOSING THIS EXPLOSION-PROOF DOOR, AND RAPTURE AND WAR NURSE WILL GUARD IT.
......
AS YOU WISH.
......
GENERAL, THAT MAGIC ITEM YOU BROUGHT...
IS IT SOMETHING WE CAN'T USE STRAIGHT AWAY?
IT TAKES SOME TIME TO ADJUST TO THE HUMAN BODY.
AND AS SOON AS YOU EQUIP IT, YOUR MAGIC DROPS.

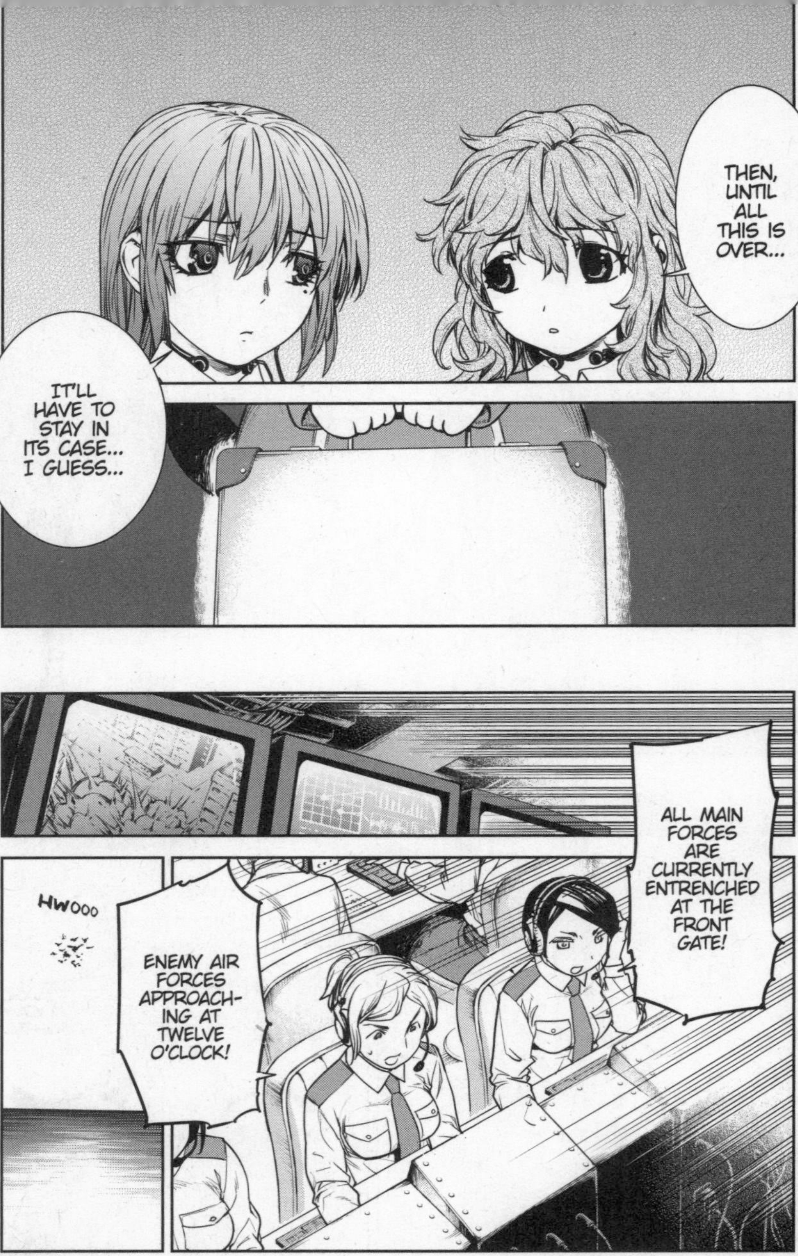
THEN, UNTIL ALL THIS IS OVER...
IT'LL HAVE TO STAY IN ITS CASE... I GUESS...
ALL MAIN FORCES ARE CURRENTLY ENTRENCHED AT THE FRONT GATE!
ENEMY AIR FORCES APPROACH-ING AT TWELVE O'CLOCK!
HWOOO

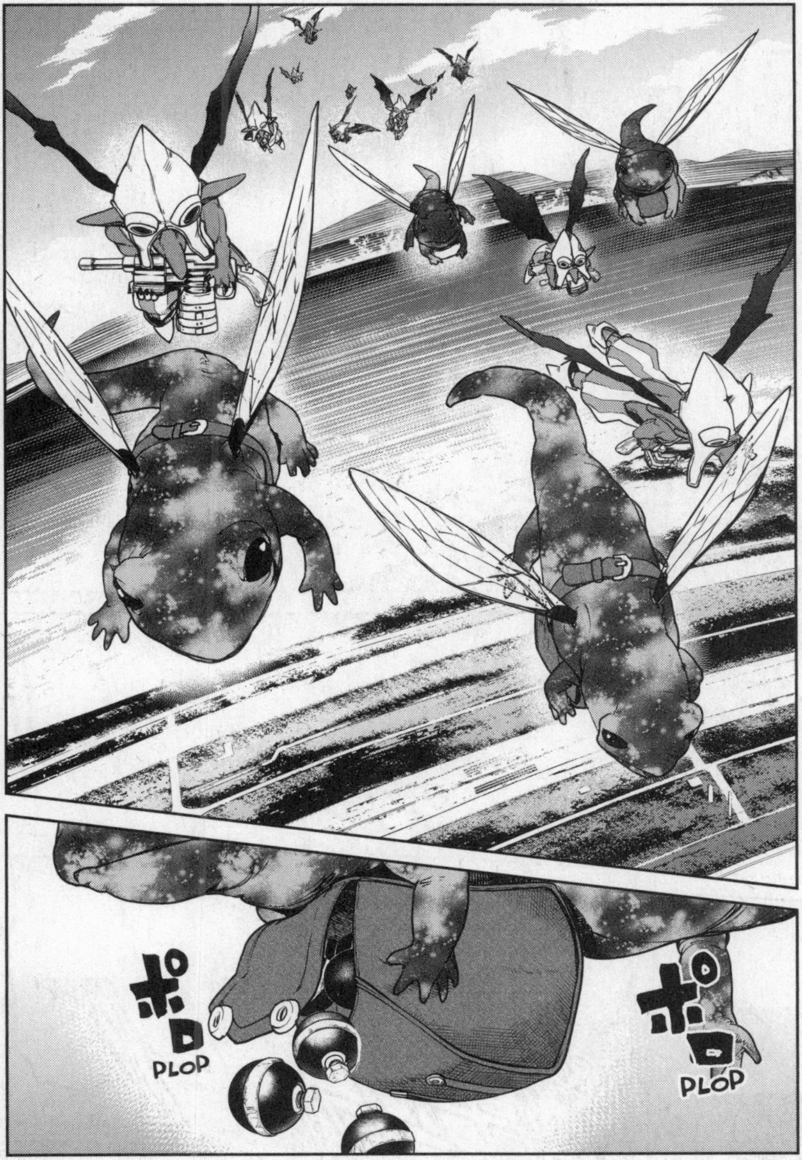
ポロ
PLOP
ポロ
PLOP

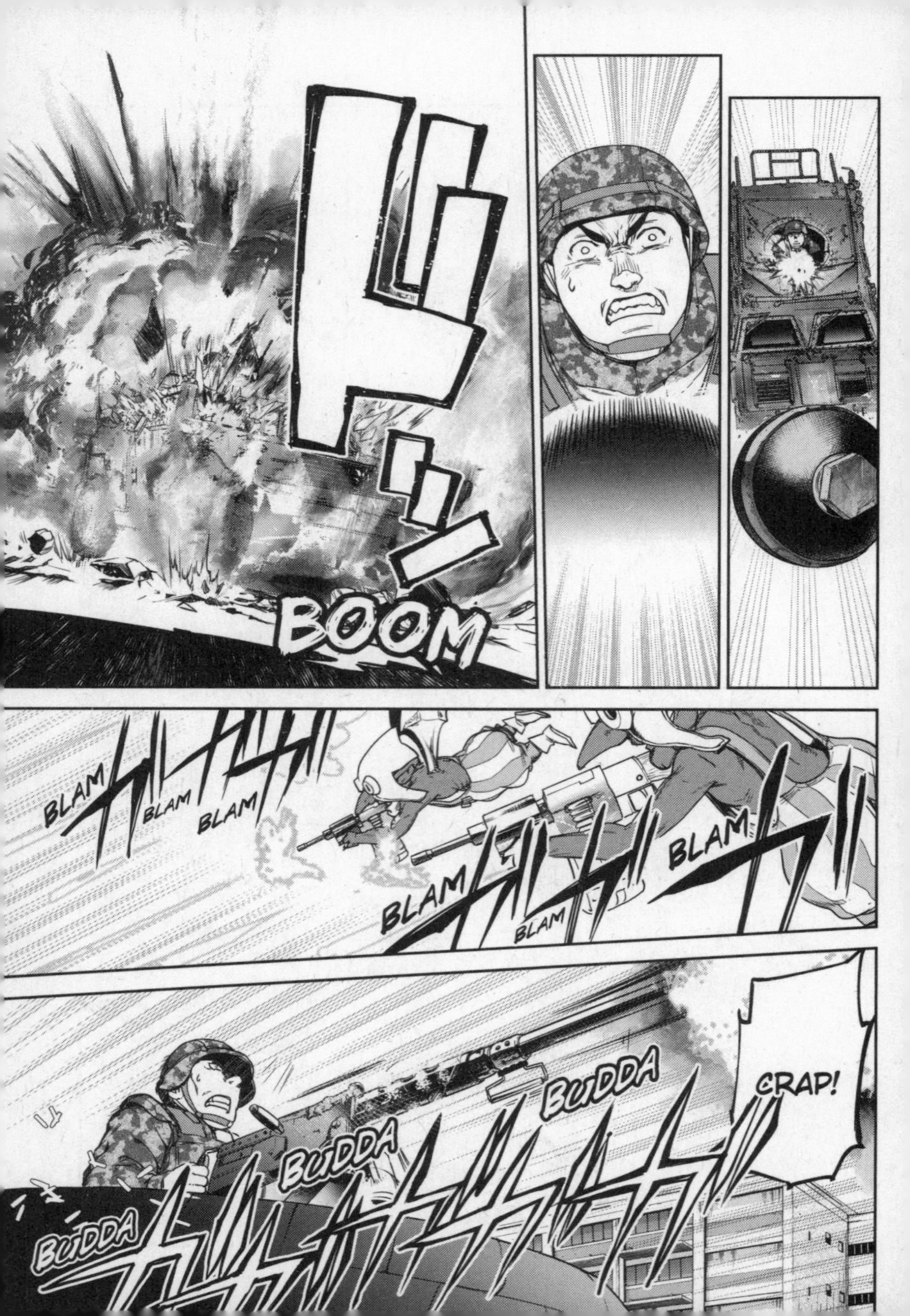
BOOM
BLAM
BLAM
BLAM
BLAM
BLAM
BLAM
CRAP!
BUDDA
BUDDA
BUDDA

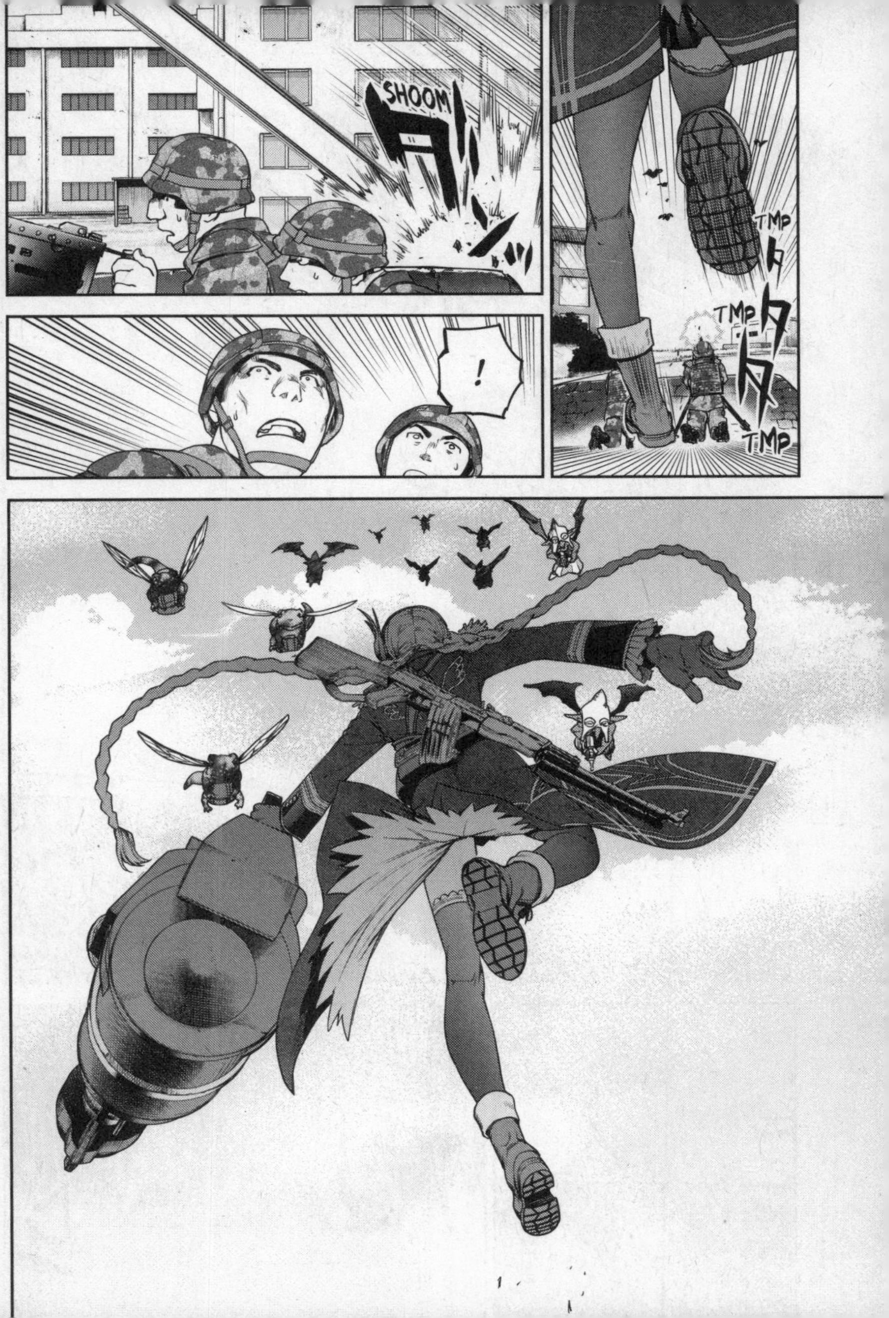
TMP
TMP
TMP
SHOOM
!

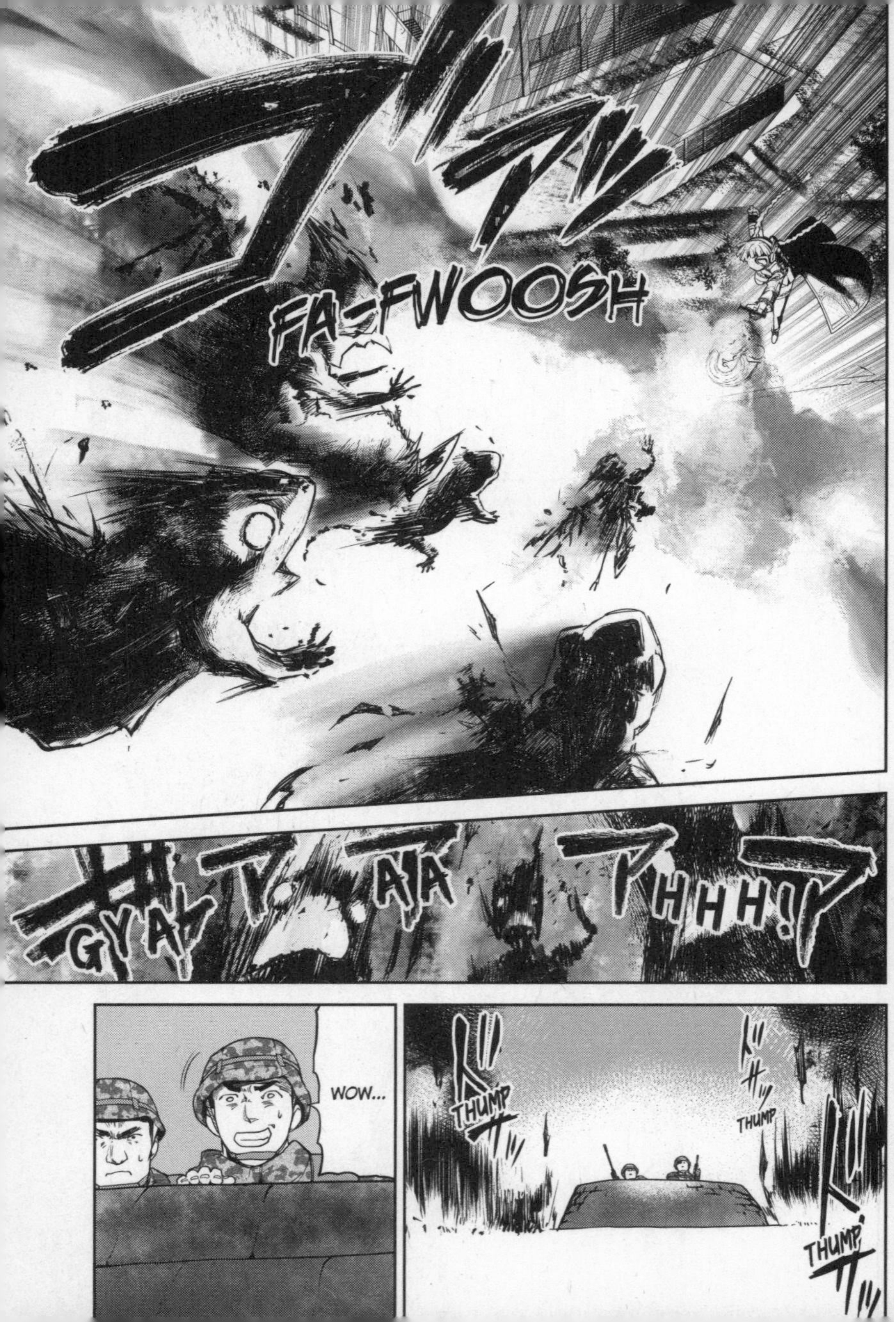
FA-FWOOSH
GYAAAAAHHH!
THUMP
THUMP
THUMP
WOW...

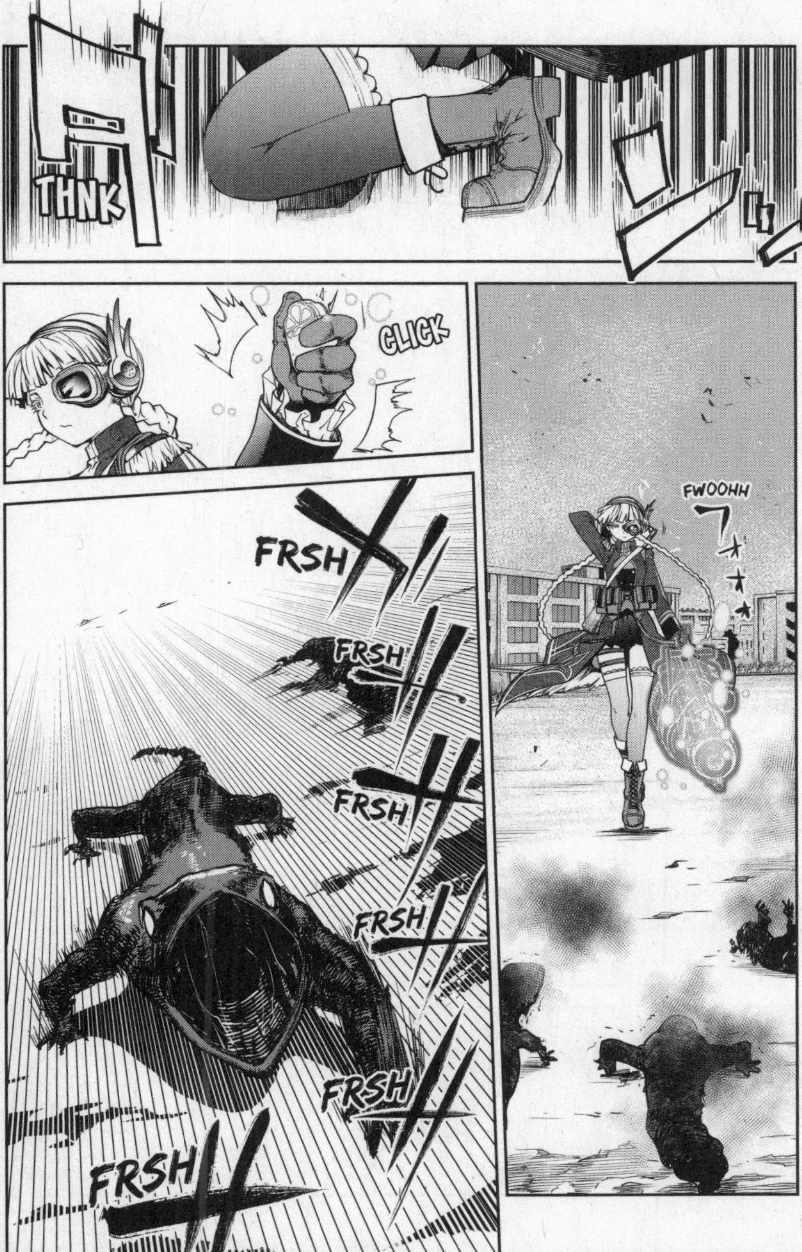
THNK
FWOOHH
CLICK
FRSH
FRSH
FRSH
FRSH
FRSH
FRSH

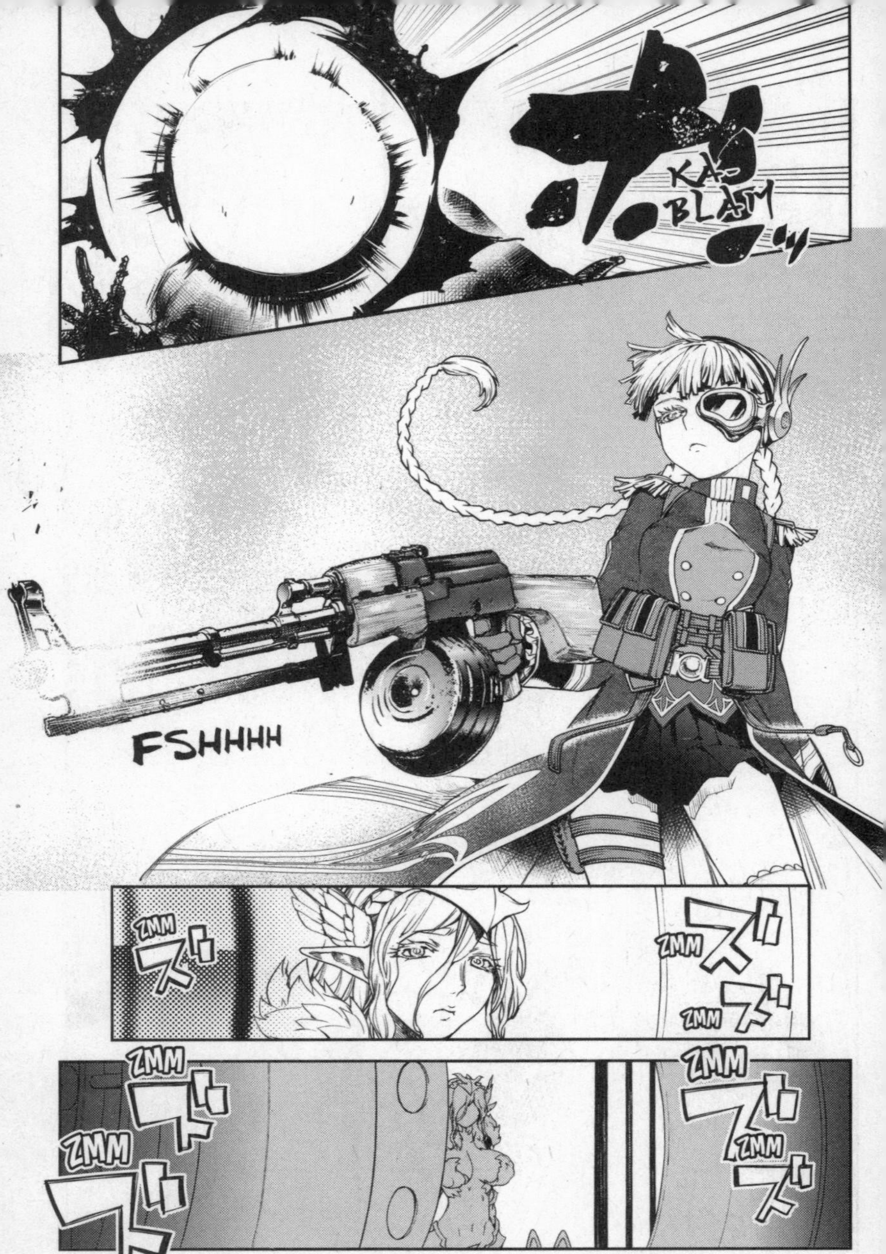
KA-BLAM
FSHHHH
ZMM
ZMM
ZMM
ZMM
ZMM
ZMM
ZMM

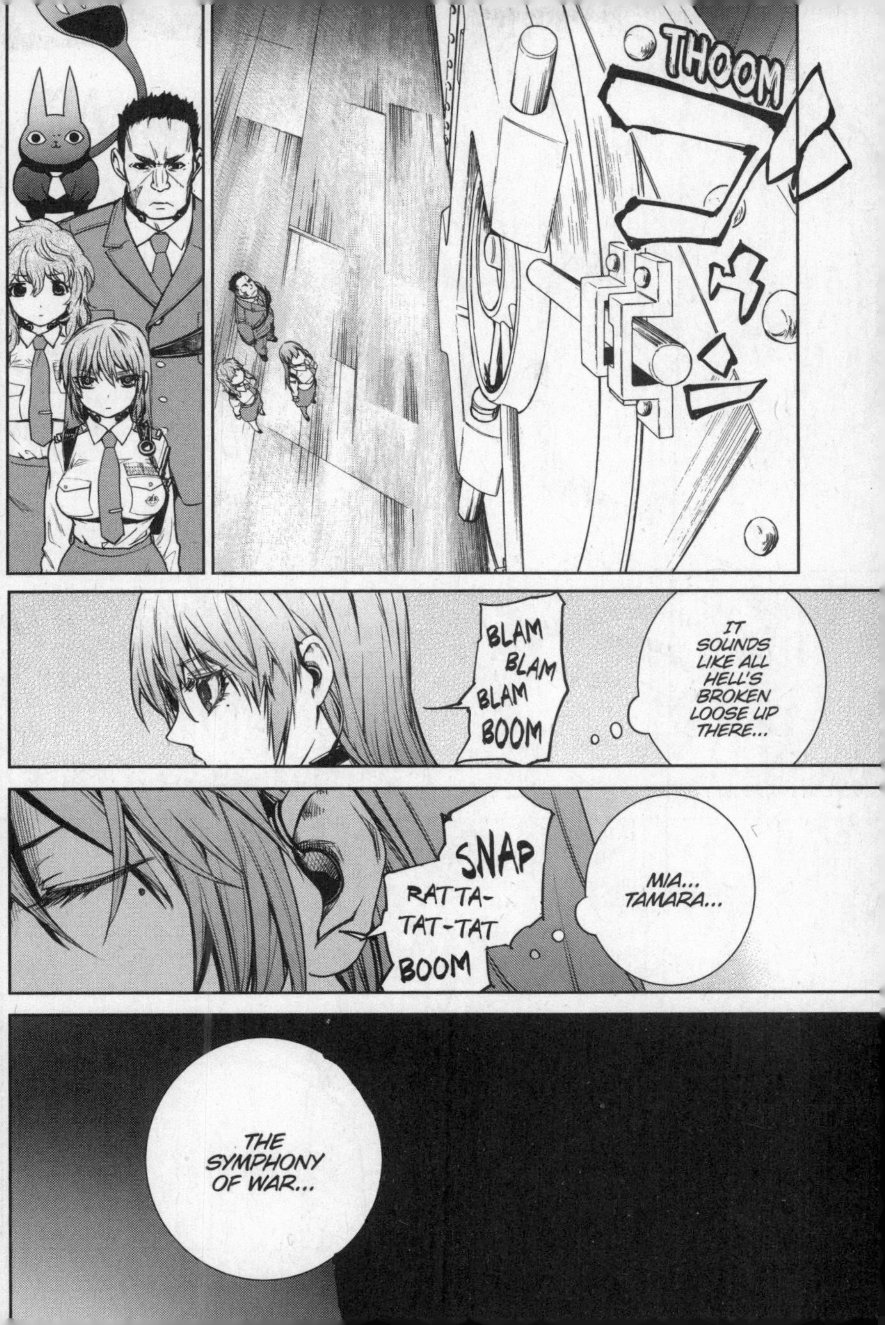
THOOM
IT SOUNDS LIKE ALL HELL'S BROKEN LOOSE UP THERE...
BLAM BLAM BLAM BOOM
MIA... TAMARA...
SNAP RATTA-TAT-TAT BOOM
THE SYMPHONY OF WAR...

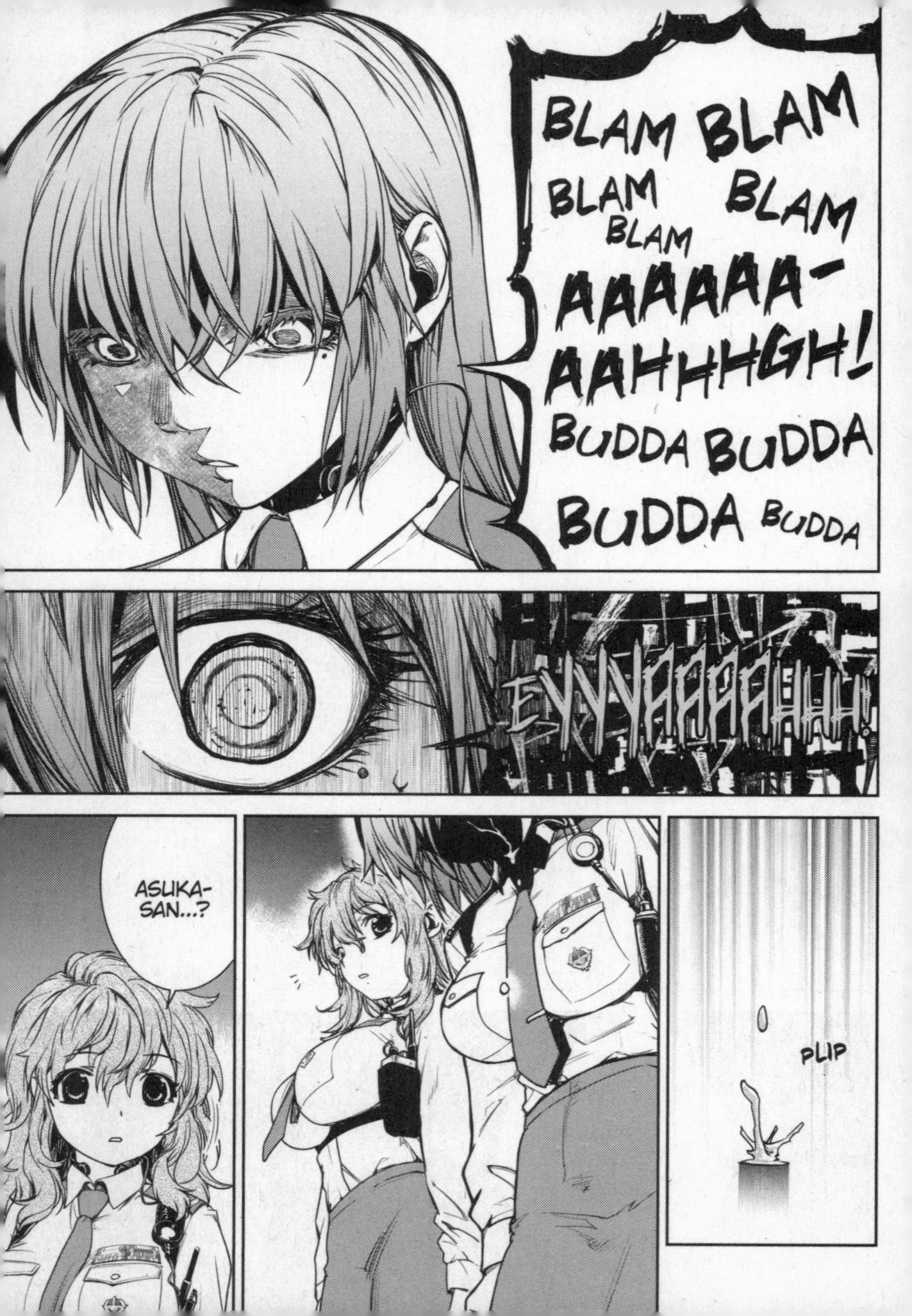
BLAM BLAM
BLAM BLAM
BLAM
AAAAAA-AAHHHGH!
BUDDA BUDDA
BUDDA BUDDA
EYYAAAAHHH!
PLIP
ASUKA-SAN...?

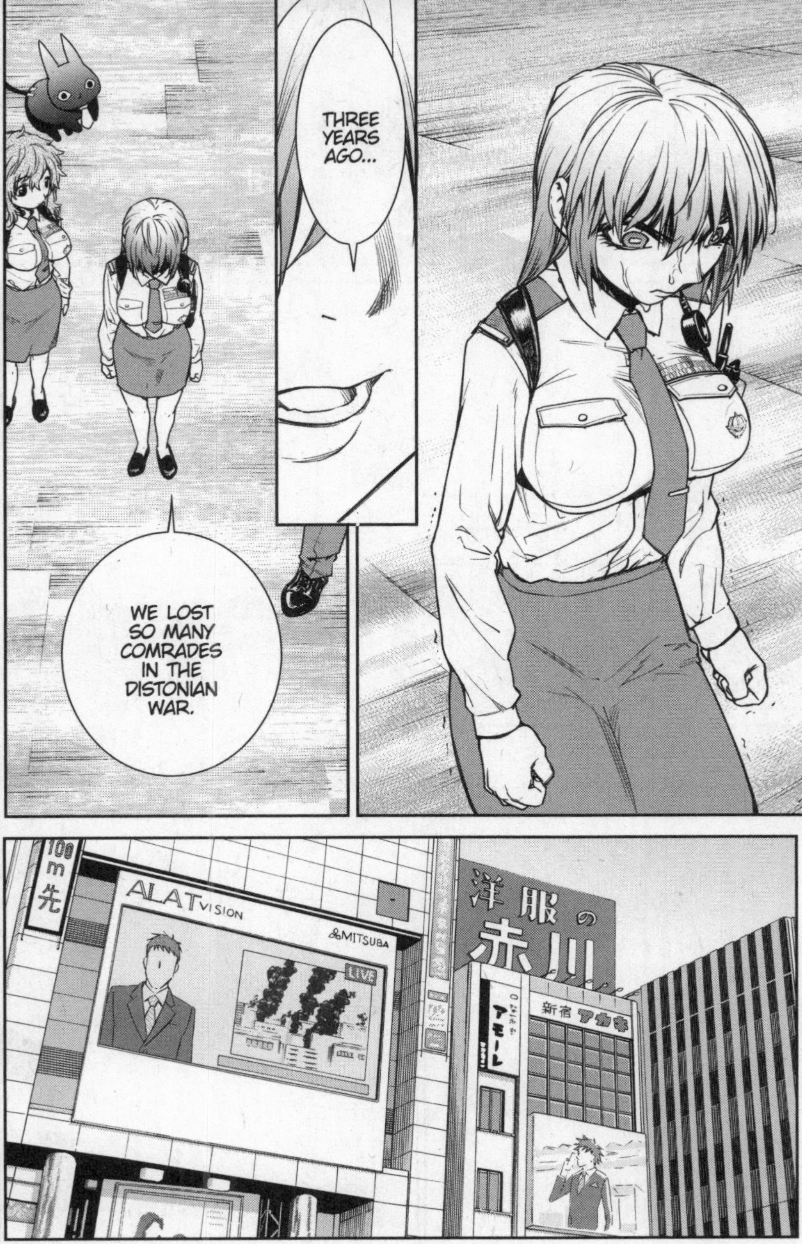
THREE YEARS AGO...
WE LOST SO MANY COMRADES IN THE DISTONIAN WAR.
100m先
ALAT VISION
MITSUBA
LIVE
洋服の赤川
新宿
アモール

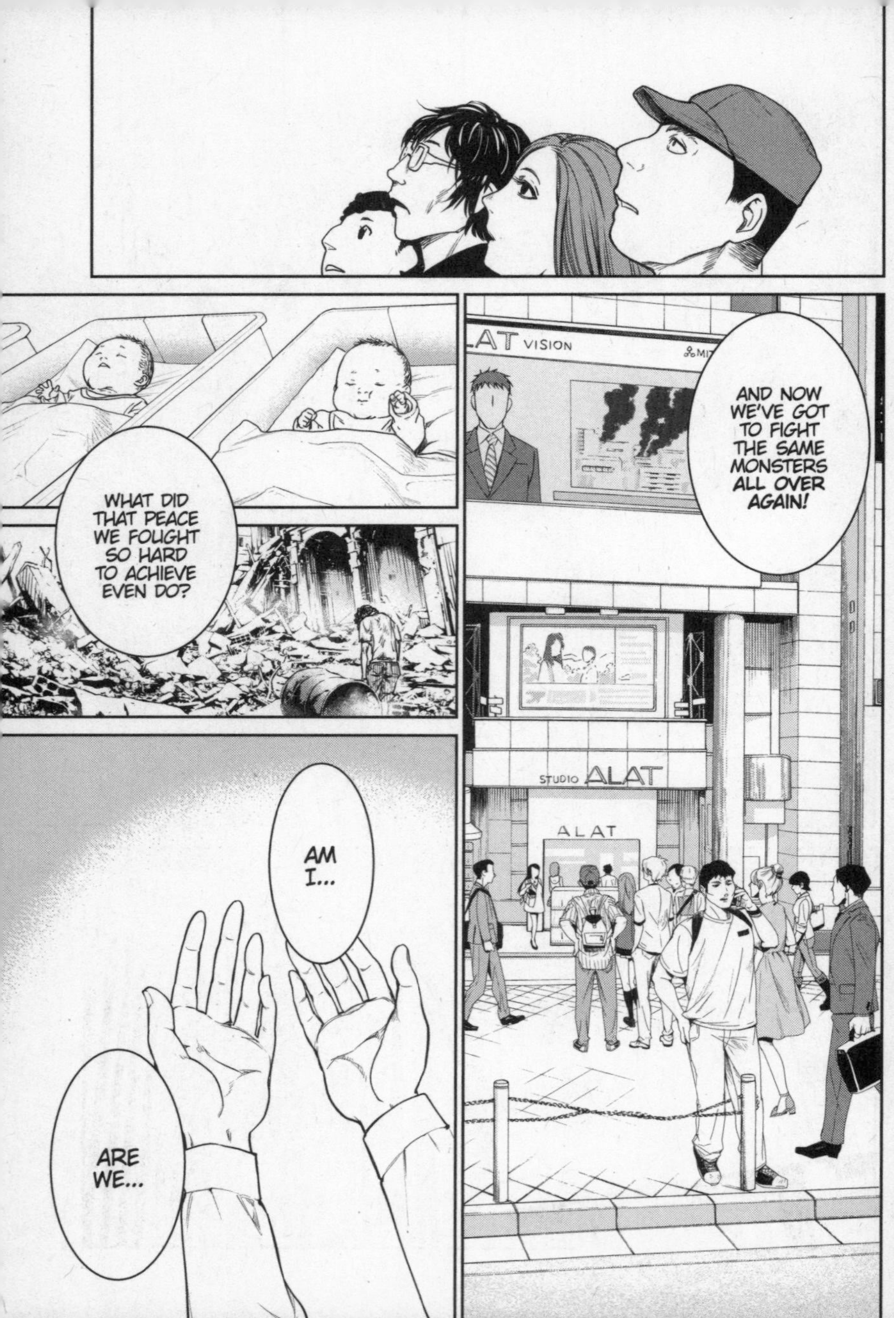
ALAT VISION
AND NOW WE'VE GOT TO FIGHT THE SAME MONSTERS ALL OVER AGAIN!
STUDIO ALAT
ALAT
WHAT DID THAT PEACE WE FOUGHT SO HARD TO ACHIEVE EVEN DO?
AM I...
ARE WE...

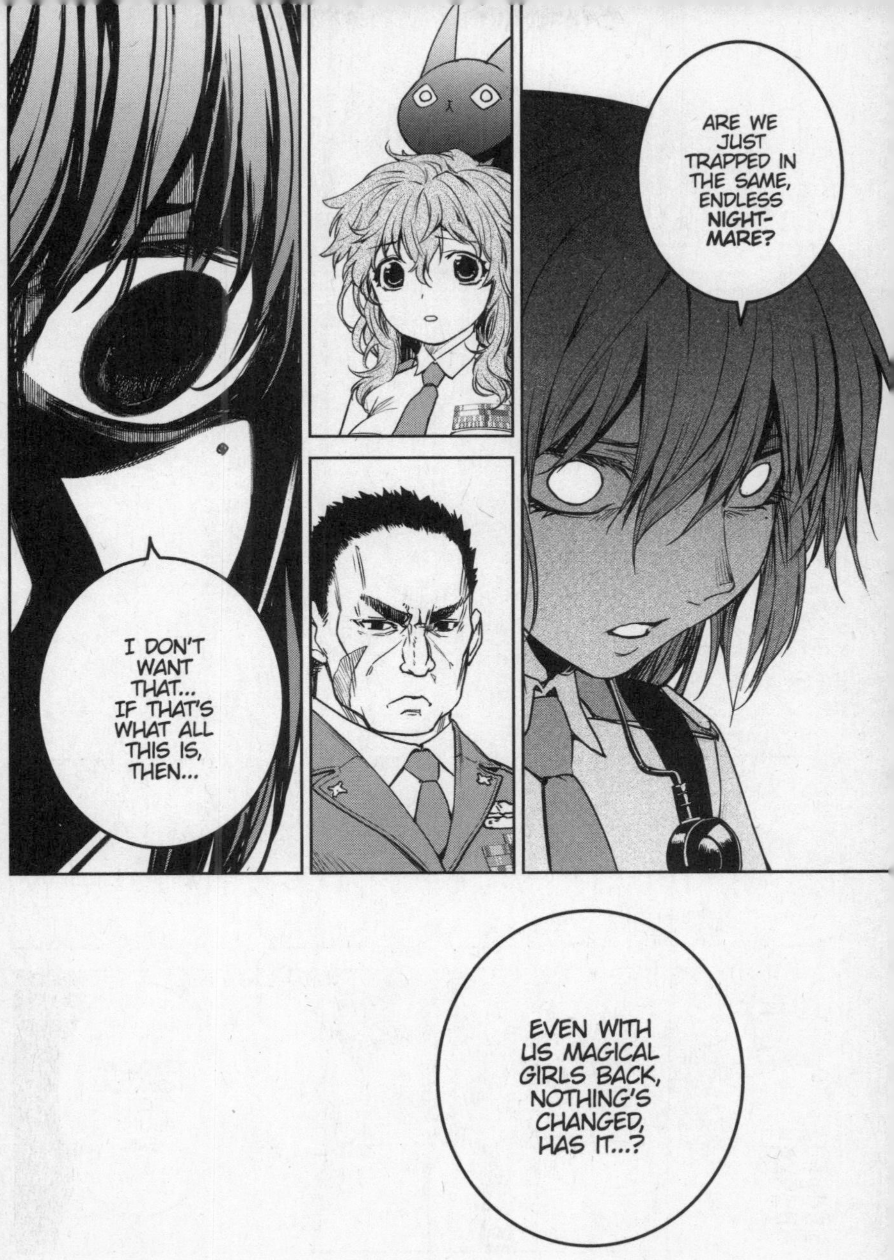
ARE WE JUST TRAPPED IN THE SAME, ENDLESS NIGHT-MARE?
I DON'T WANT THAT... IF THAT'S WHAT ALL THIS IS, THEN...
EVEN WITH US MAGICAL GIRLS BACK, NOTHING'S CHANGED, HAS IT...?

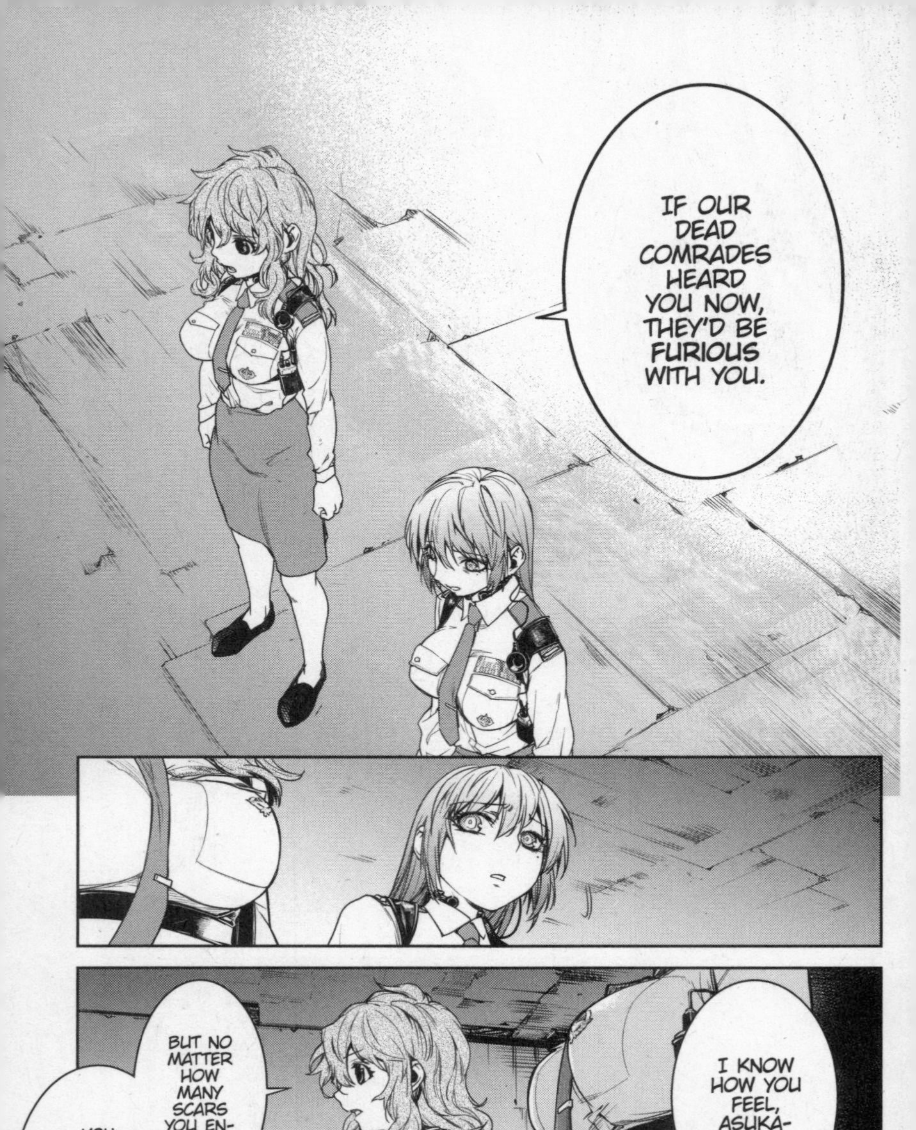
IF OUR DEAD COMRADES HEARD YOU NOW, THEY'D BE FURIOUS WITH YOU.
I KNOW HOW YOU FEEL, ASUKA-SAN.
BUT NO MATTER HOW MANY SCARS YOU ENDURED...
YOU ALWAYS MARCHED BACK TO THE BATTLEFIELD.

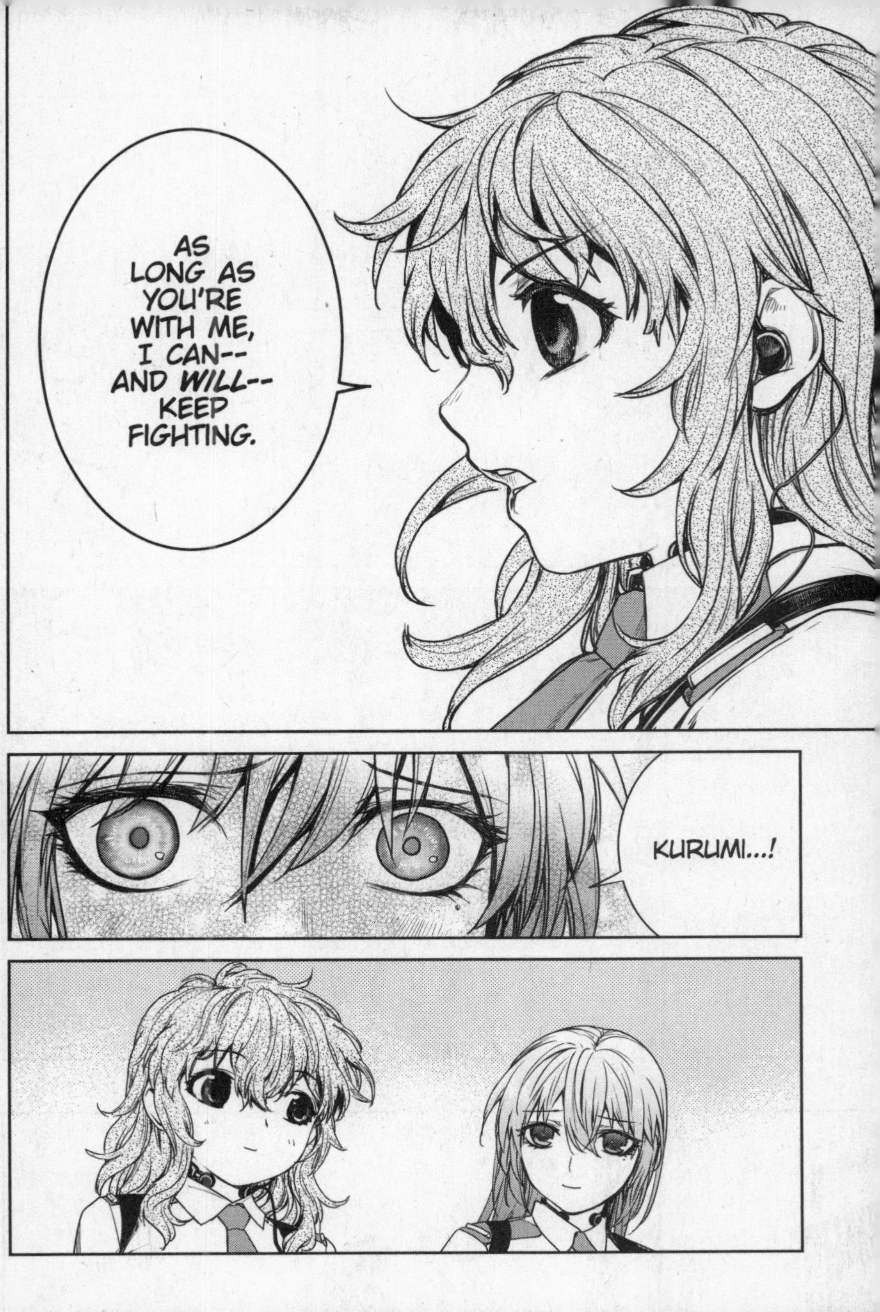
AS LONG AS YOU'RE WITH ME, I CAN-- AND WILL-- KEEP FIGHTING.
KURUMI...!

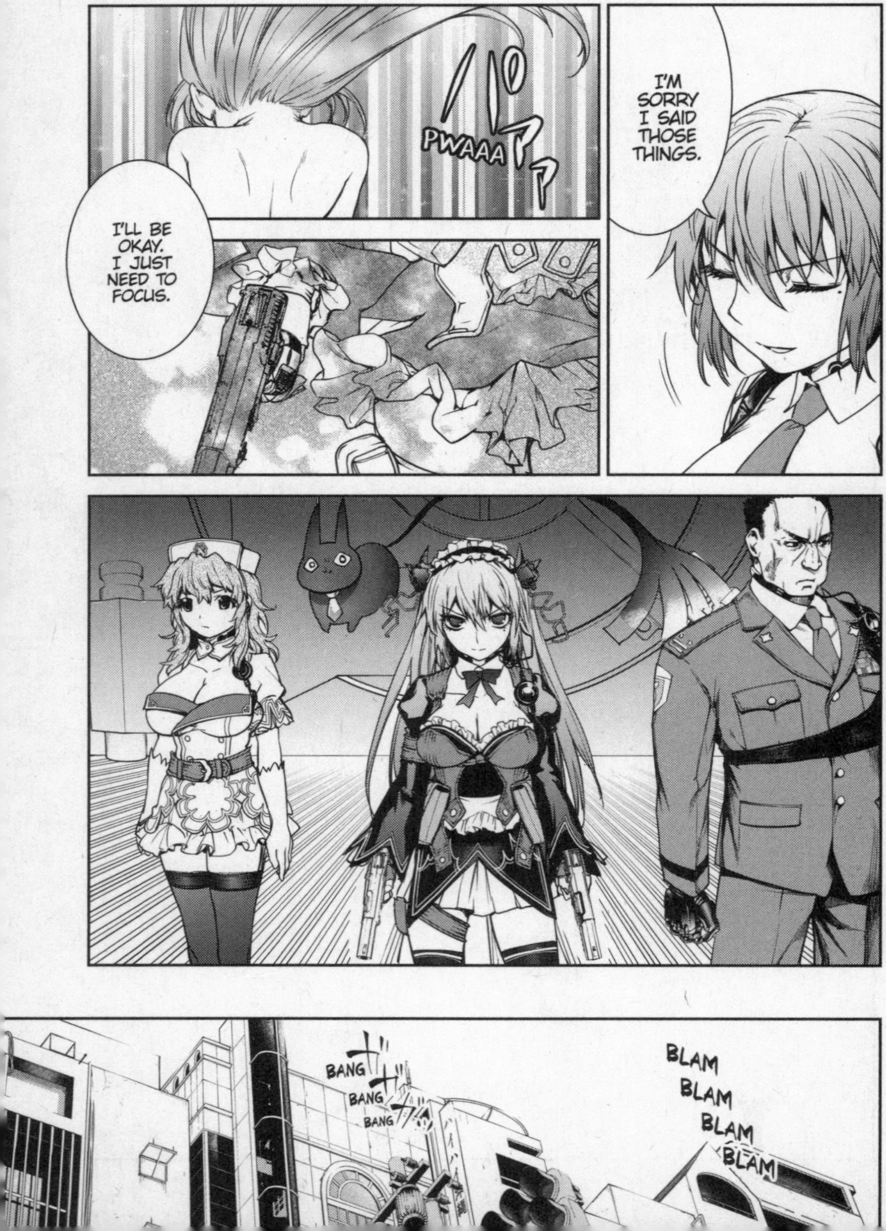
I'M SORRY I SAID THOSE THINGS.
PWAAA
I'LL BE OKAY. I JUST NEED TO FOCUS.
BLAM
BLAM
BLAM
BLAM
BANG
BANG
BANG

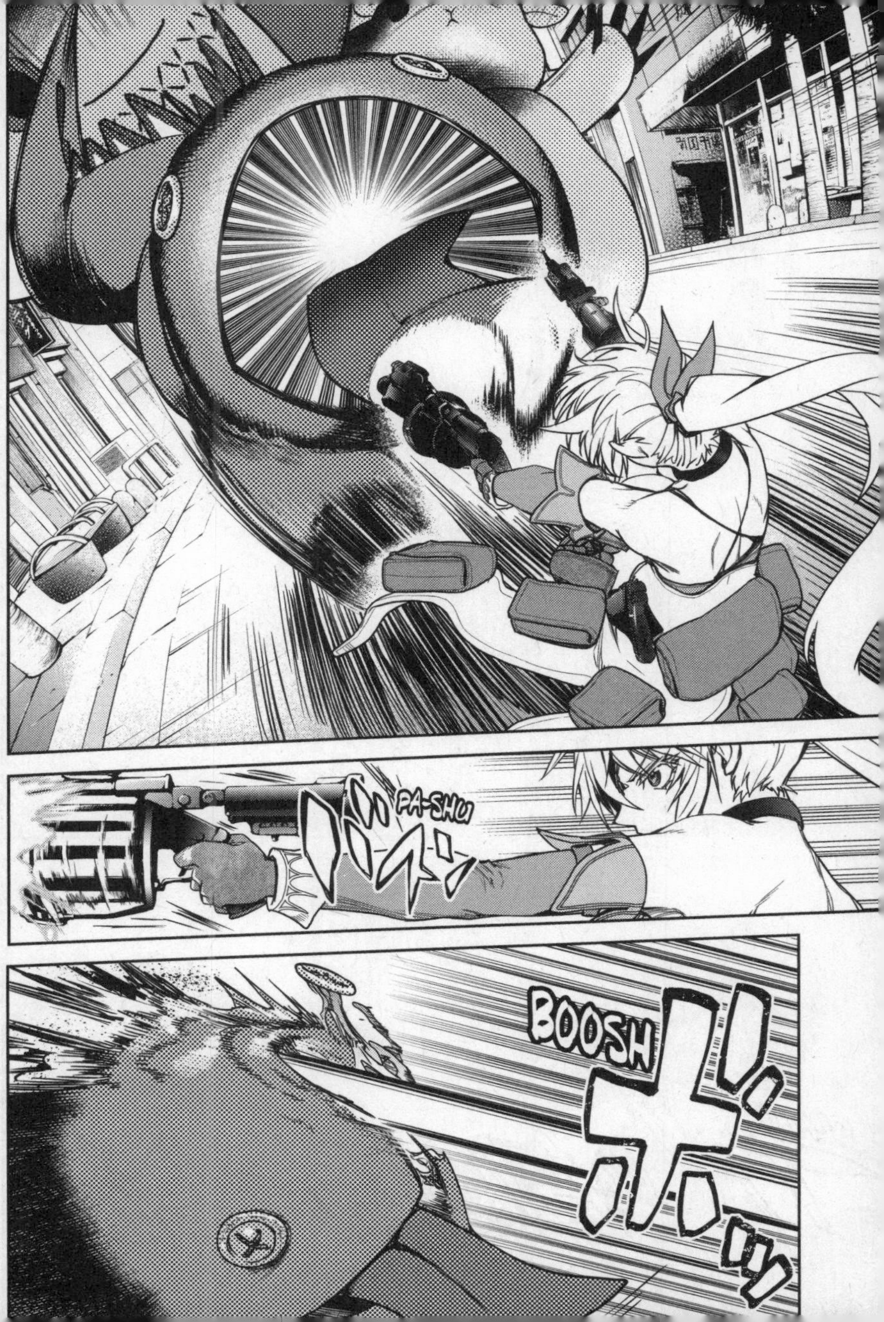
PA-SHU
BOOSH

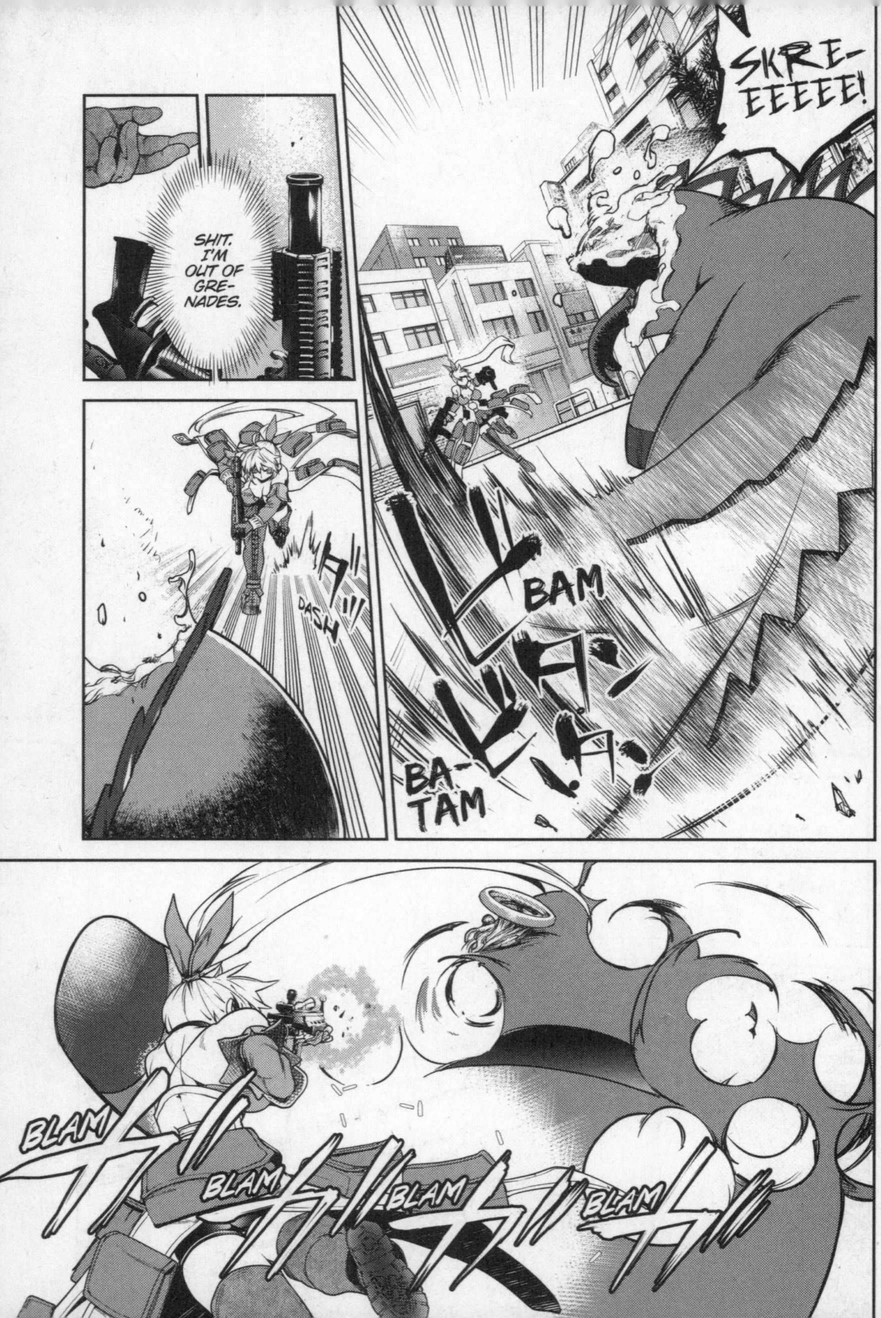
SKRE-EEEEEE!
BAM
BA-TAM
SHIT. I'M OUT OF GRE-NADES.
DASH
BLAM
BLAM
BLAM
BLAM

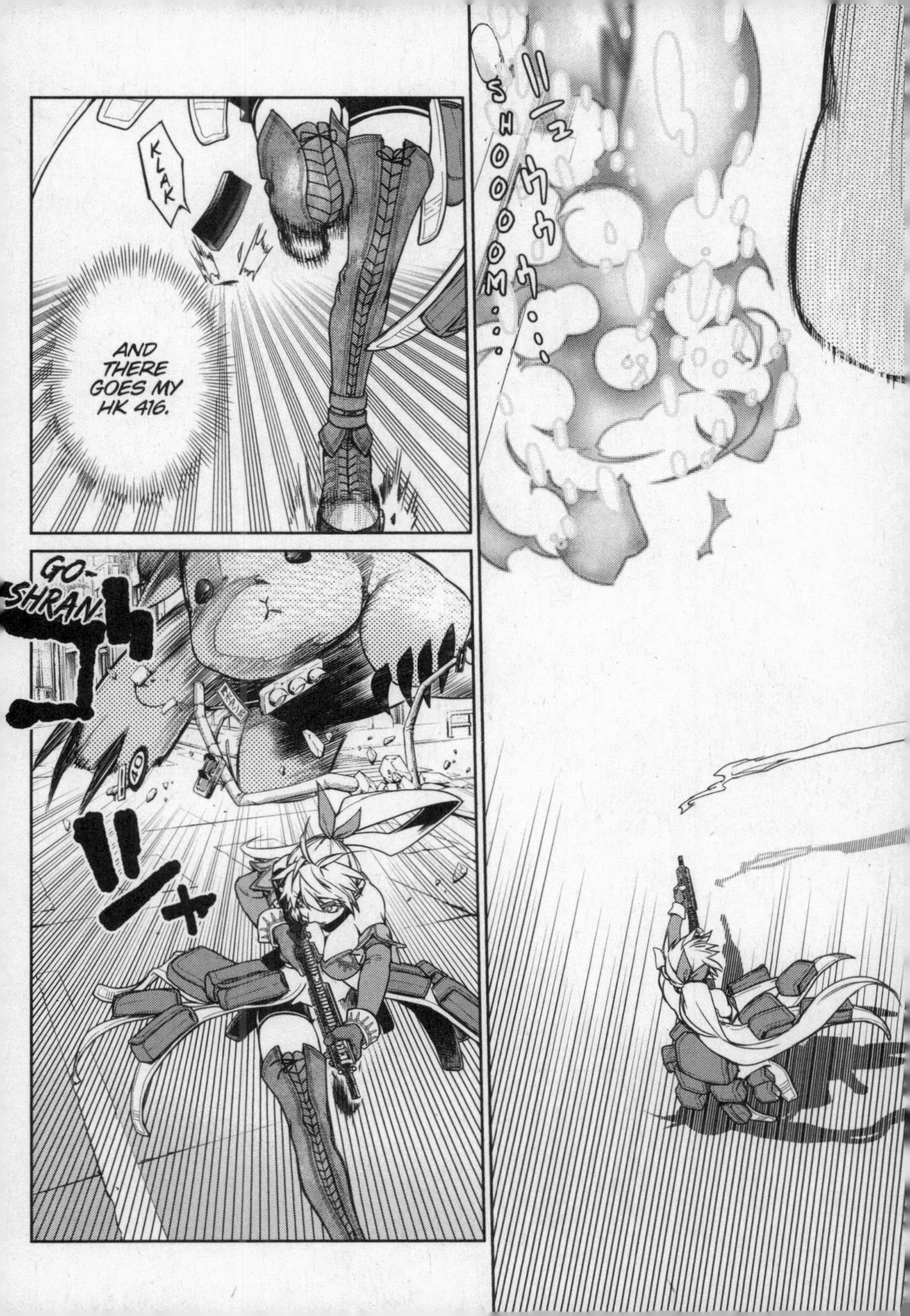
SHOOOOM...
KLAK
AND THERE GOES MY HK 416.
GO-SHRAN

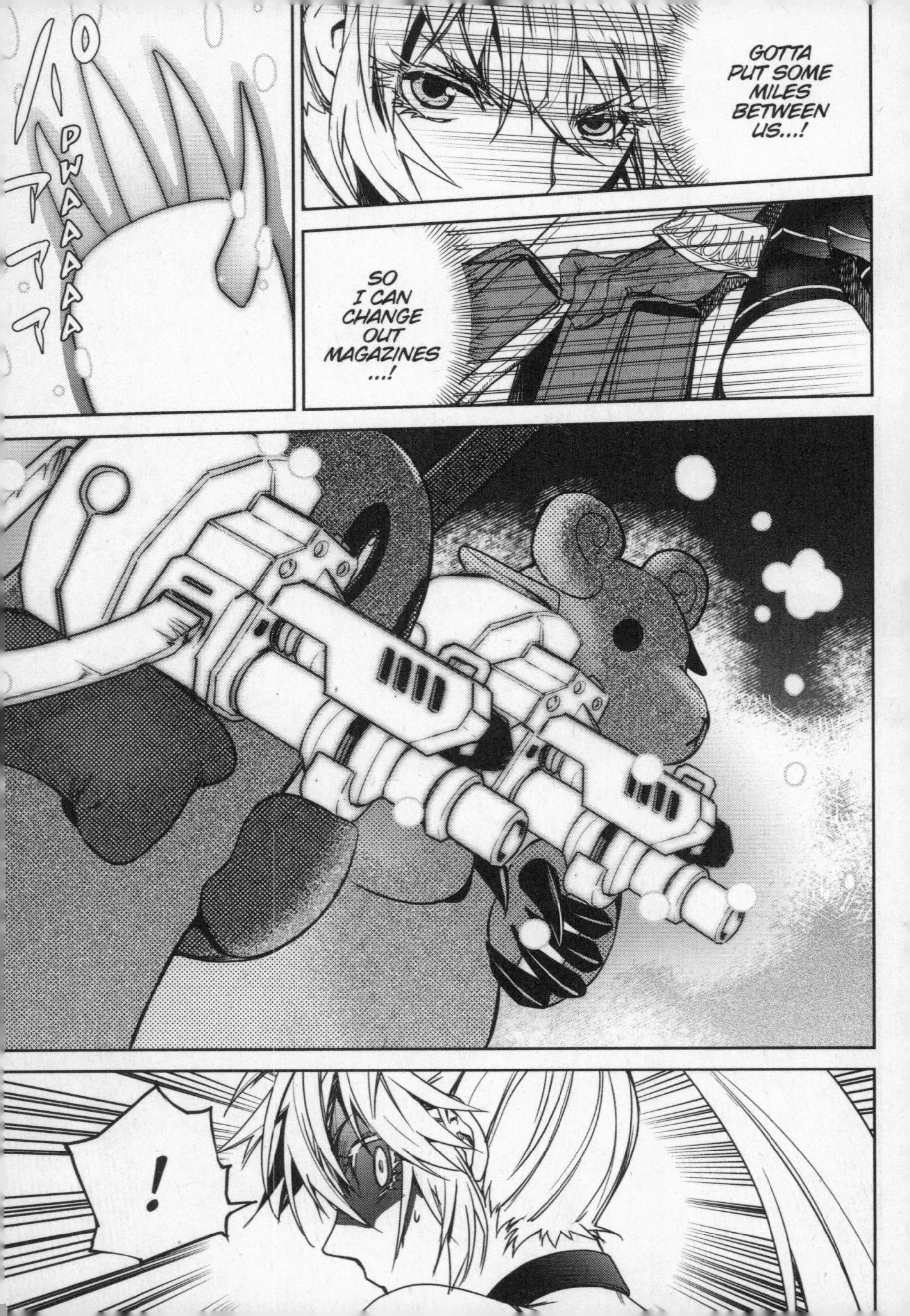
GOTTA PUT SOME MILES BETWEEN US...!
SO I CAN CHANGE OUT MAGAZINES ...!
PWAAAAAA
!

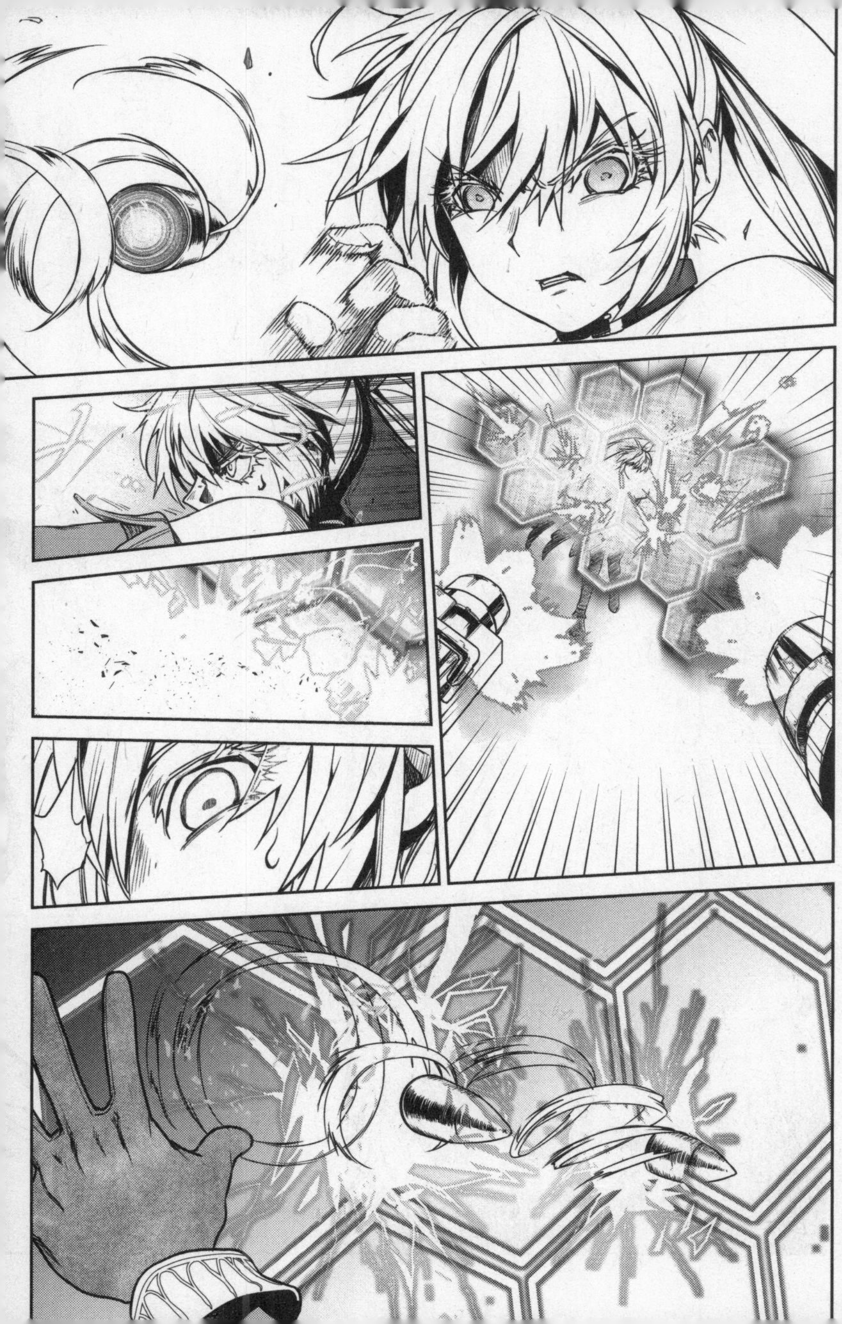

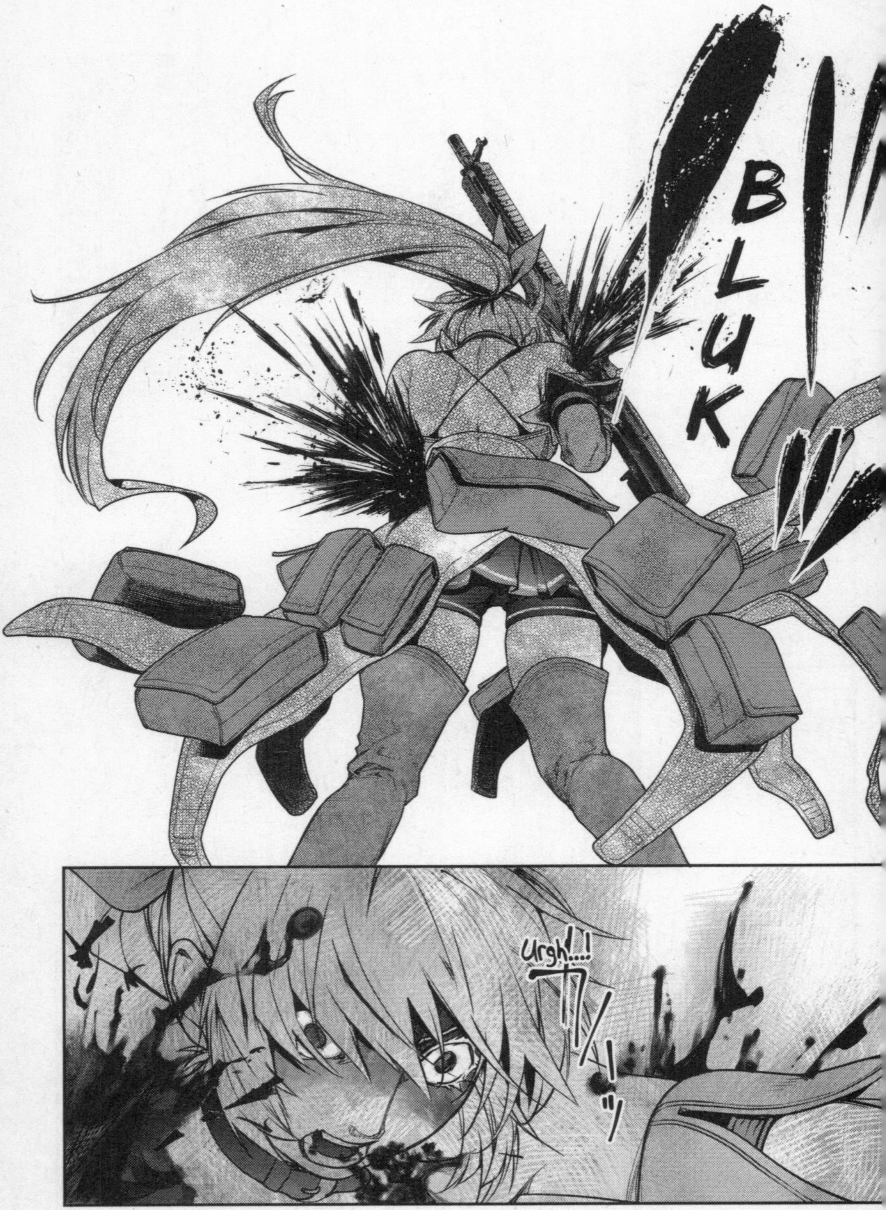
BLUK
Urgh...!

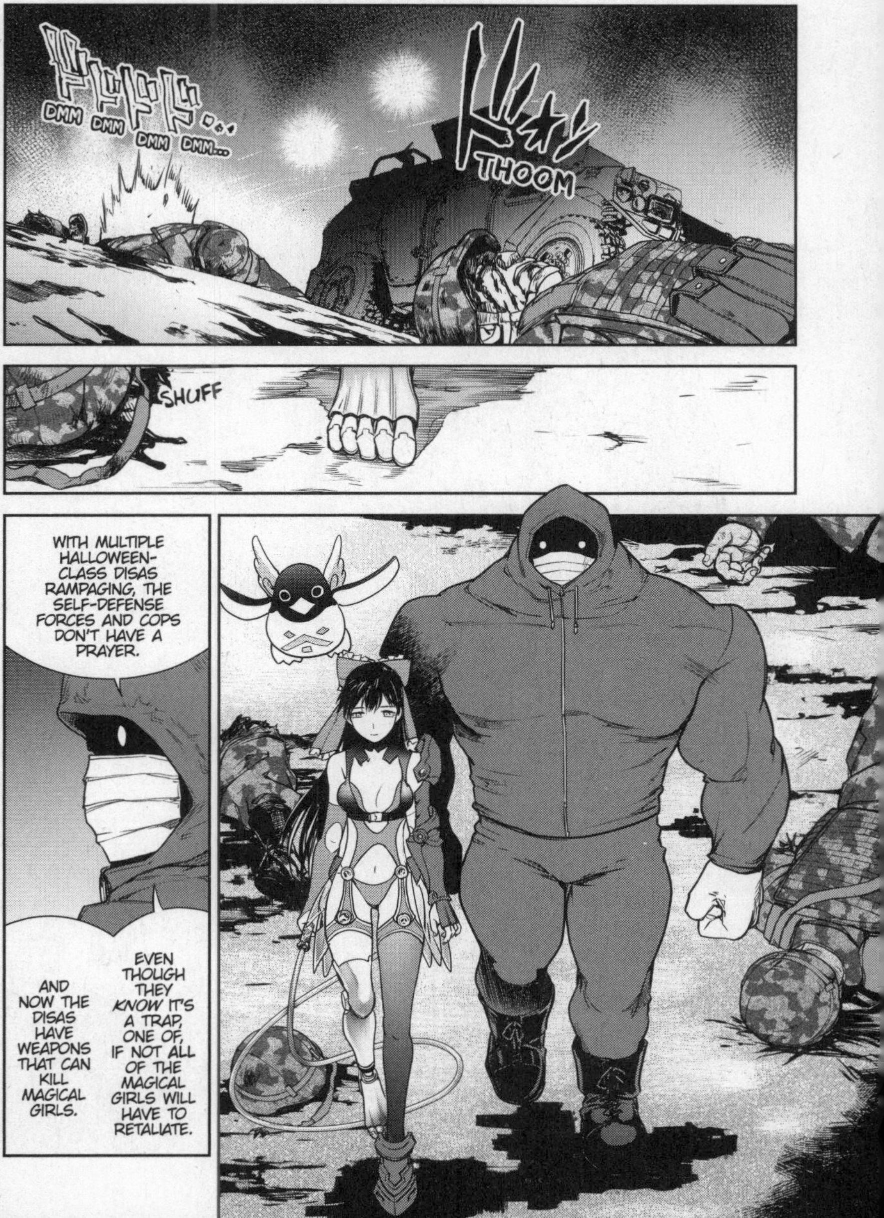
THOOM
DMM DMM DMM DMM...
SHUFF
WITH MULTIPLE HALLOWEEN-CLASS DISAS RAMPAGING, THE SELF-DEFENSE FORCES AND COPS DON'T HAVE A PRAYER.
EVEN THOUGH THEY *KNOW* IT'S A TRAP, ONE OF, IF NOT ALL OF THE MAGICAL GIRLS WILL HAVE TO RETALIATE.
AND NOW THE DISAS HAVE WEAPONS THAT CAN KILL MAGICAL GIRLS.

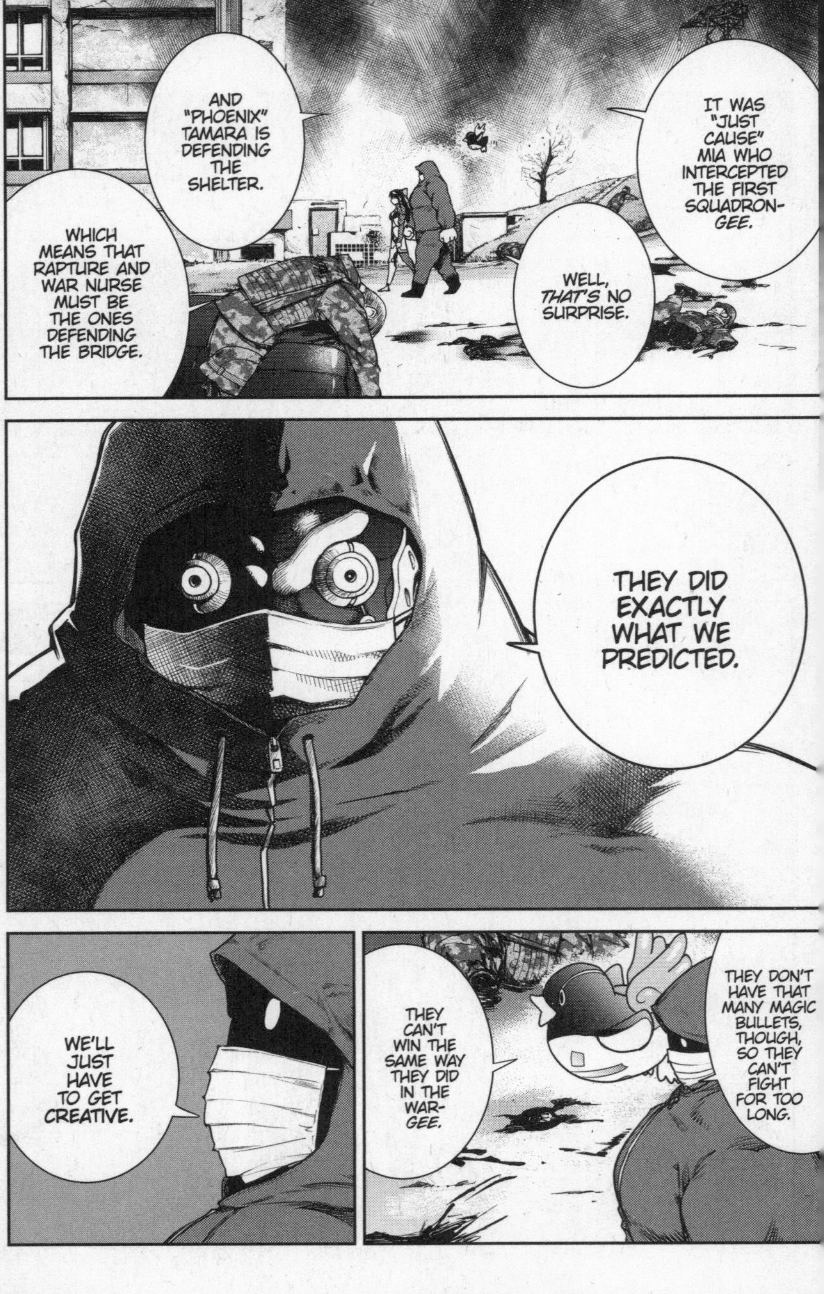
IT WAS "JUST CAUSE" MIA WHO INTERCEPTED THE FIRST SQUADRON-GEE.
WELL, *THAT'S* NO SURPRISE.
AND "PHOENIX" TAMARA IS DEFENDING THE SHELTER.
WHICH MEANS THAT RAPTURE AND WAR NURSE MUST BE THE ONES DEFENDING THE BRIDGE.
THEY DID EXACTLY WHAT WE PREDICTED.
THEY DON'T HAVE THAT MANY MAGIC BULLETS, THOUGH, SO THEY CAN'T FIGHT FOR TOO LONG.
THEY CAN'T WIN THE SAME WAY THEY DID IN THE WAR-GEE.
WE'LL JUST HAVE TO GET CREATIVE.

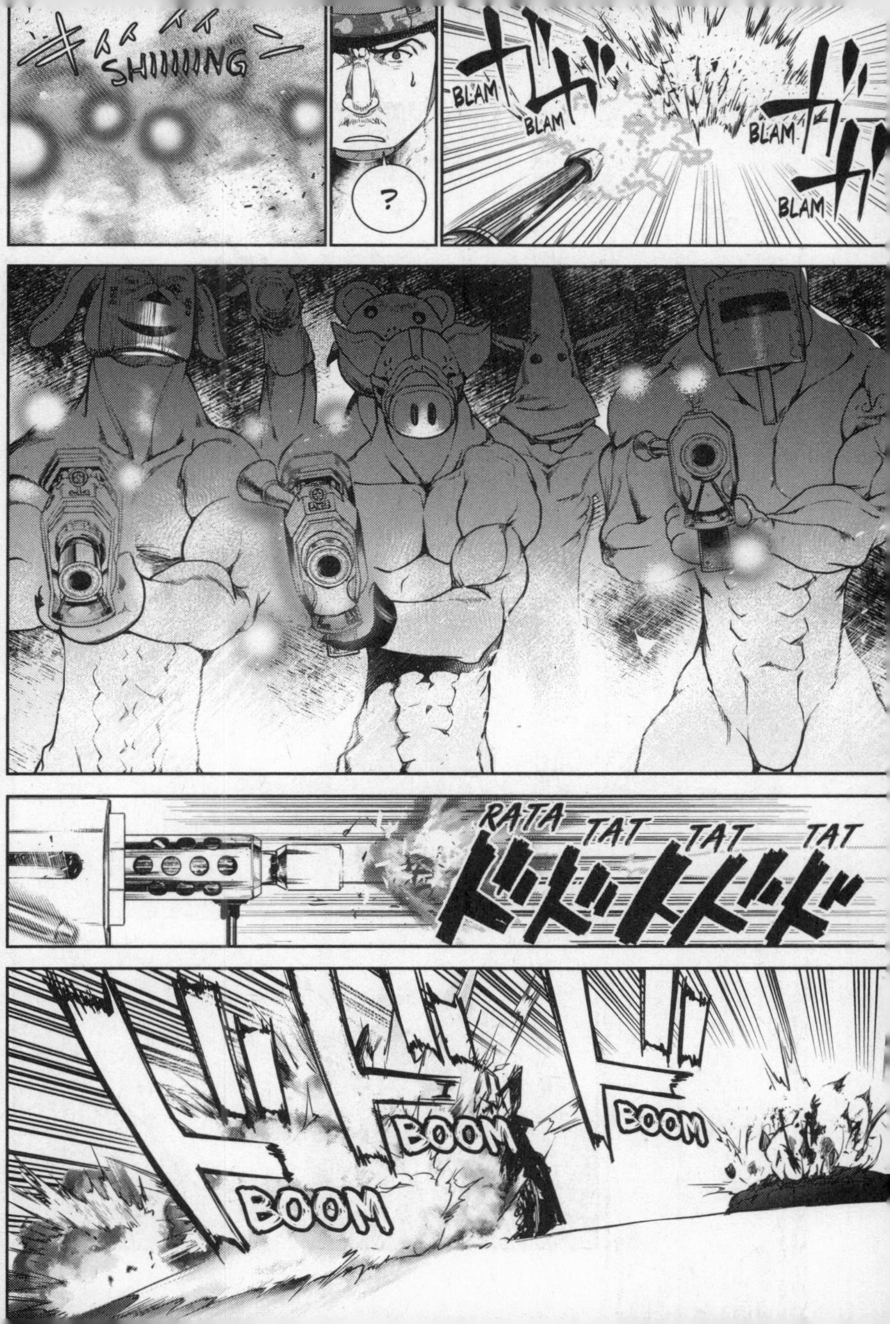
BLAM
BLAM
BLAM
BLAM
?
SHIIIIING
RATA TAT TAT TAT
BOOM
BOOM
BOOM

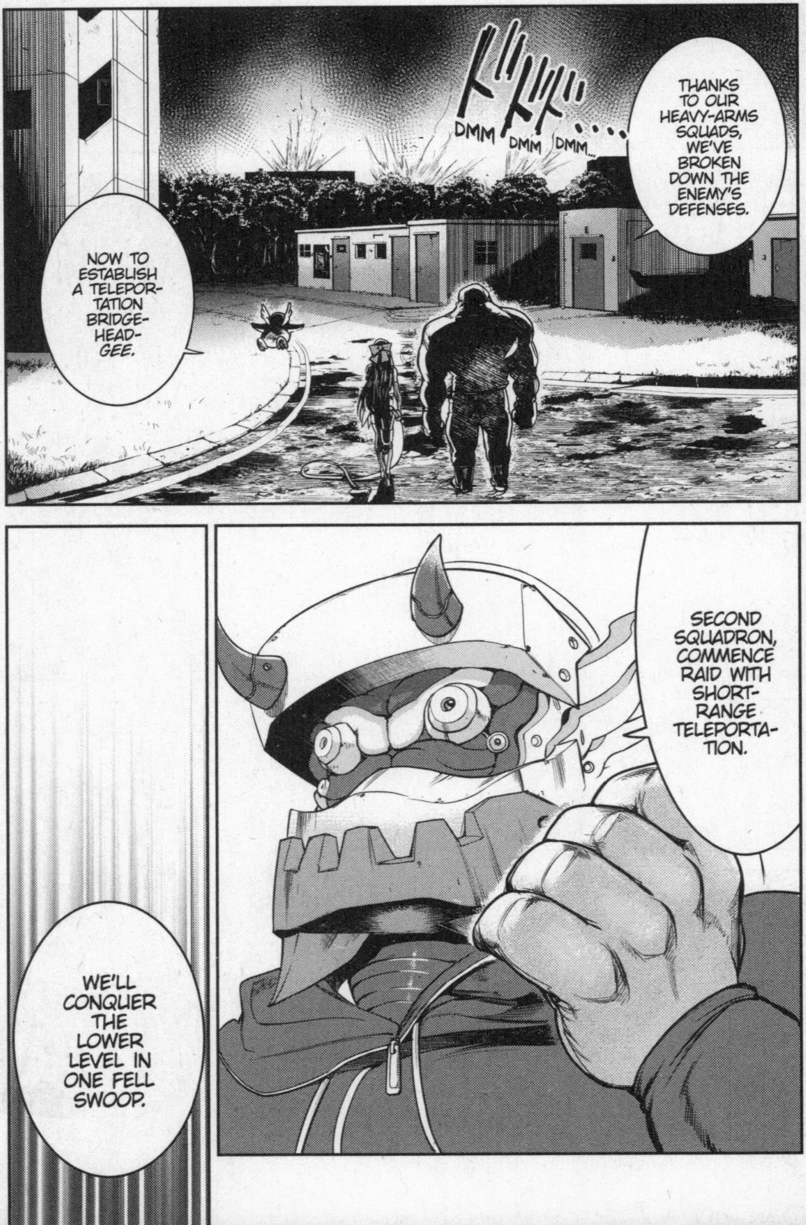
THANKS TO OUR HEAVY-ARMS SQUADS, WE'VE BROKEN DOWN THE ENEMY'S DEFENSES.
DMM DMM DMM...
NOW TO ESTABLISH A TELEPORTATION BRIDGEHEAD-GEE.
SECOND SQUADRON, COMMENCE RAID WITH SHORT-RANGE TELEPORTATION.
WE'LL CONQUER THE LOWER LEVEL IN ONE FELL SWOOP.

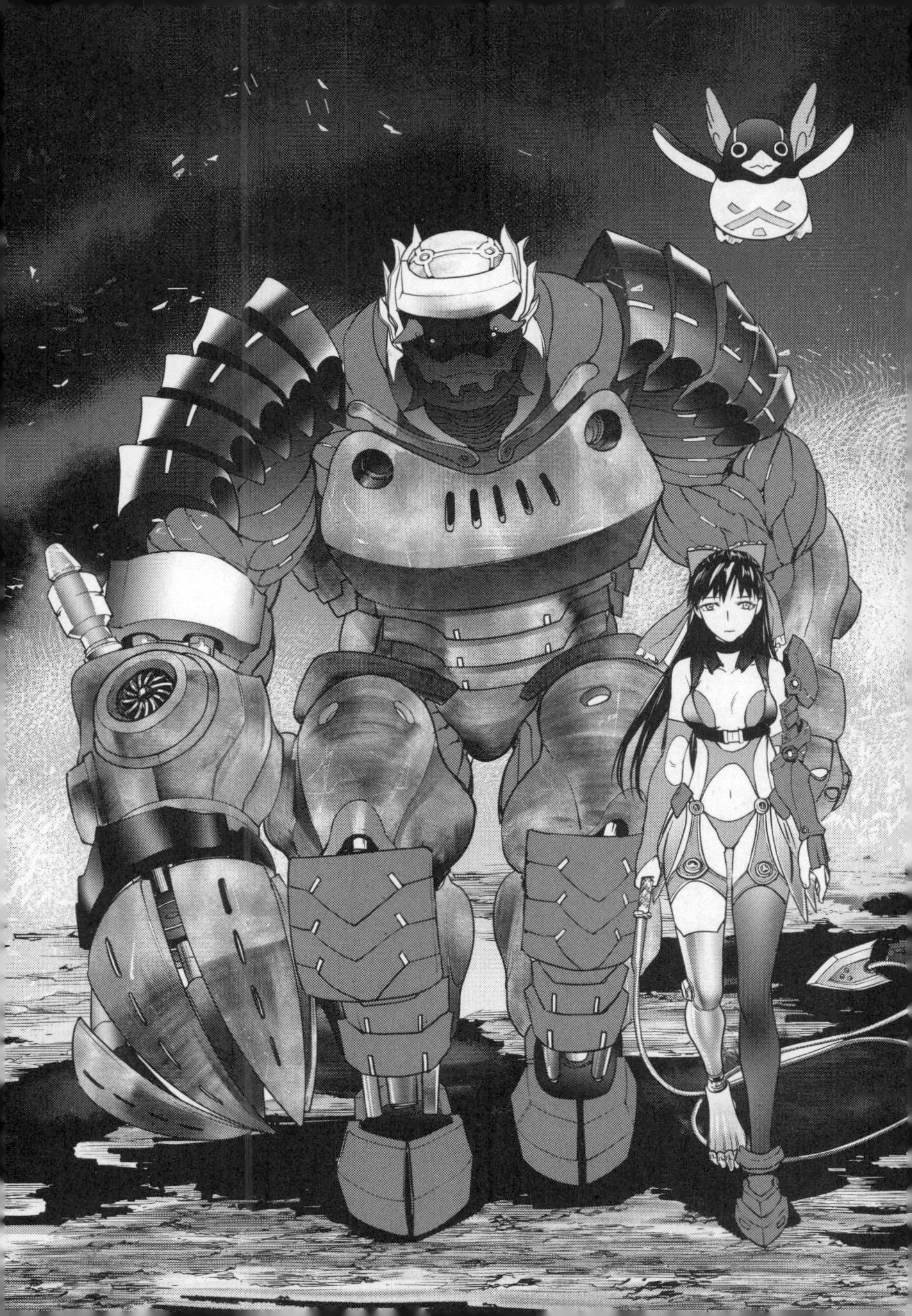

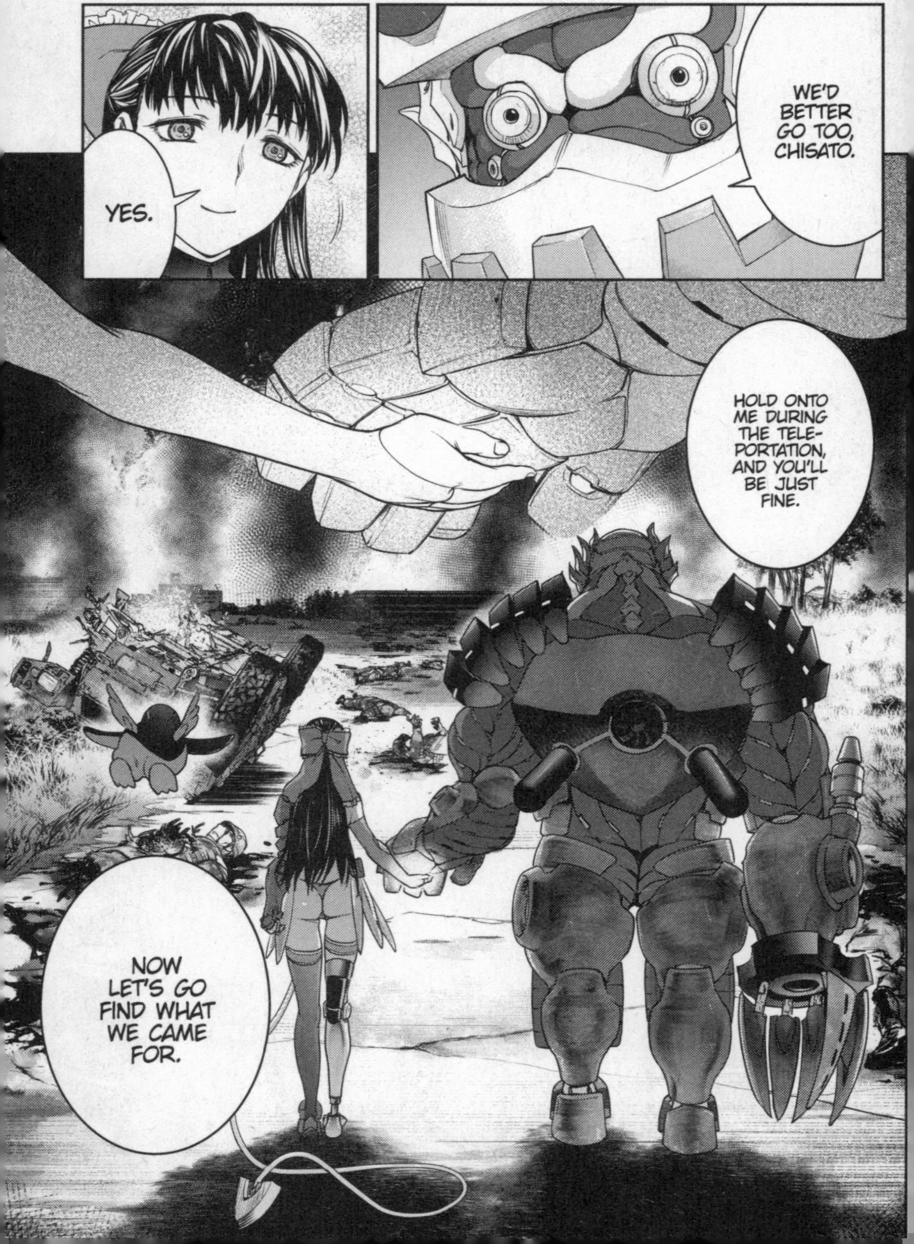
WE'D BETTER GO TOO, CHISATO.
YES.
HOLD ONTO ME DURING THE TELE-PORTATION, AND YOU'LL BE JUST FINE.
NOW LET'S GO FIND WHAT WE CAME FOR.

魔法少女特殊戦あすか

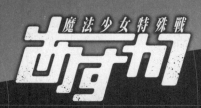

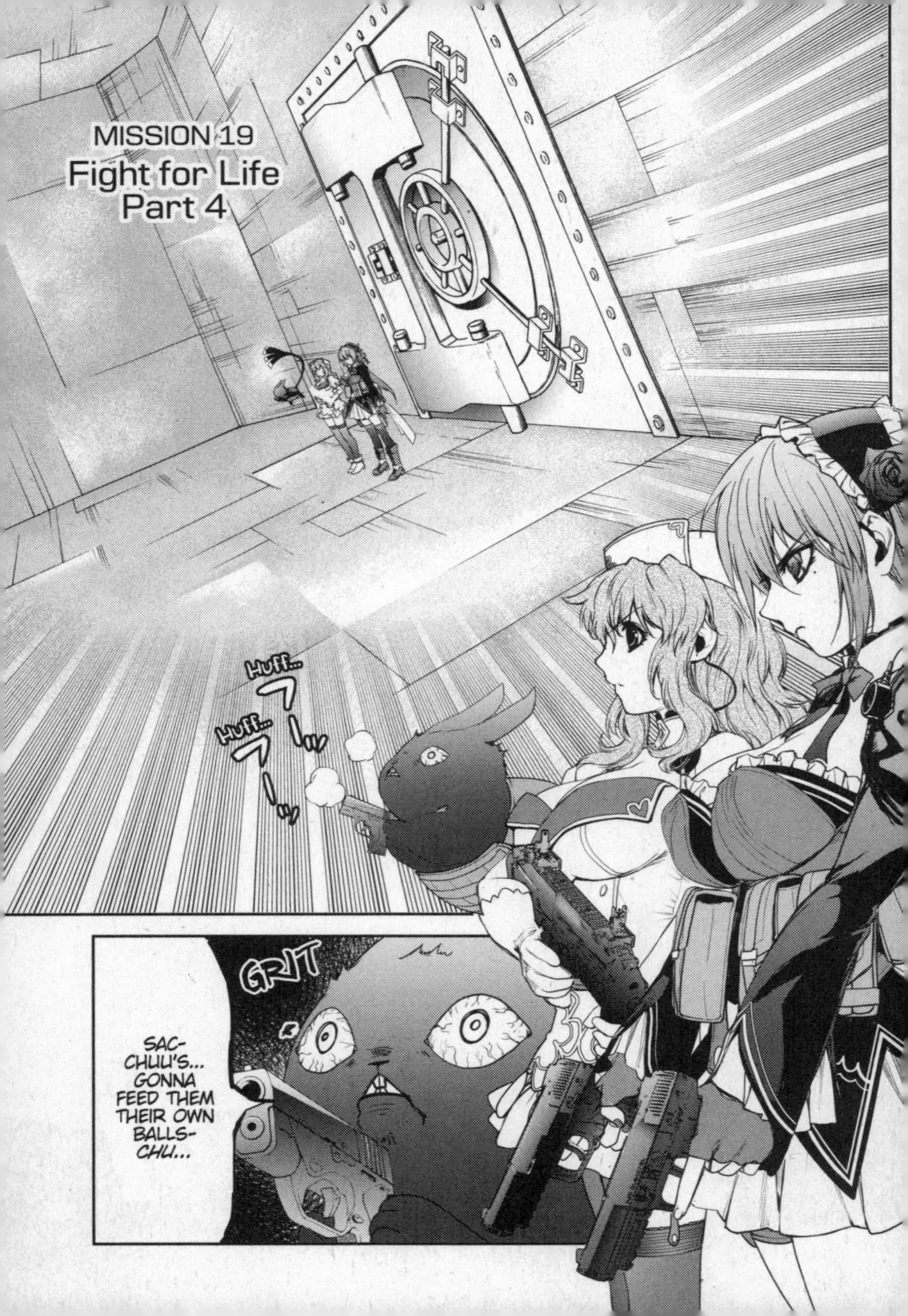
MISSION 19
Fight for Life
Part 4
Huff...
Huff...
GRIT
SAC-CHUU'S... GONNA FEED THEM THEIR OWN BALLS-CHU...

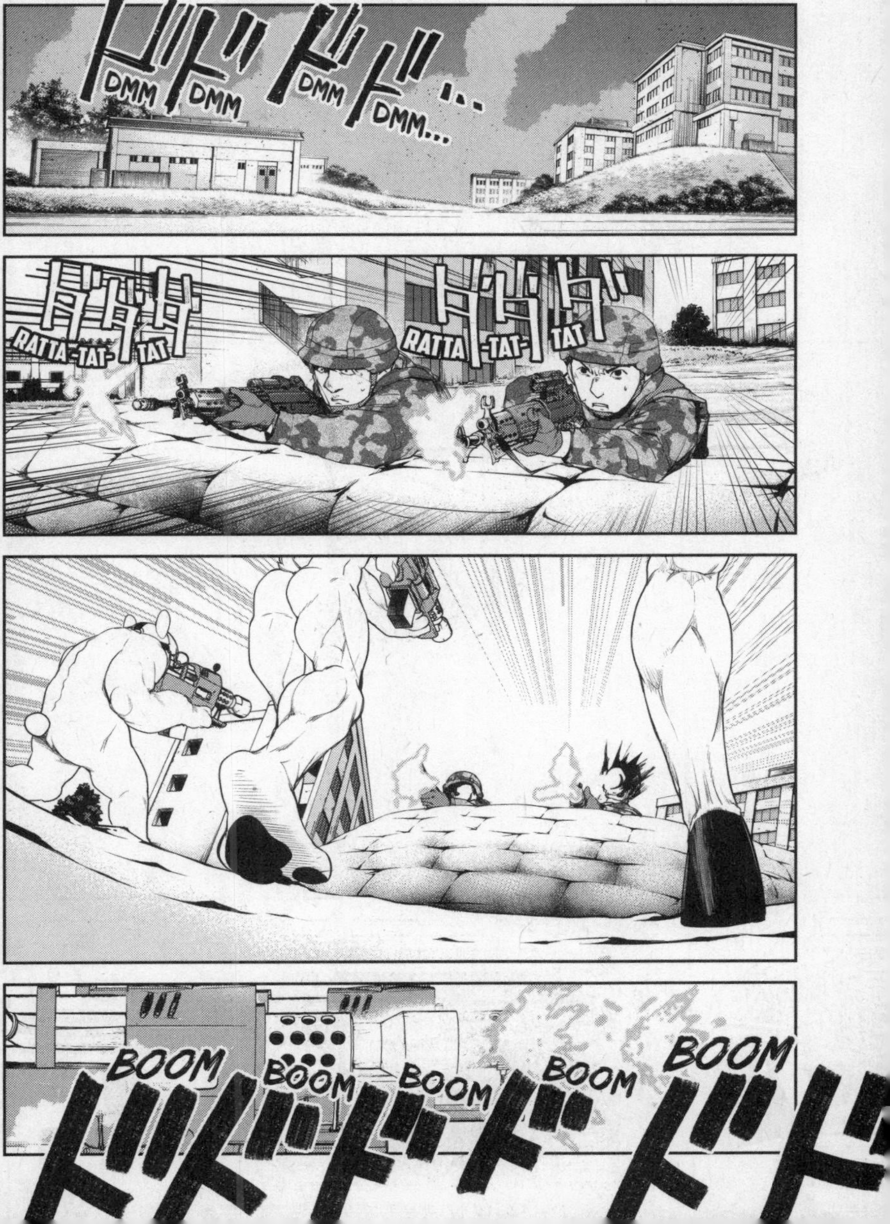
DMM DMM
DMM DMM...
RATTA-TAT-TAT
RATTA-TAT-TAT
BOOM BOOM BOOM BOOM BOOM

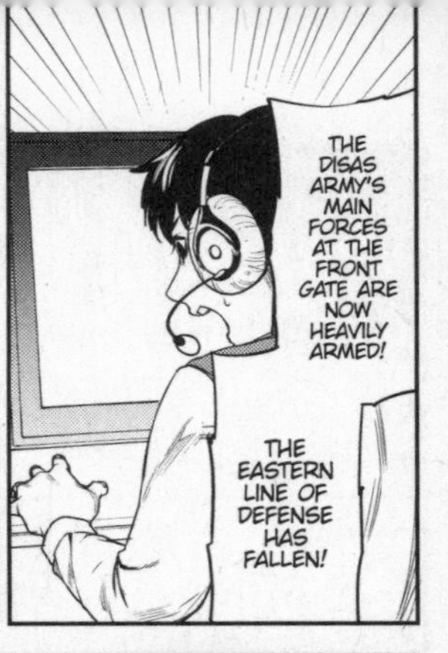
THE DISAS ARMY'S MAIN FORCES AT THE FRONT GATE ARE NOW HEAVILY ARMED!
THE EASTERN LINE OF DEFENSE HAS FALLEN!

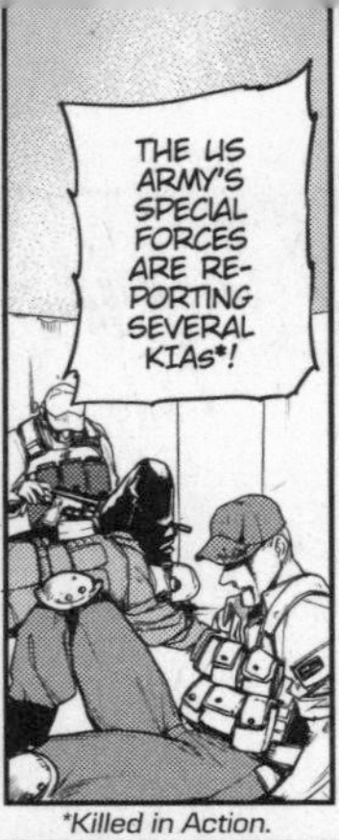
THE US ARMY'S SPECIAL FORCES ARE REPORTING SEVERAL KIAs*!

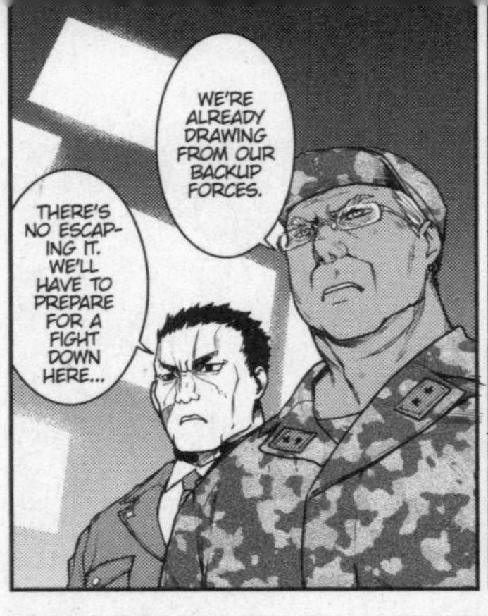
WE'RE ALREADY DRAWING FROM OUR BACKUP FORCES.
THERE'S NO ESCAPING IT. WE'LL HAVE TO PREPARE FOR A FIGHT DOWN HERE...

*Killed in Action.

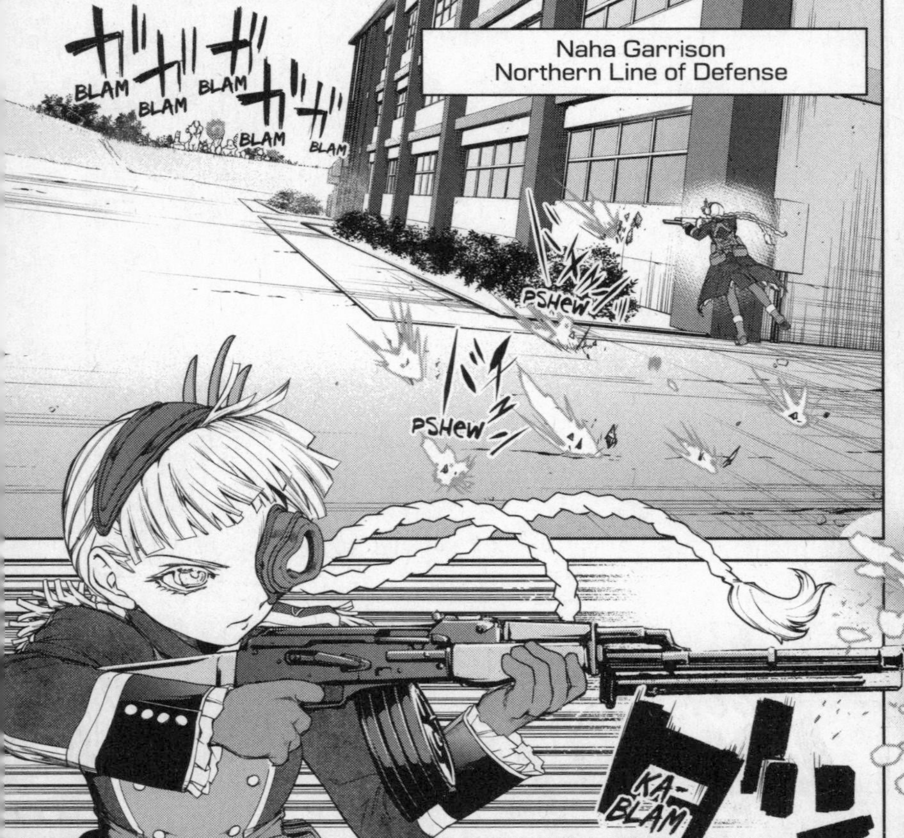
Naha Garrison
Northern Line of Defense
BLAM
BLAM
BLAM
BLAM
BLAM
PSHEW
PSHEW
KA-BLAM

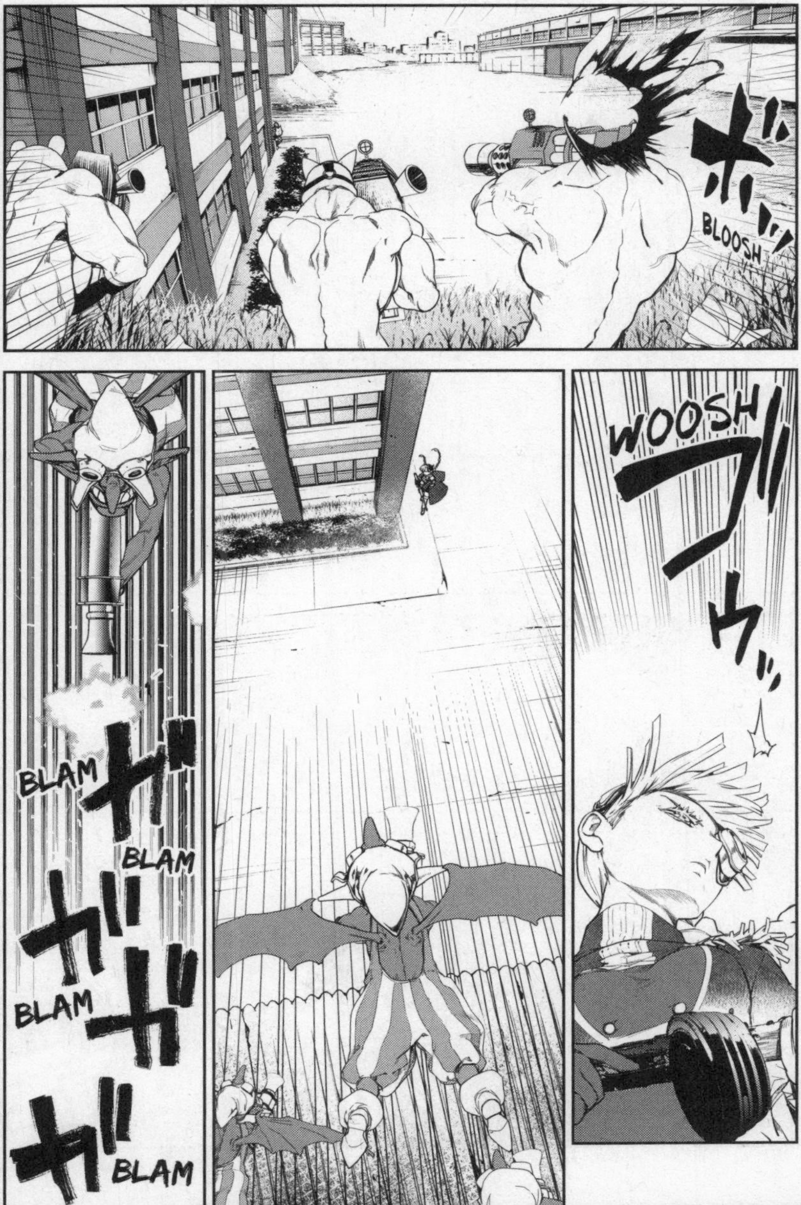

ボッ
BLOOSH
WOOSH
ブゥッ
BLAM
ガ
BLAM
ガ
BLAM
ガ
BLAM
ガ

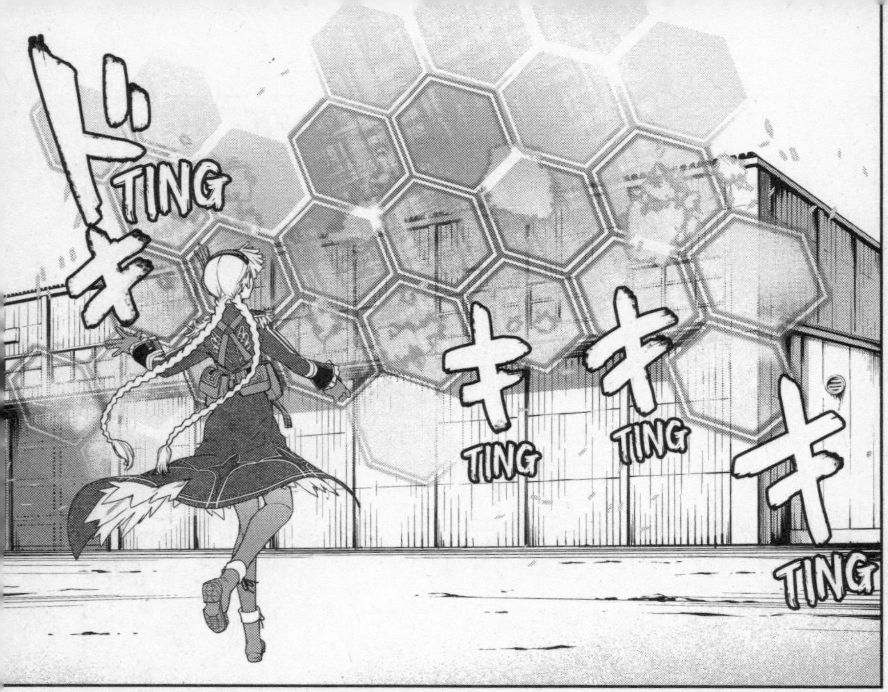
TING
TING
TING
TING
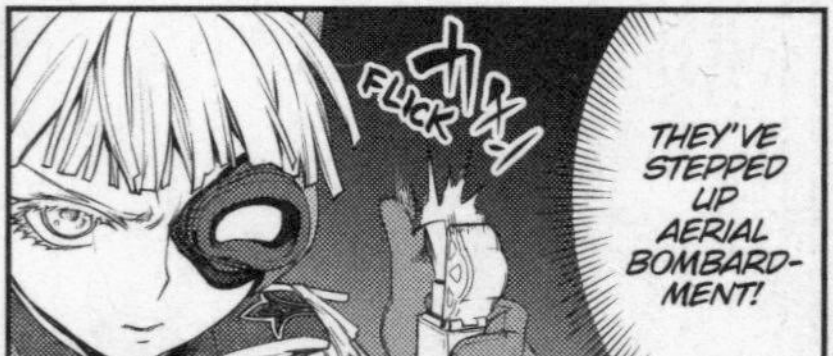
FLICK
THEY'VE STEPPED UP AERIAL BOMBARD-MENT!
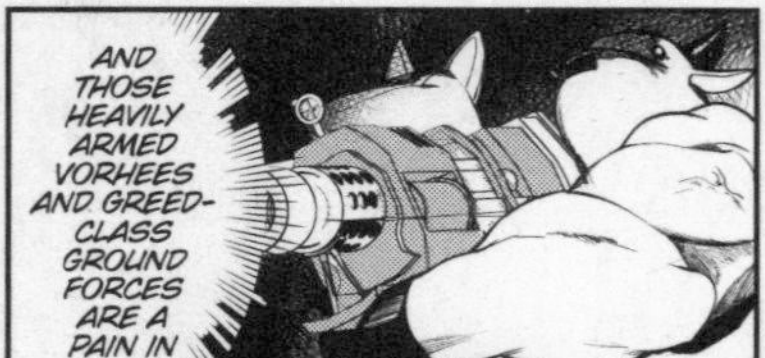
AND THOSE HEAVILY ARMED VORHEES AND GREED-CLASS GROUND FORCES ARE A PAIN IN MY ASS!
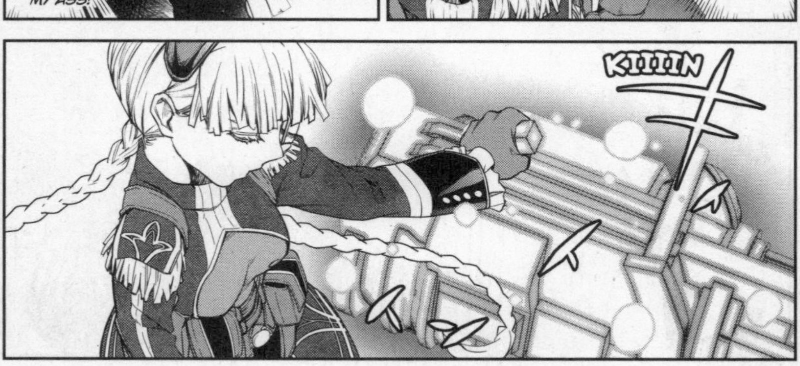
KIIIIN

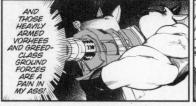

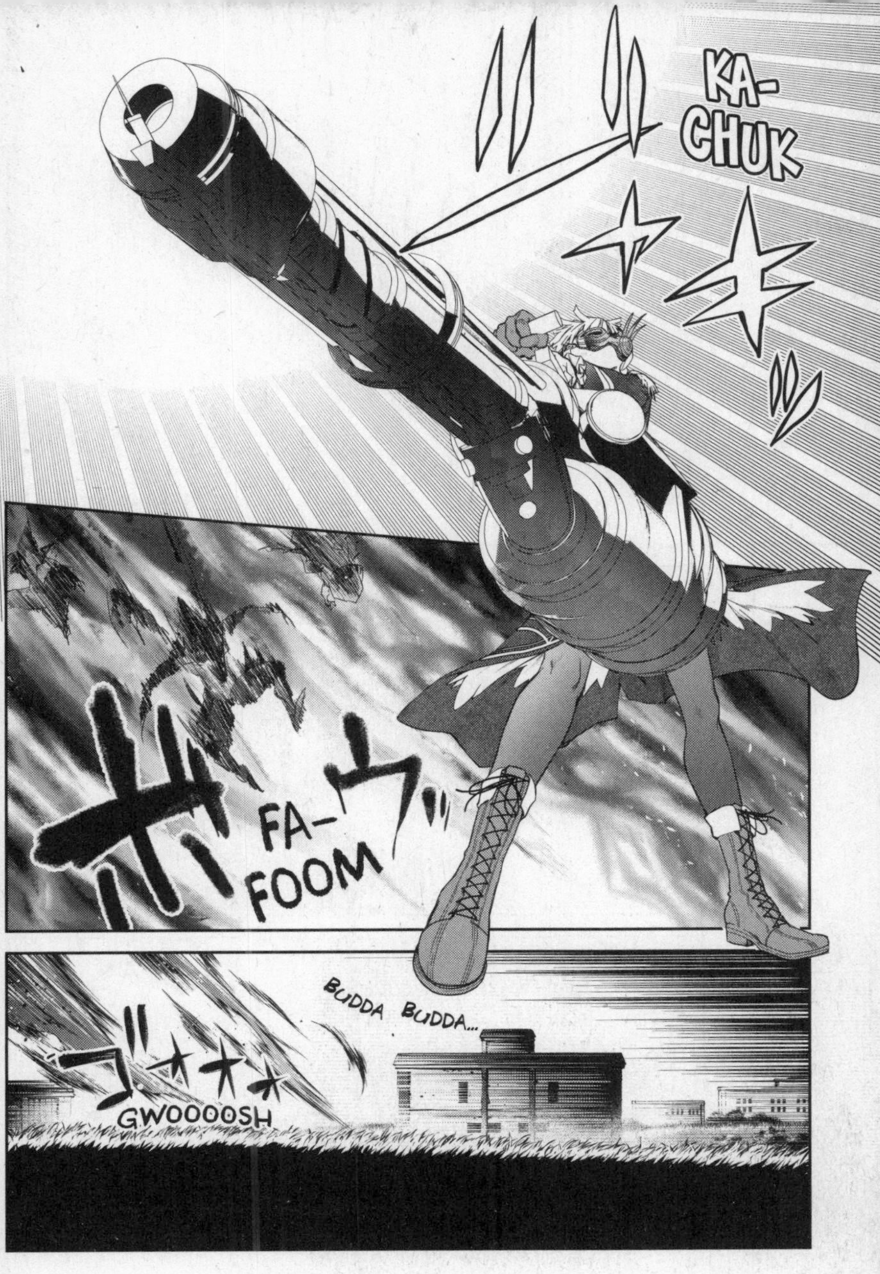
KA-
CHUK
FA-
FOOM
BUDDA BUDDA...
GWOOOOSH

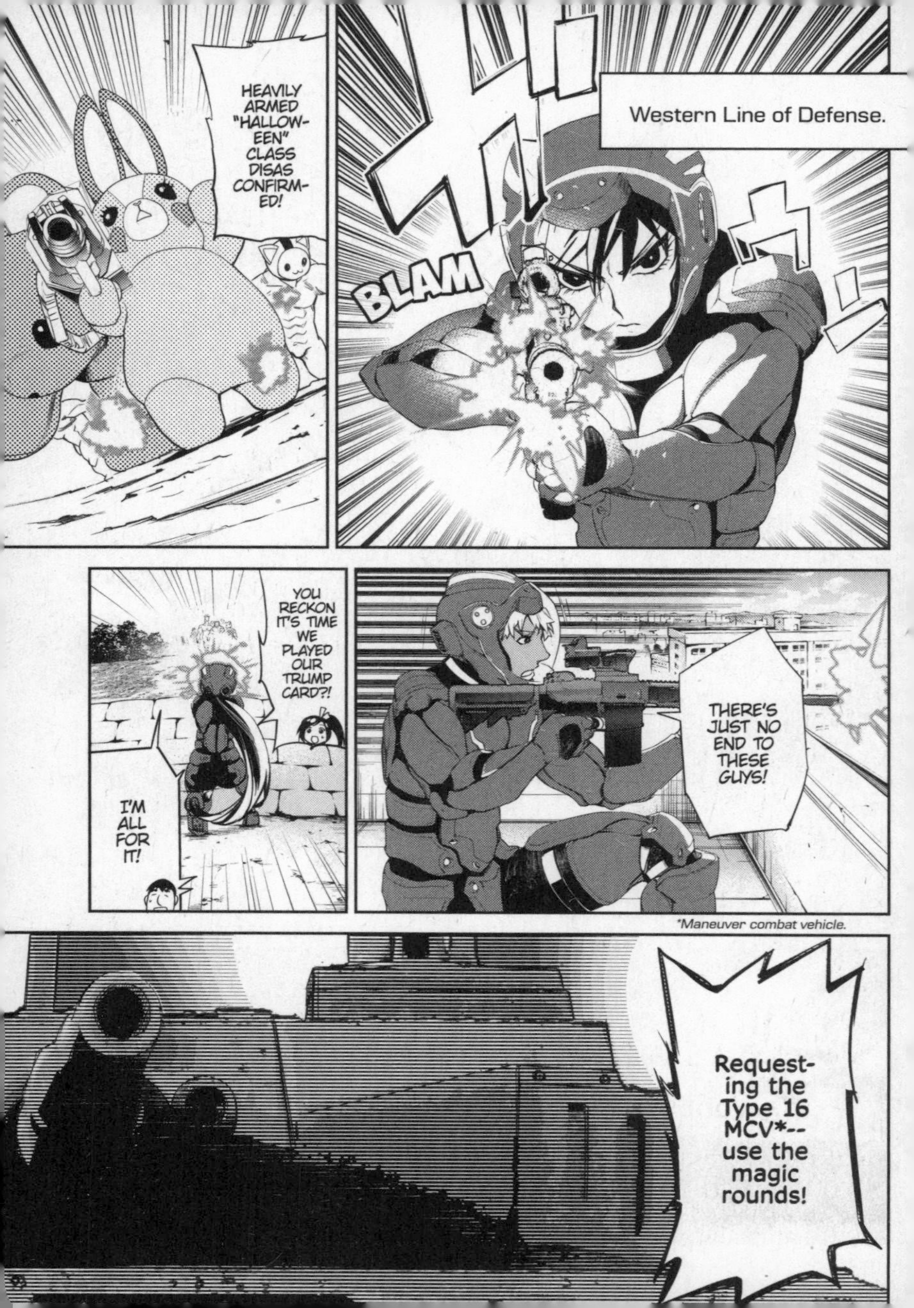
Western Line of Defense.
BLAM
HEAVILY ARMED "HALLOWEEN" CLASS DISAS CONFIRMED!
THERE'S JUST NO END TO THESE GUYS!
YOU RECKON IT'S TIME WE PLAYED OUR TRUMP CARD?!
I'M ALL FOR IT!
Requesting the Type 16 MCV*-- use the magic rounds!

*Maneuver combat vehicle.

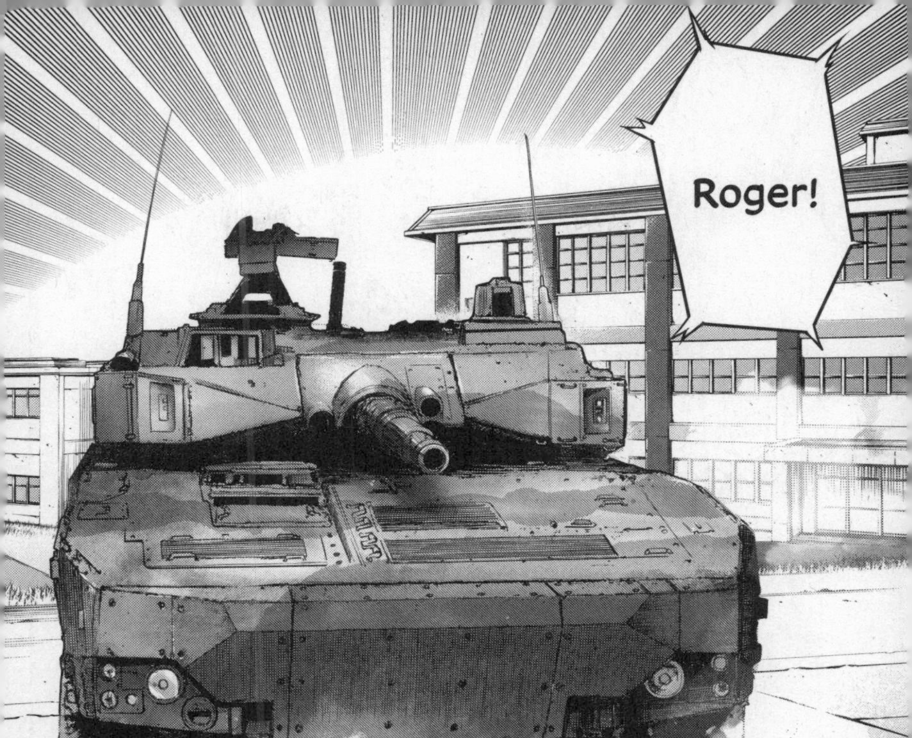
Roger!
トッドッドドド
RUMMMMBLE
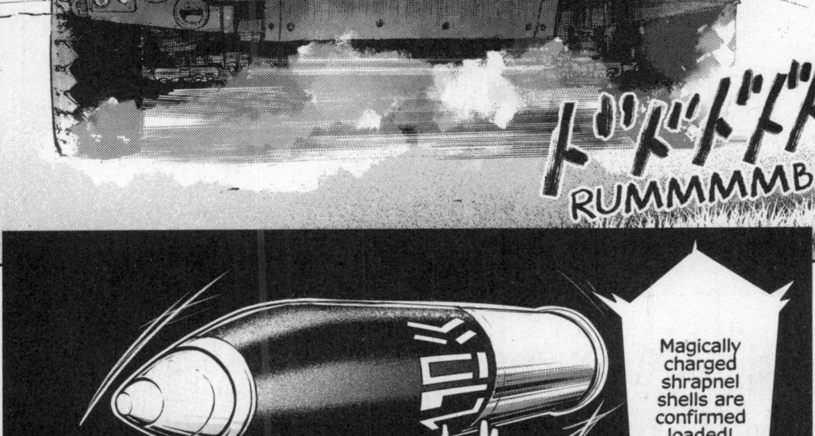
Magically charged shrapnel shells are confirmed loaded!
ガッコン
KA-CLUNK

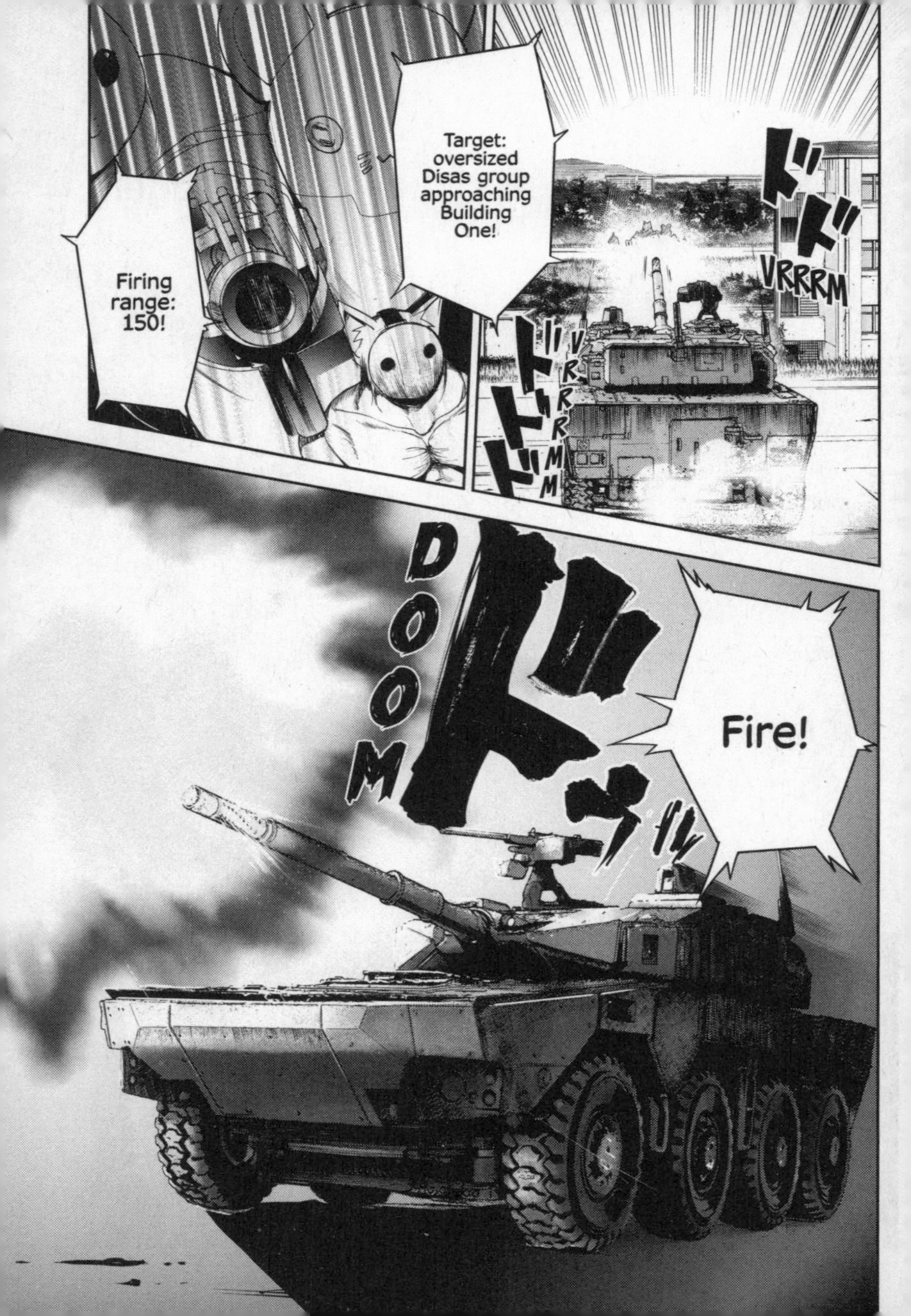
ドドド
VRRRM
ドドドド
VRRRMM
Target: oversized Disas group approaching Building One!
Firing range: 150!
Fire!
ドッ
DOOOM

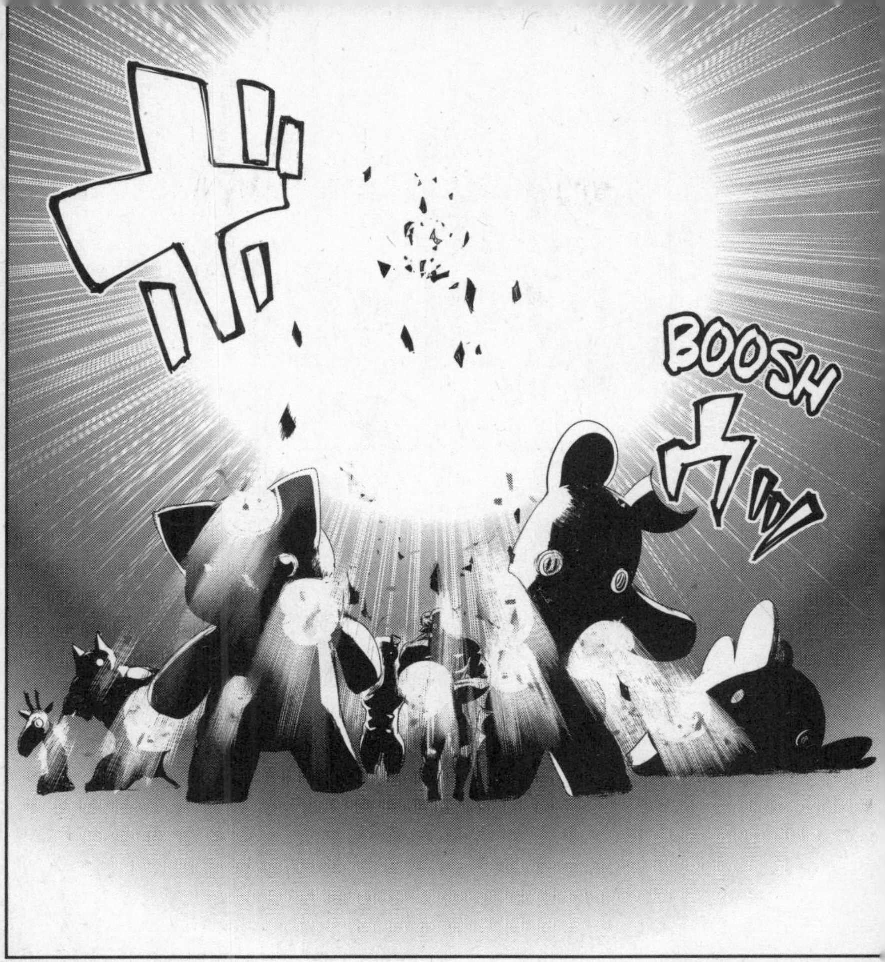
BOOSH
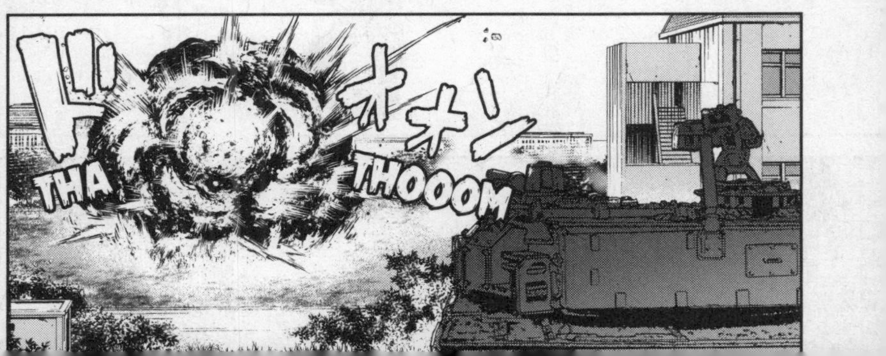
THA
THOOOM

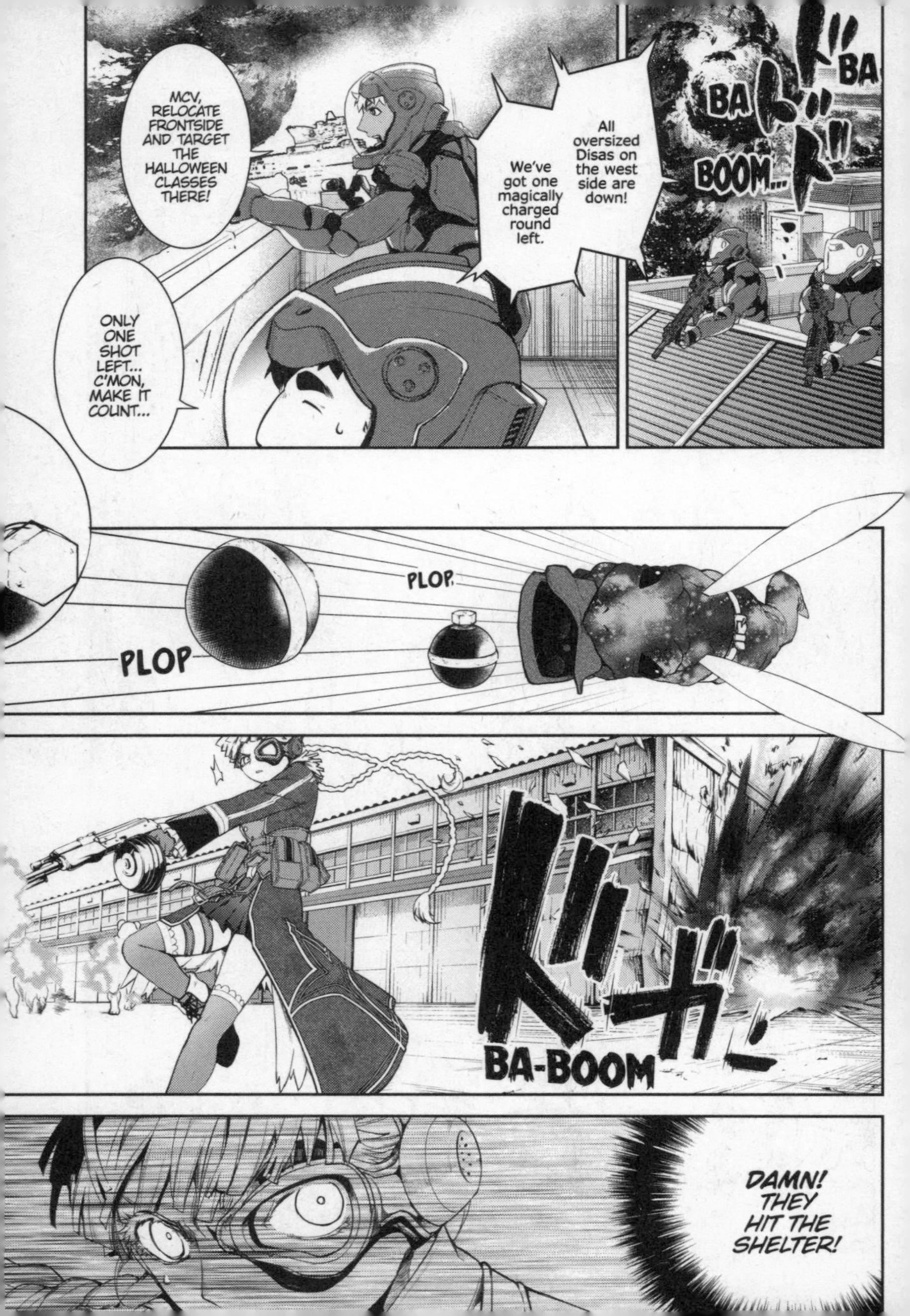

BA BA BOOM...
All oversized Disas on the west side are down!
We've got one magically charged round left.
MCV, RELOCATE FRONTSIDE AND TARGET THE HALLOWEEN CLASSES THERE!
ONLY ONE SHOT LEFT... C'MON, MAKE IT COUNT...
PLOP.
PLOP
BA-BOOM
DAMN! THEY HIT THE SHELTER!

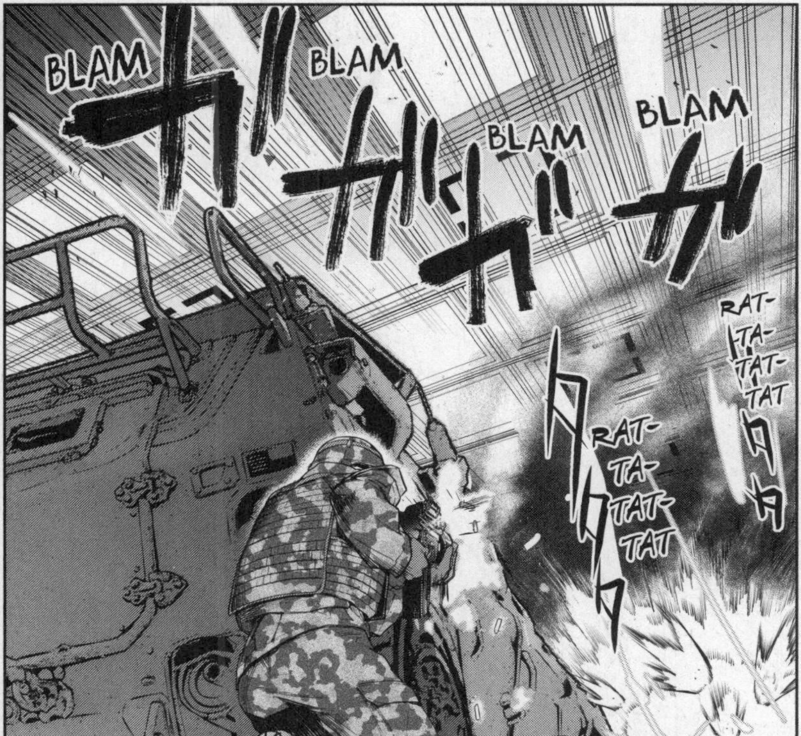
BLAM
BLAM
BLAM
BLAM
RAT-TA-TAT-TAT
RAT-TA-TAT-TAT
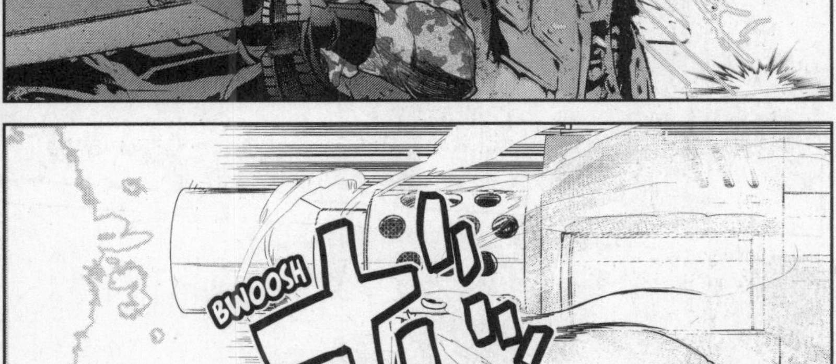
BWOOSH

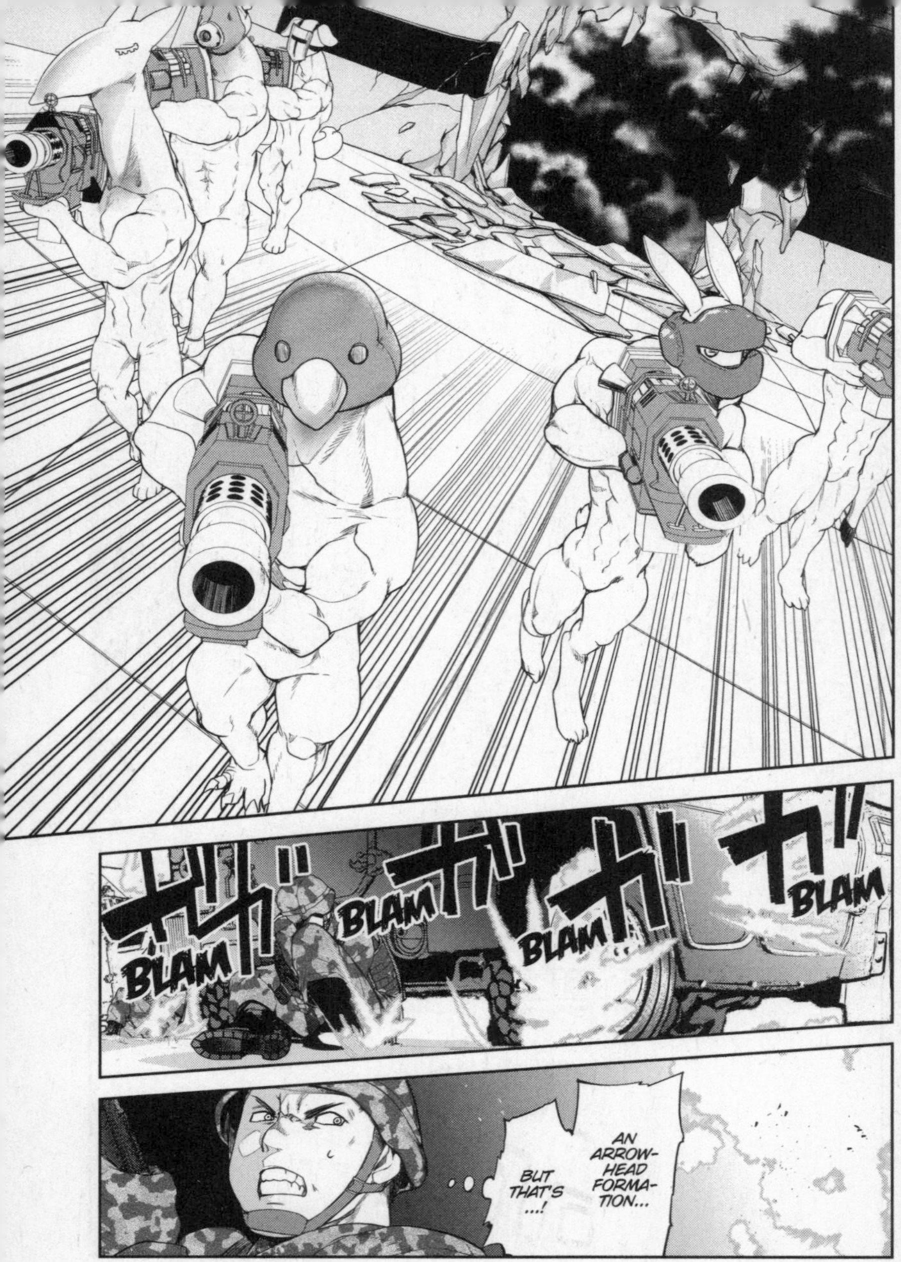

BLAM
BLAM
BLAM
BLAM
AN ARROW-HEAD FORMA-TION...
BUT THAT'S ...!

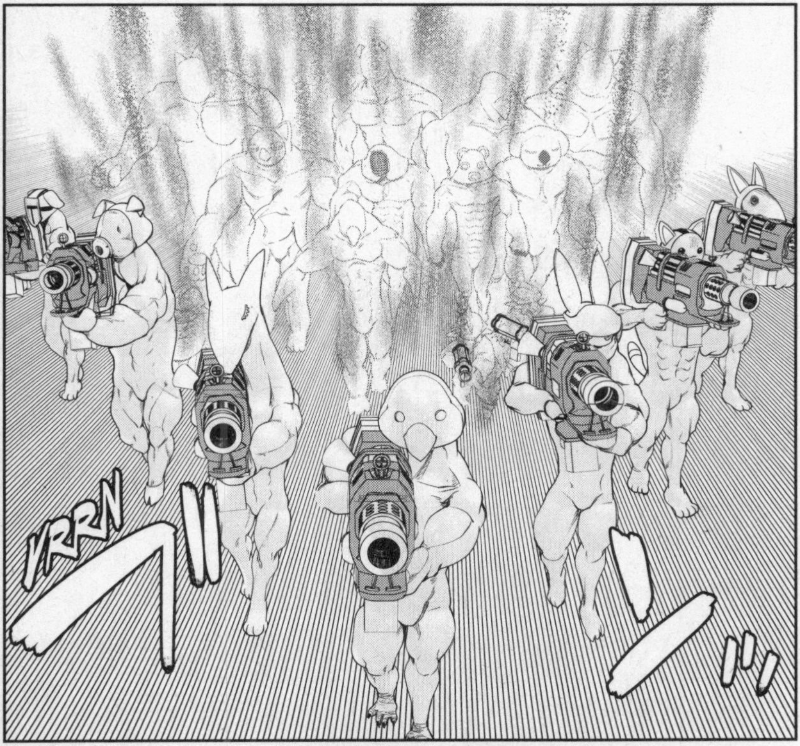
VRRN

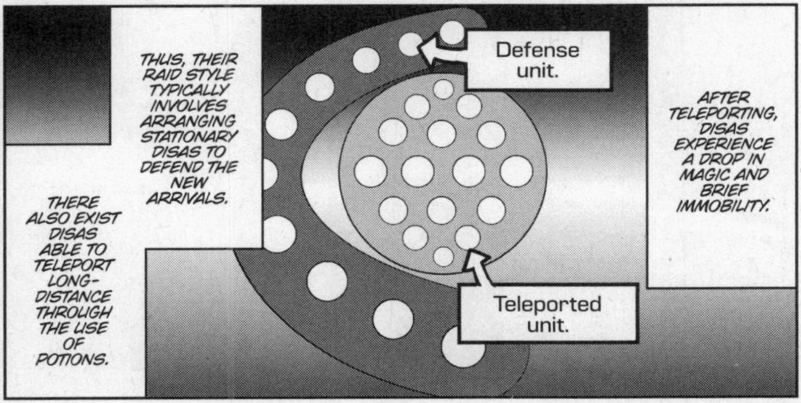
AFTER TELEPORTING, DISAS EXPERIENCE A DROP IN MAGIC AND BRIEF IMMOBILITY.
THUS, THEIR RAID STYLE TYPICALLY INVOLVES ARRANGING STATIONARY DISAS TO DEFEND THE NEW ARRIVALS.
Defense unit.
Teleported unit.
THERE ALSO EXIST DISAS ABLE TO TELEPORT LONG-DISTANCE THROUGH THE USE OF POTIONS.

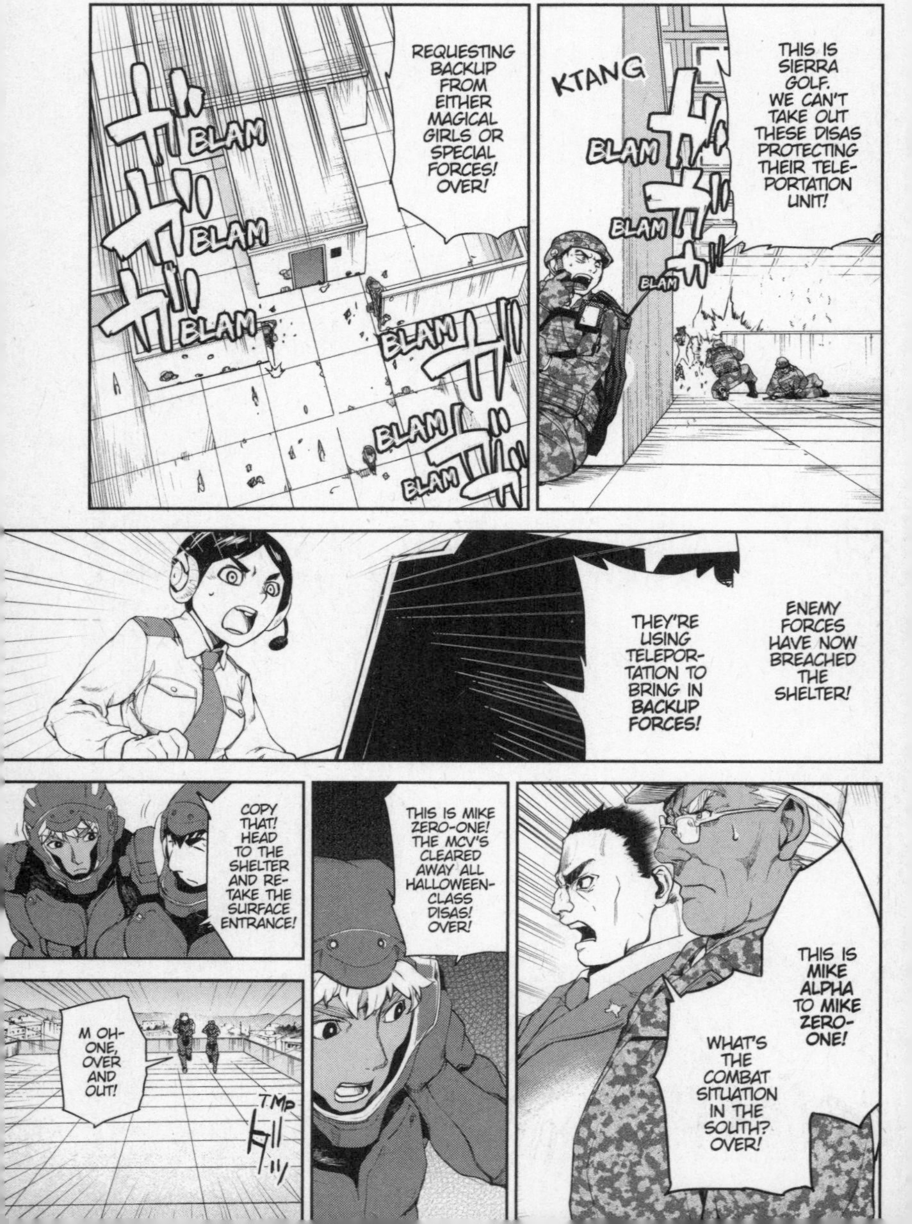
KTANG
THIS IS SIERRA GOLF. WE CAN'T TAKE OUT THESE DISAS PROTECTING THEIR TELE-PORTATION UNIT!
BLAM
BLAM
BLAM
REQUESTING BACKUP FROM EITHER MAGICAL GIRLS OR SPECIAL FORCES! OVER!
BLAM
BLAM
BLAM
BLAM
BLAM
BLAM
ENEMY FORCES HAVE NOW BREACHED THE SHELTER!
THEY'RE USING TELEPOR-TATION TO BRING IN BACKUP FORCES!
THIS IS MIKE ALPHA TO MIKE ZERO-ONE!
WHAT'S THE COMBAT SITUATION IN THE SOUTH? OVER!
THIS IS MIKE ZERO-ONE! THE MCV'S CLEARED AWAY ALL HALLOWEEN-CLASS DISAS! OVER!
COPY THAT! HEAD TO THE SHELTER AND RE-TAKE THE SURFACE ENTRANCE!
M OH-ONE, OVER AND OUT!
TMP

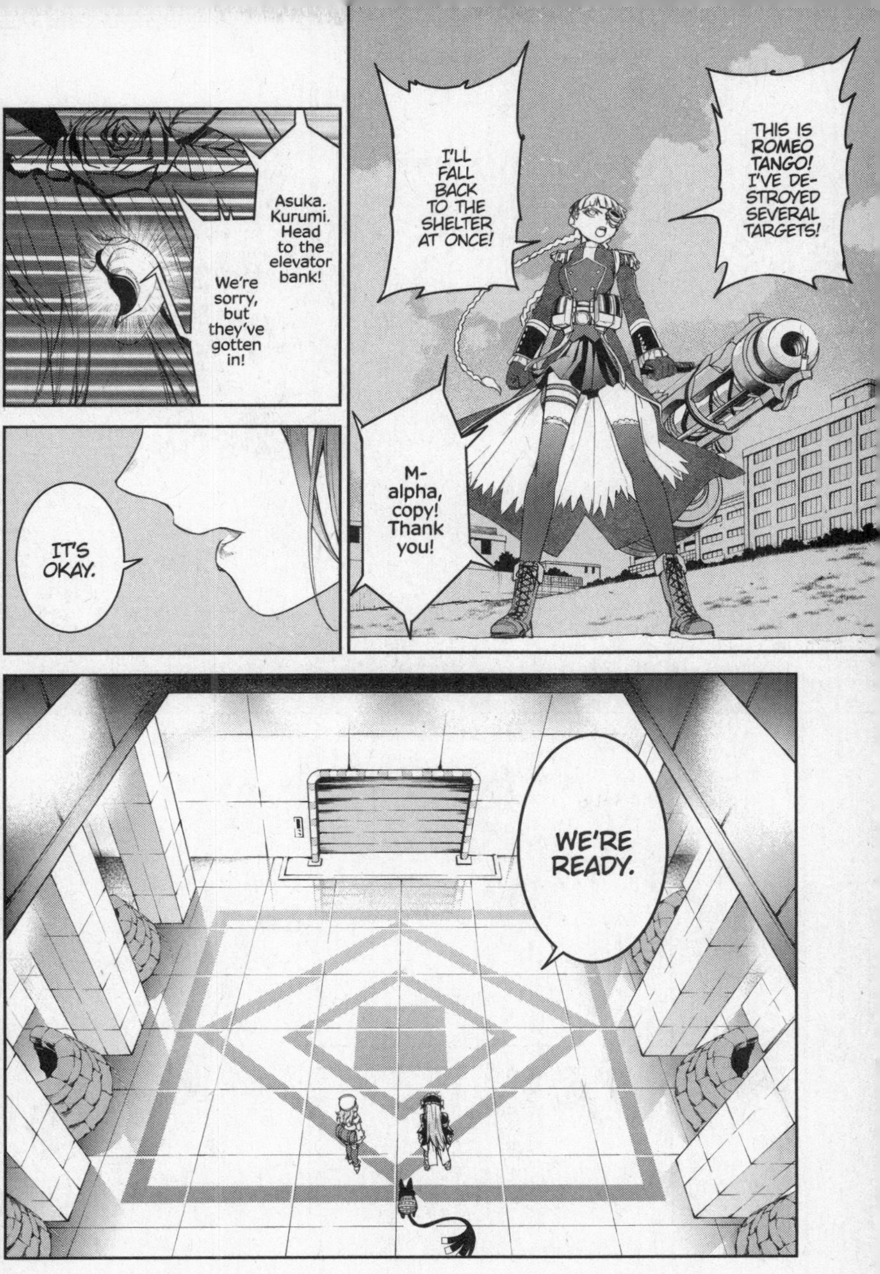
THIS IS ROMEO TANGO! I'VE DESTROYED SEVERAL TARGETS!
I'LL FALL BACK TO THE SHELTER AT ONCE!
M-alpha, copy! Thank you!
Asuka. Kurumi. Head to the elevator bank!
We're sorry, but they've gotten in!
IT'S OKAY.
WE'RE READY.

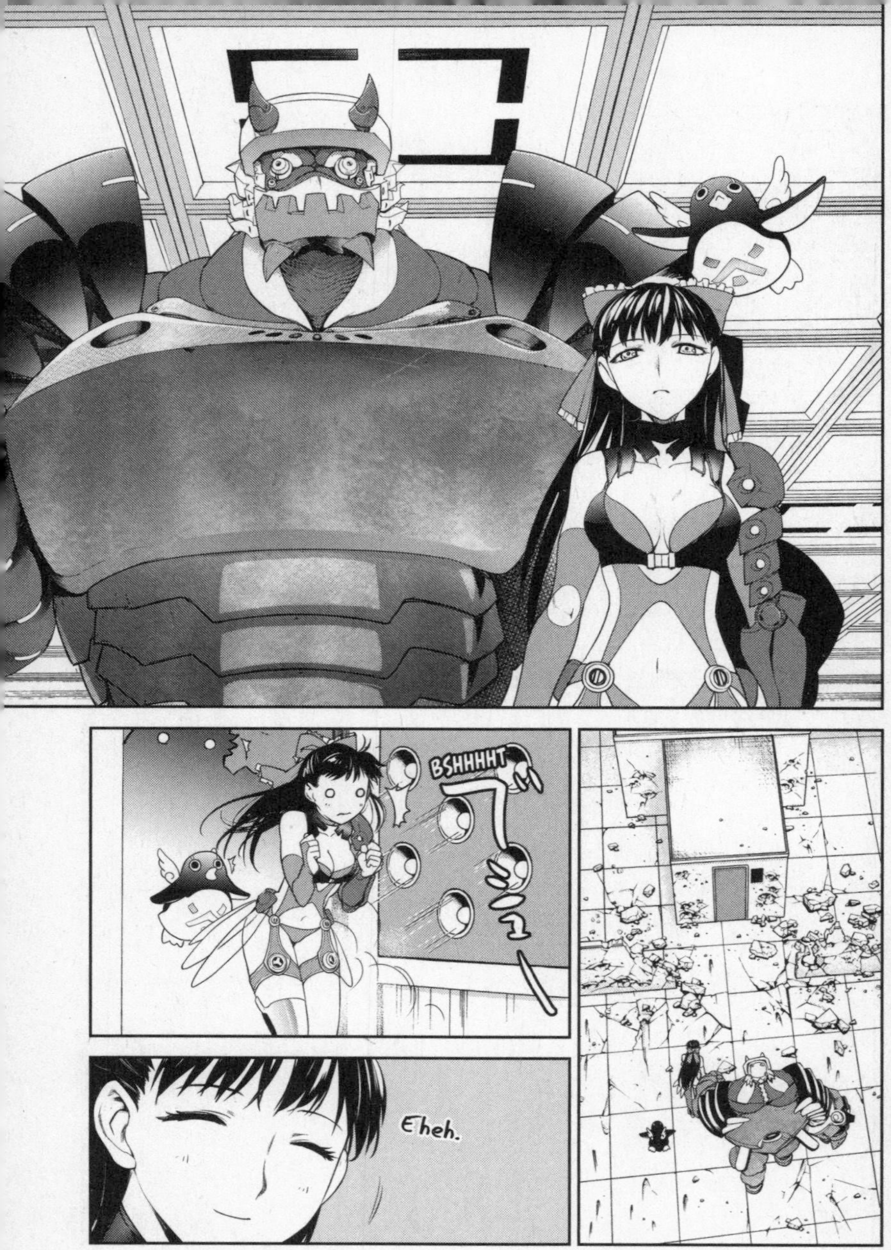
BSHHHHT
Eheh.

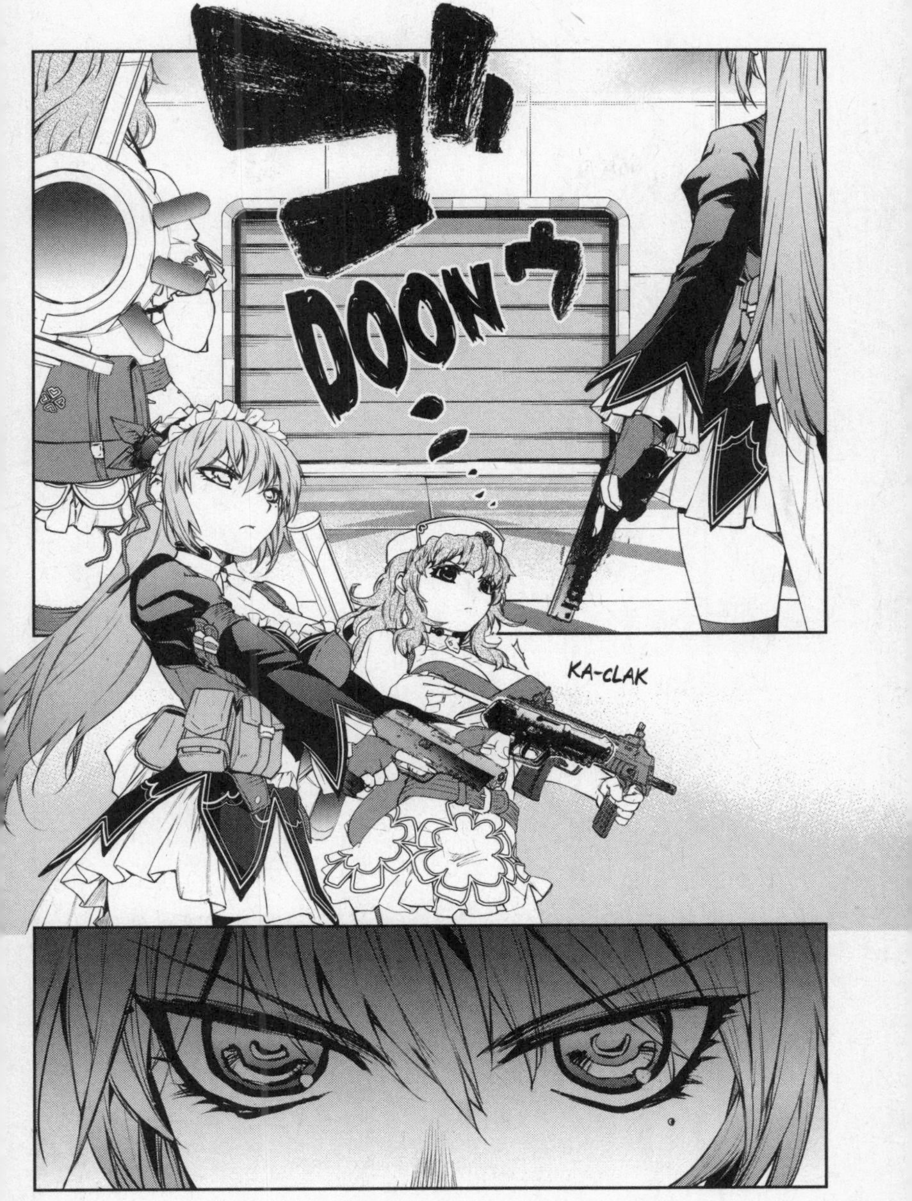
DOON
KA-CLAK

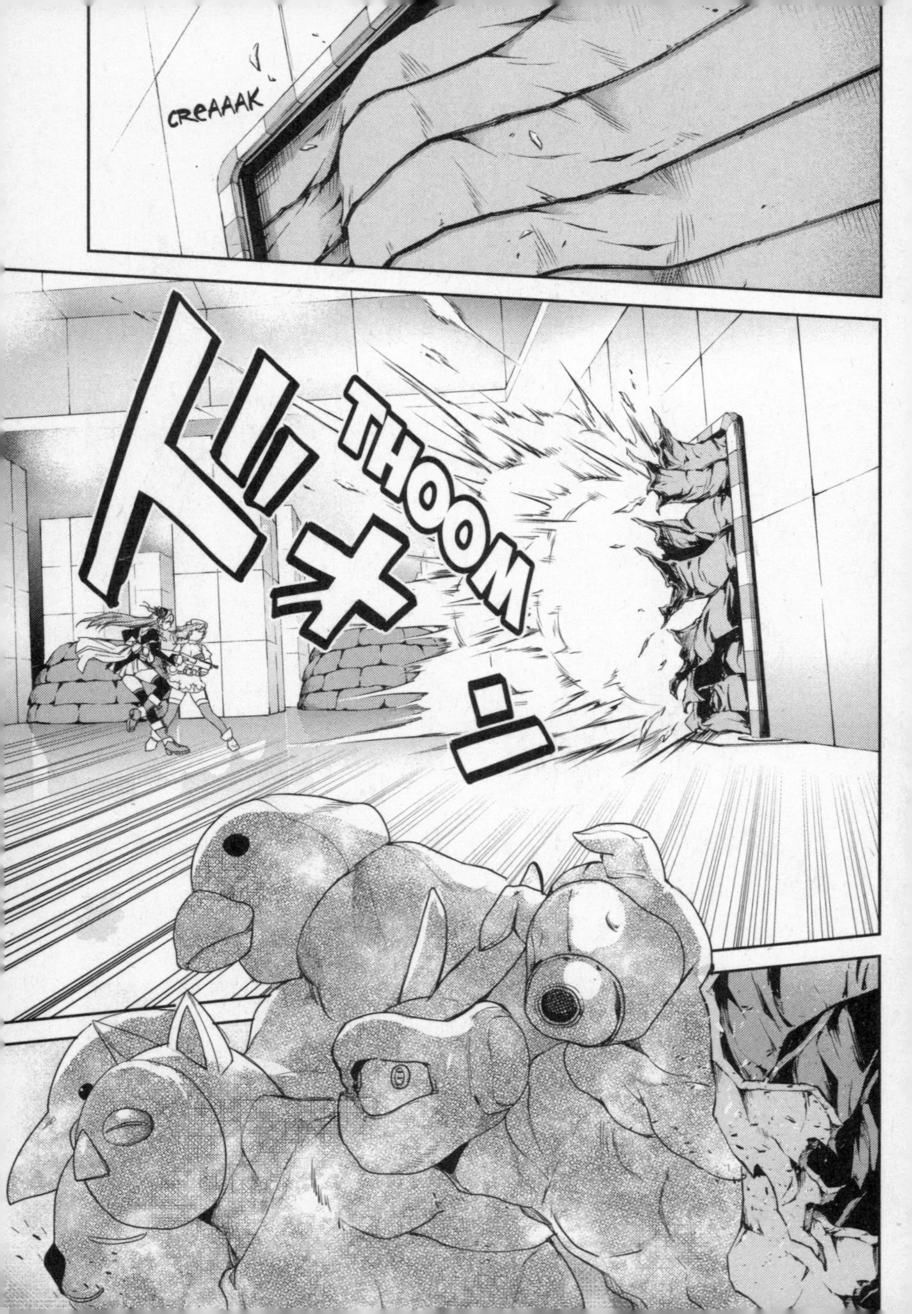
CREAAAK
THOOM

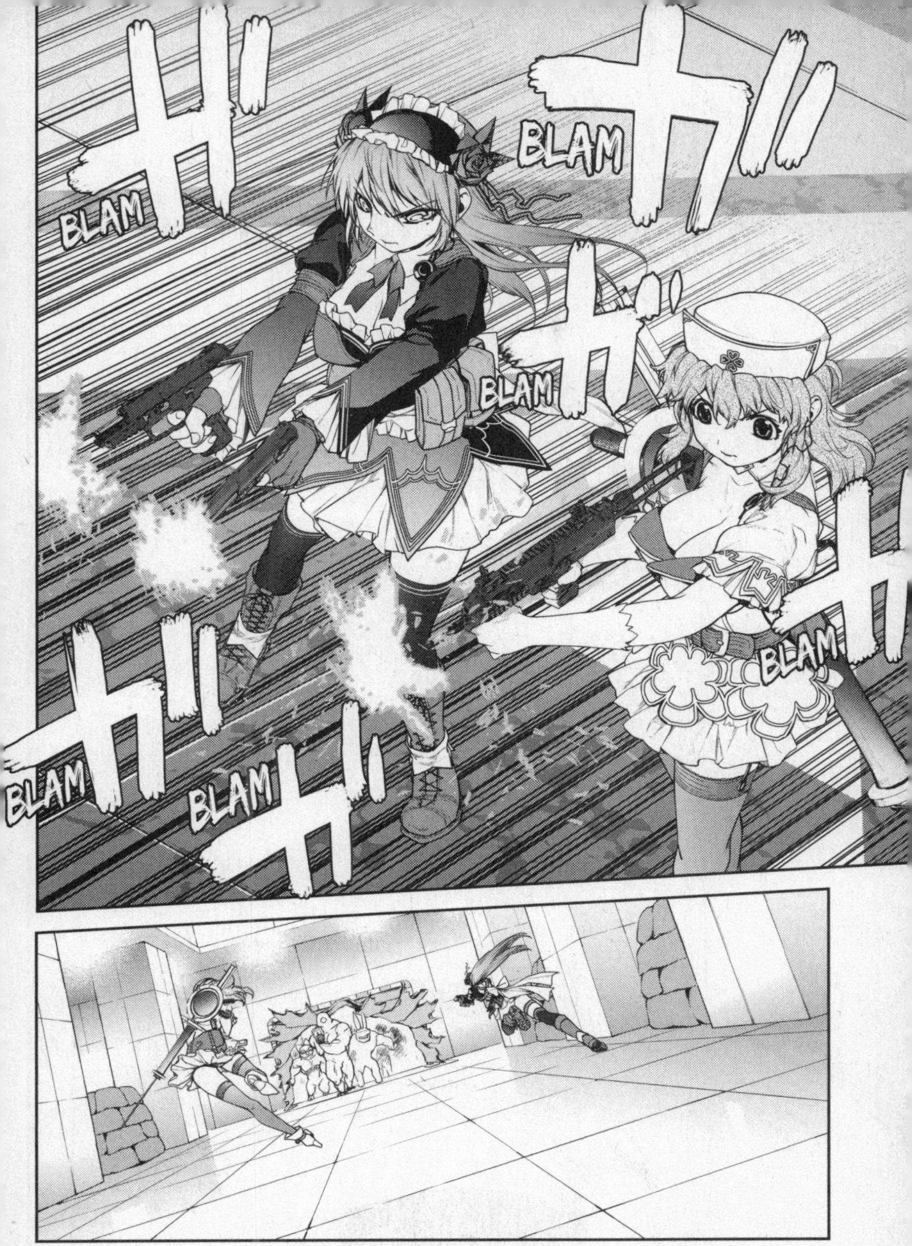
BLAM
BLAM
BLAM
BLAM
BLAM
BLAM

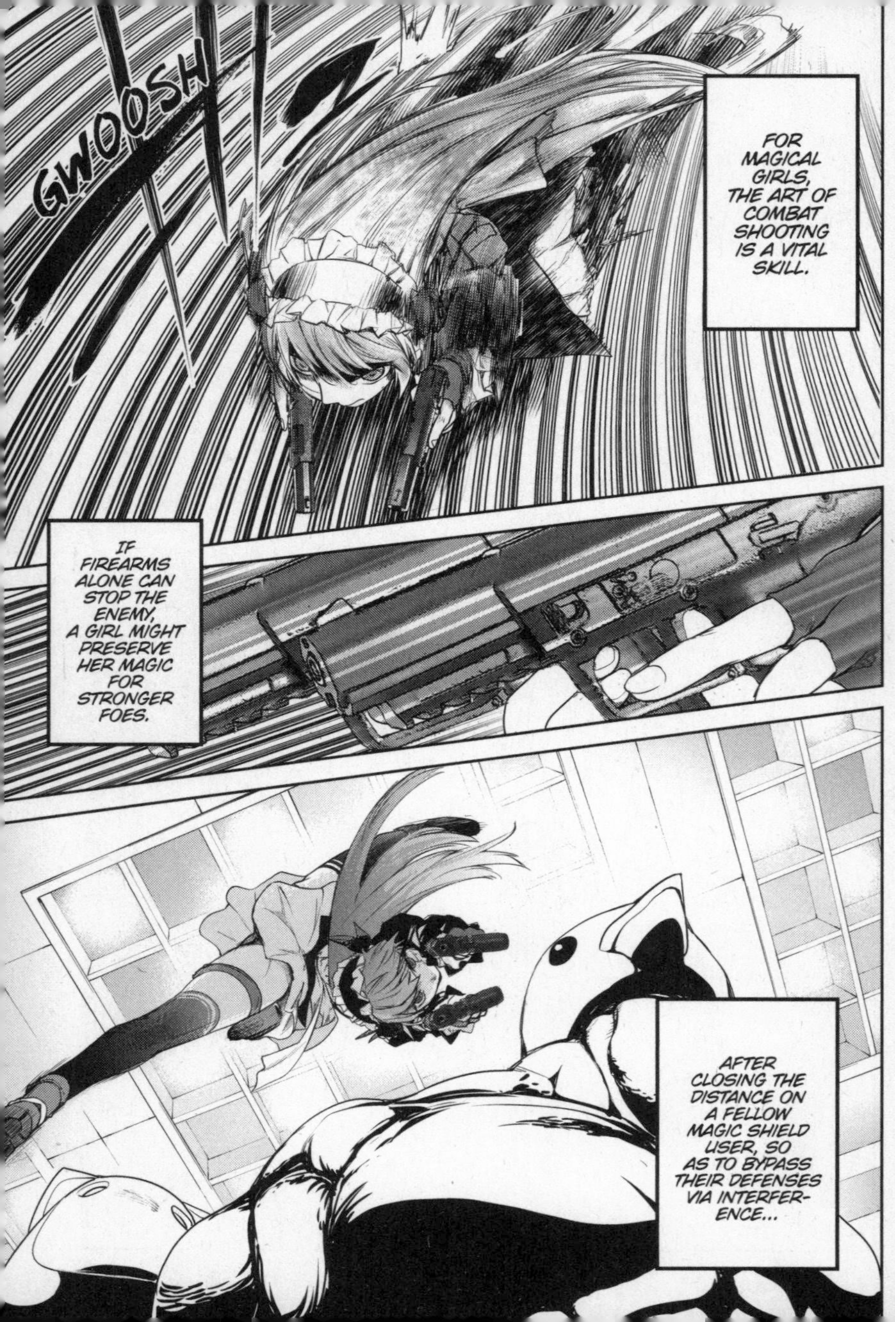
GWOOSH
FOR MAGICAL GIRLS, THE ART OF COMBAT SHOOTING IS A VITAL SKILL.
IF FIREARMS ALONE CAN STOP THE ENEMY, A GIRL MIGHT PRESERVE HER MAGIC FOR STRONGER FOES.
AFTER CLOSING THE DISTANCE ON A FELLOW MAGIC SHIELD USER, SO AS TO BYPASS THEIR DEFENSES VIA INTERFER-ENCE...

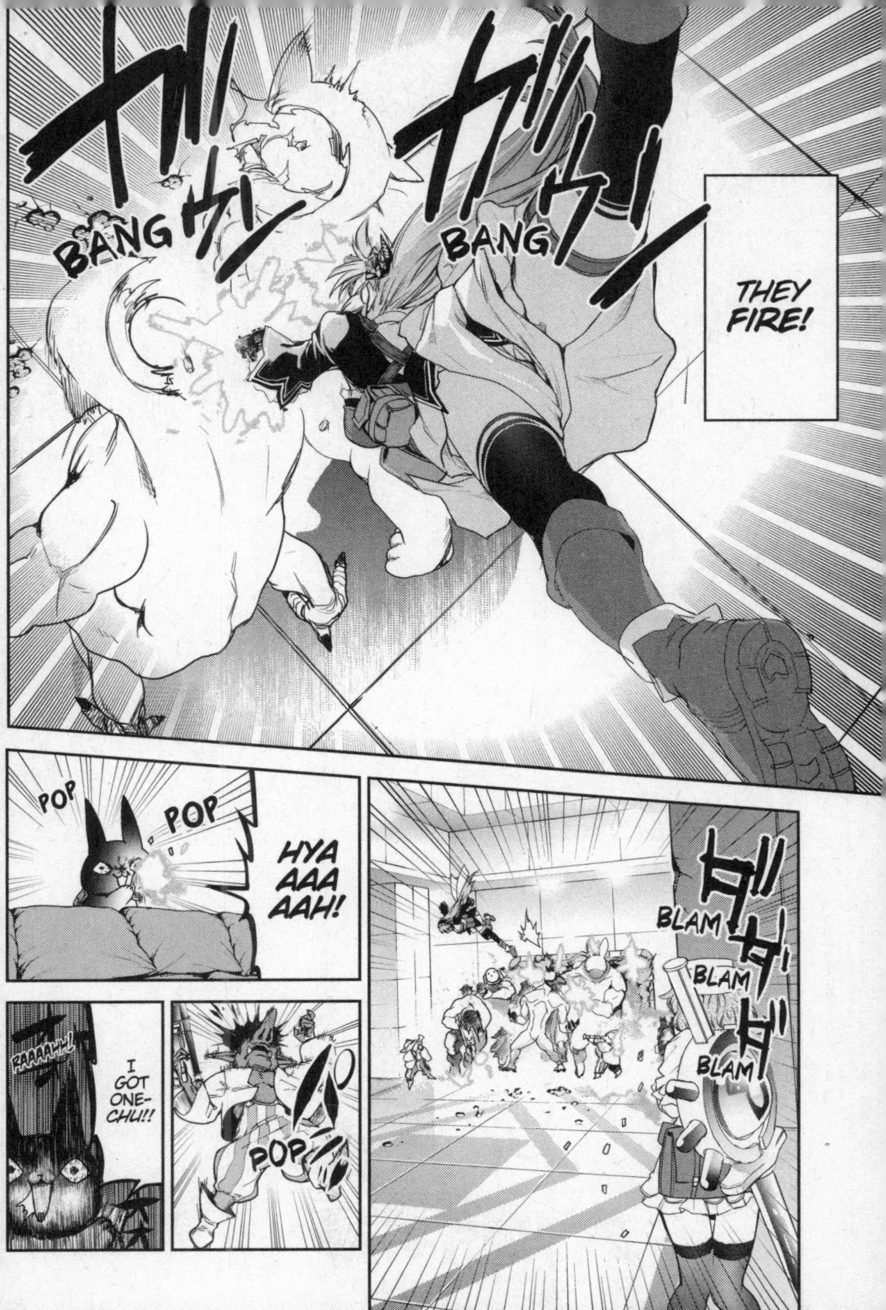
THEY FIRE!
BANG
BANG
BLAM
BLAM
BLAM
POP
POP
HYA AAA AAH!
POP
RAAAAHH!!
I GOT ONE-CHU!!

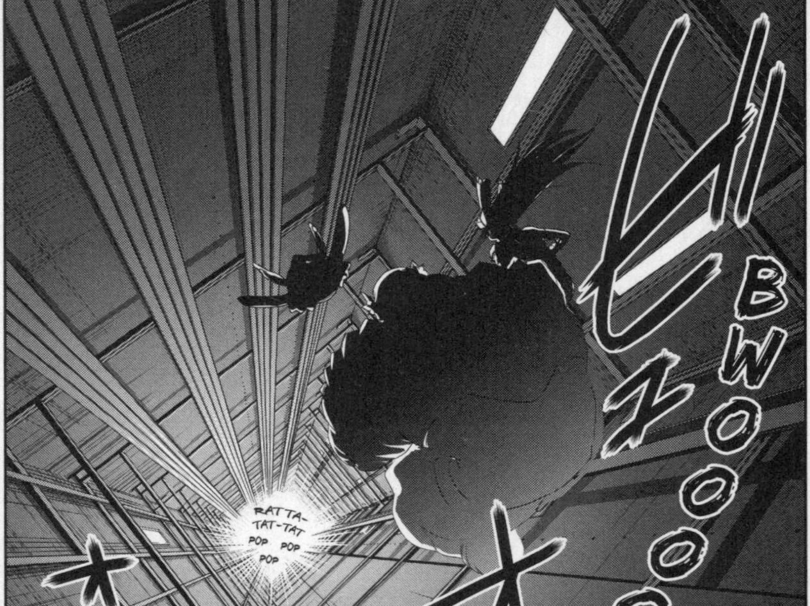
BWOOOOOSH
RATTA-TAT-TAT
POP POP POP
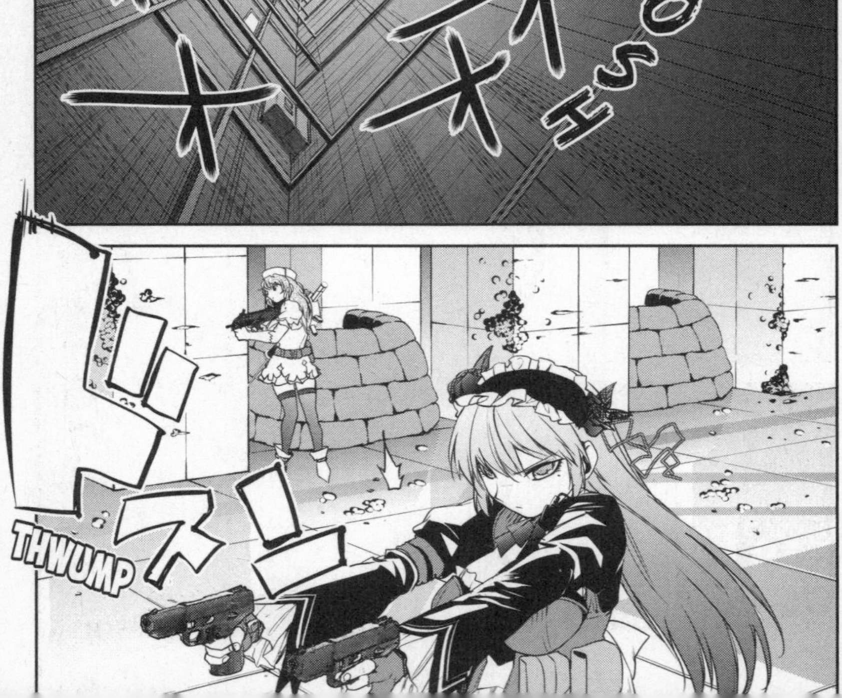
THWUMP

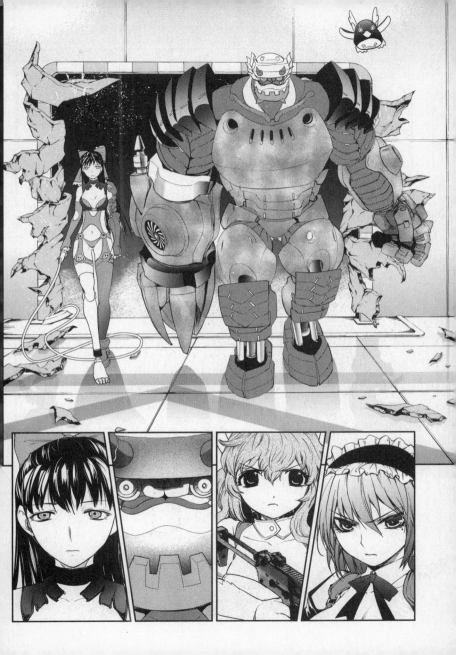

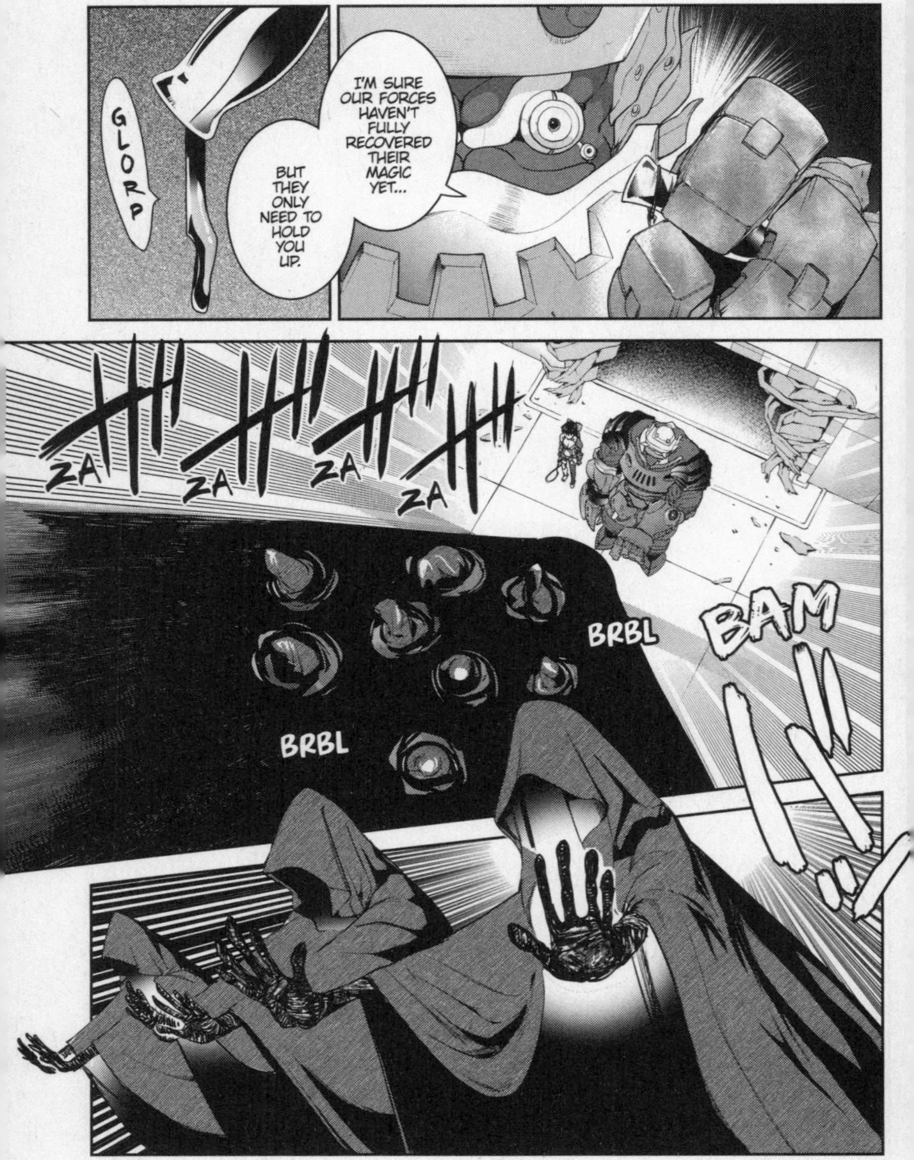
I'M SURE OUR FORCES HAVEN'T FULLY RECOVERED THEIR MAGIC YET...
BUT THEY ONLY NEED TO HOLD YOU UP.
GLORP
ZA
ZA
ZA
ZA
BAM
BRBL
BRBL

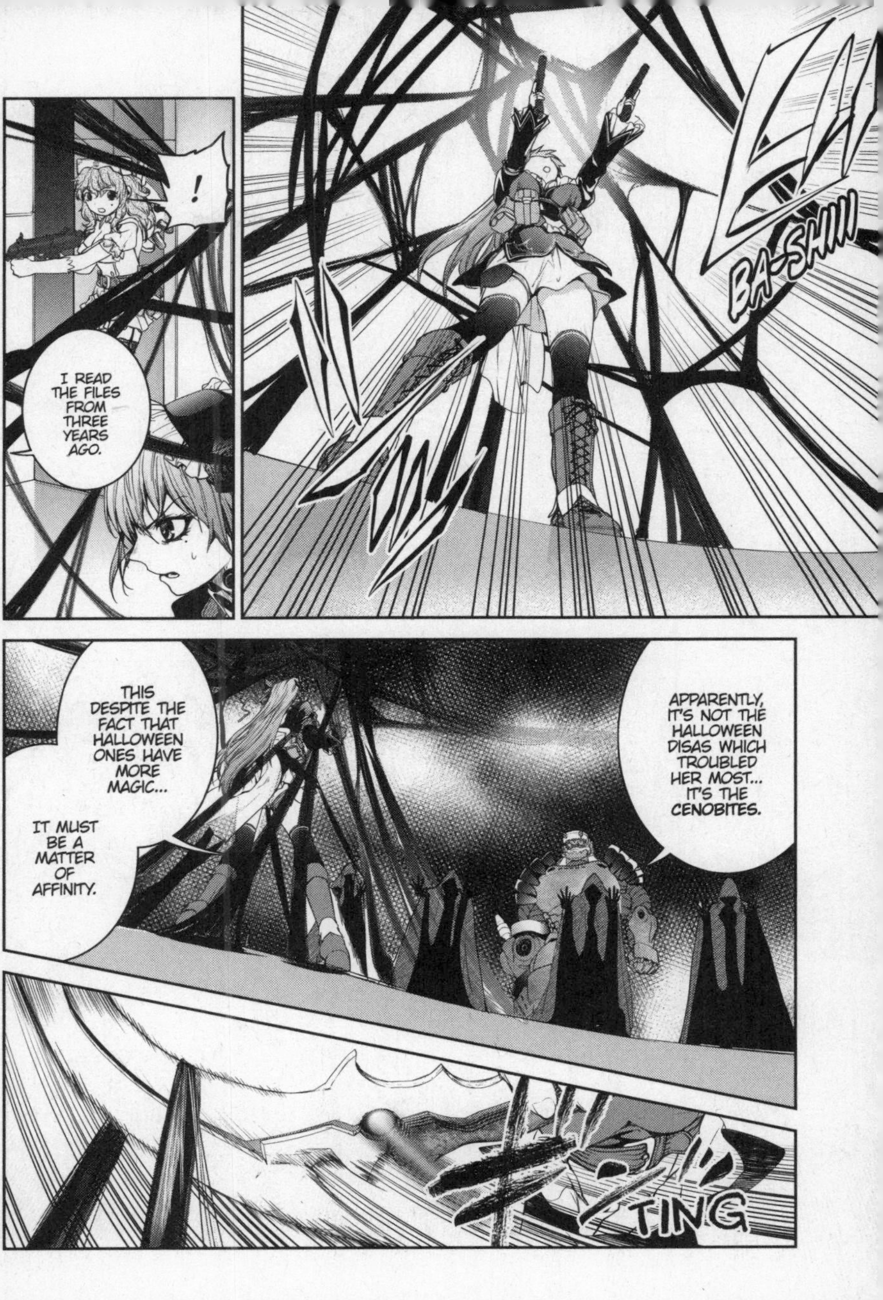
BA-SHIII
!
I READ THE FILES FROM THREE YEARS AGO.
APPARENTLY, IT'S NOT THE HALLOWEEN DISAS WHICH TROUBLED HER MOST... IT'S THE CENOBITES.
THIS DESPITE THE FACT THAT HALLOWEEN ONES HAVE MORE MAGIC...
IT MUST BE A MATTER OF AFFINITY.
TING

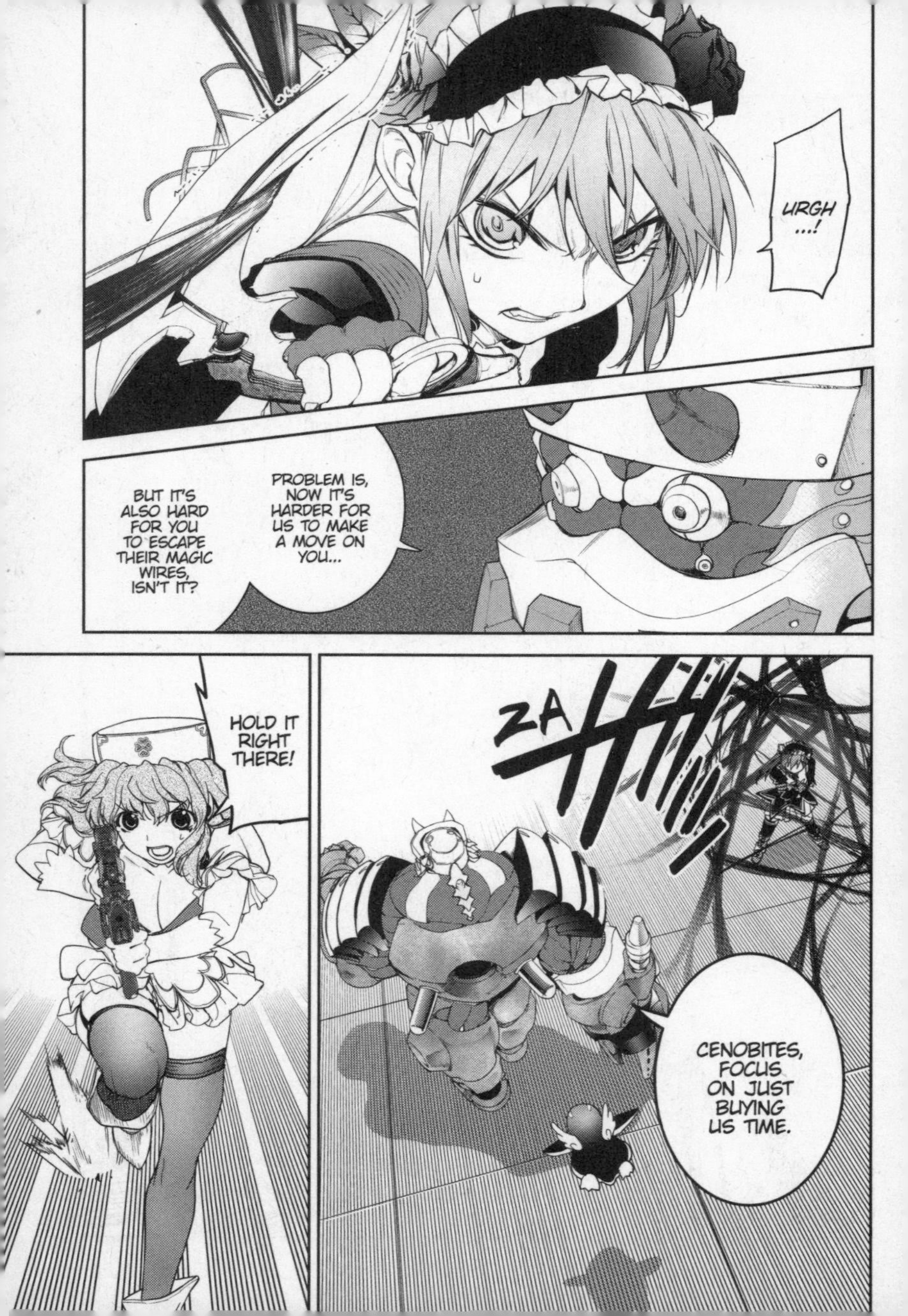
URGH ...!
PROBLEM IS, NOW IT'S HARDER FOR US TO MAKE A MOVE ON YOU...
BUT IT'S ALSO HARD FOR YOU TO ESCAPE THEIR MAGIC WIRES, ISN'T IT?
ZA
CENOBITES, FOCUS ON JUST BUYING US TIME.
HOLD IT RIGHT THERE!

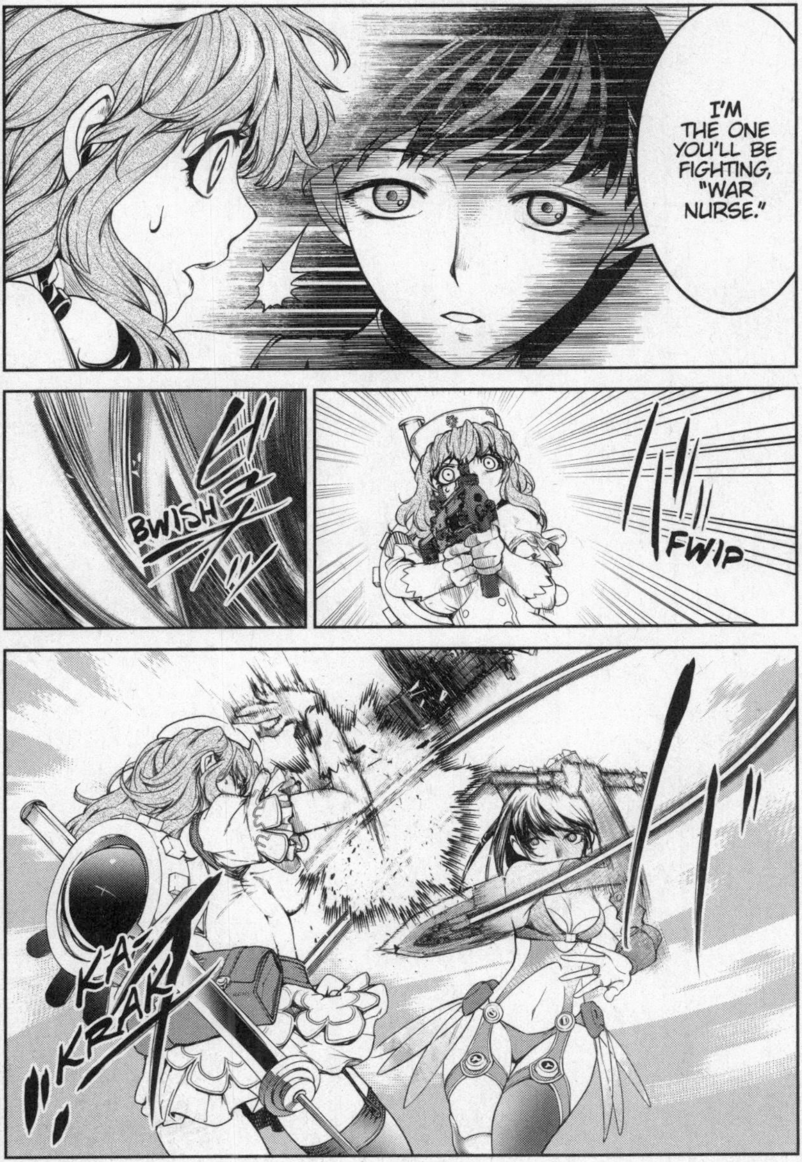
I'M THE ONE YOU'LL BE FIGHTING, "WAR NURSE."
FWIP
BWISH
KA-KRAK

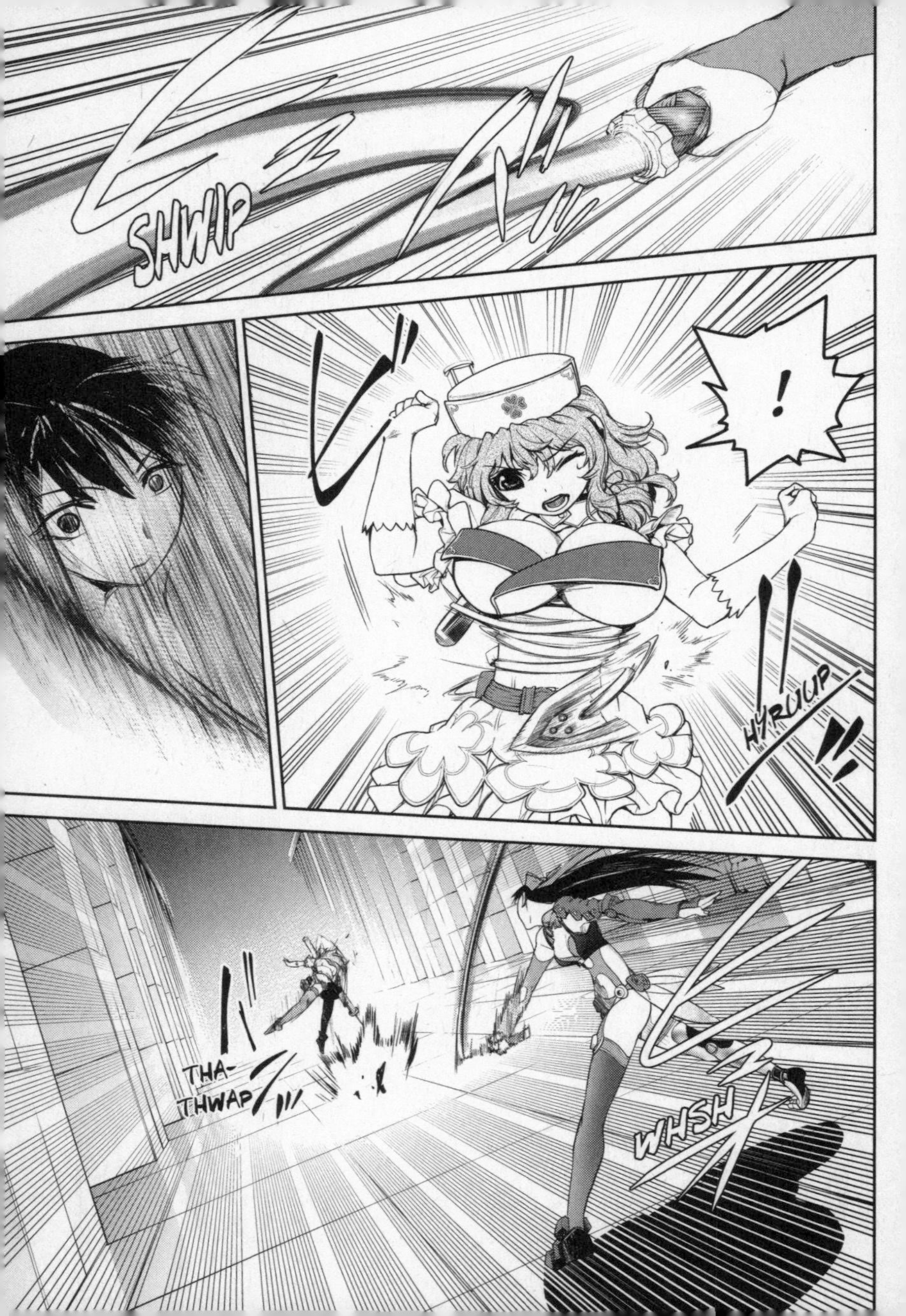
SHWIP
!
HYRUUP
WHSH
THA-
THWAP

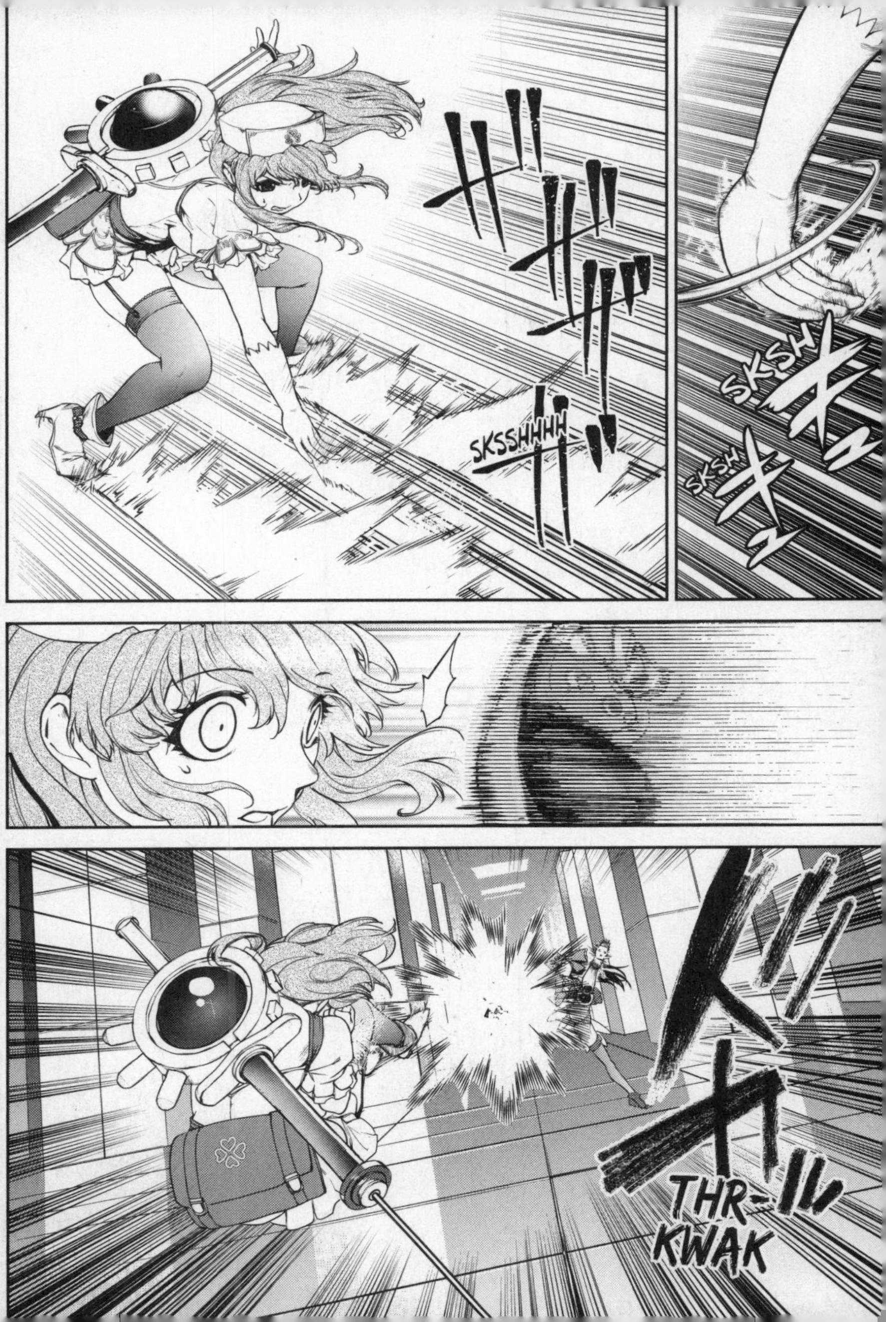
SKSH
SKSH
SKSSHHHH
THR-
KWAK

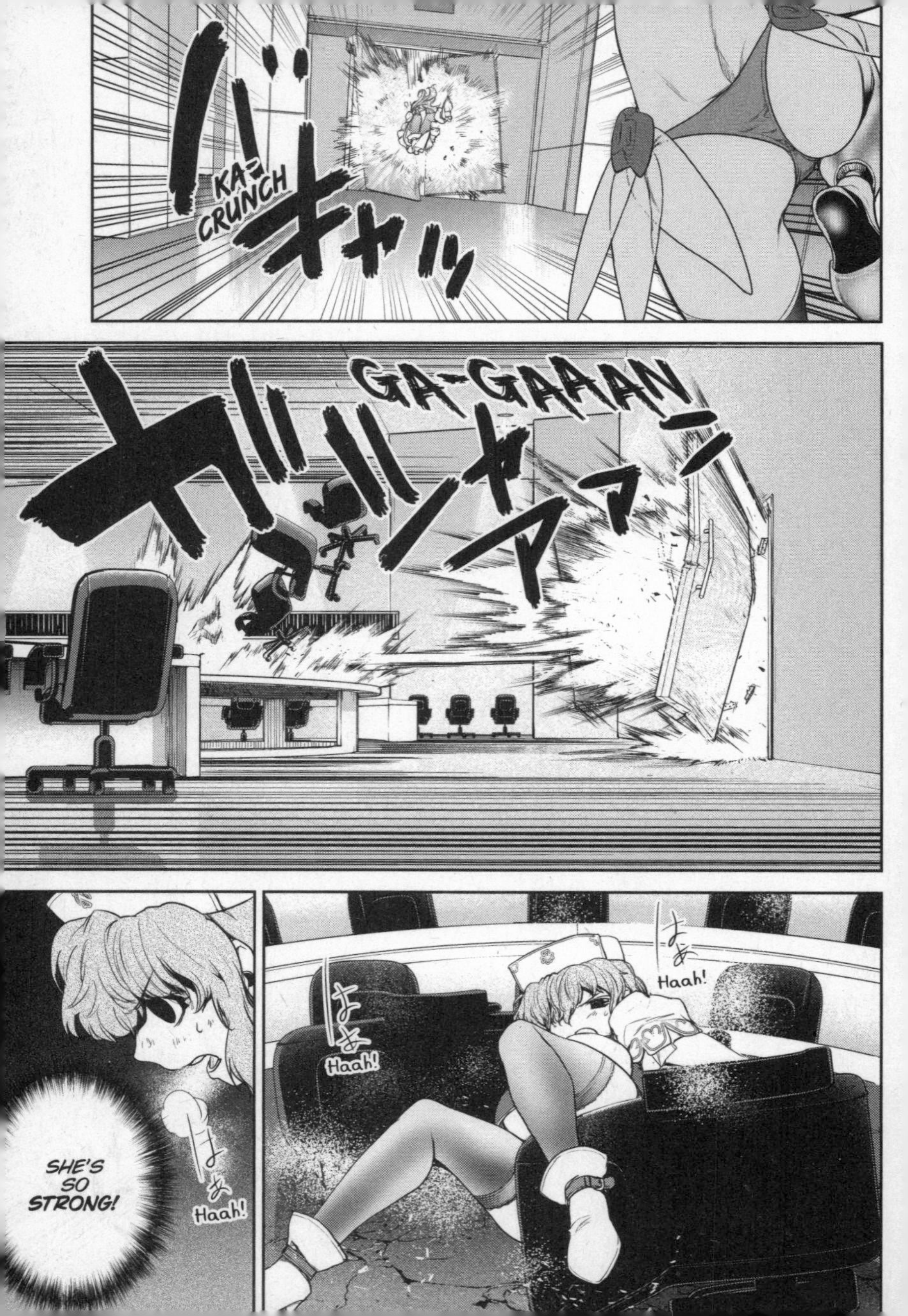
KA-CRUNCH
GA-GAAAN
Haah!
Haah!
Haah!
SHE'S SO STRONG!

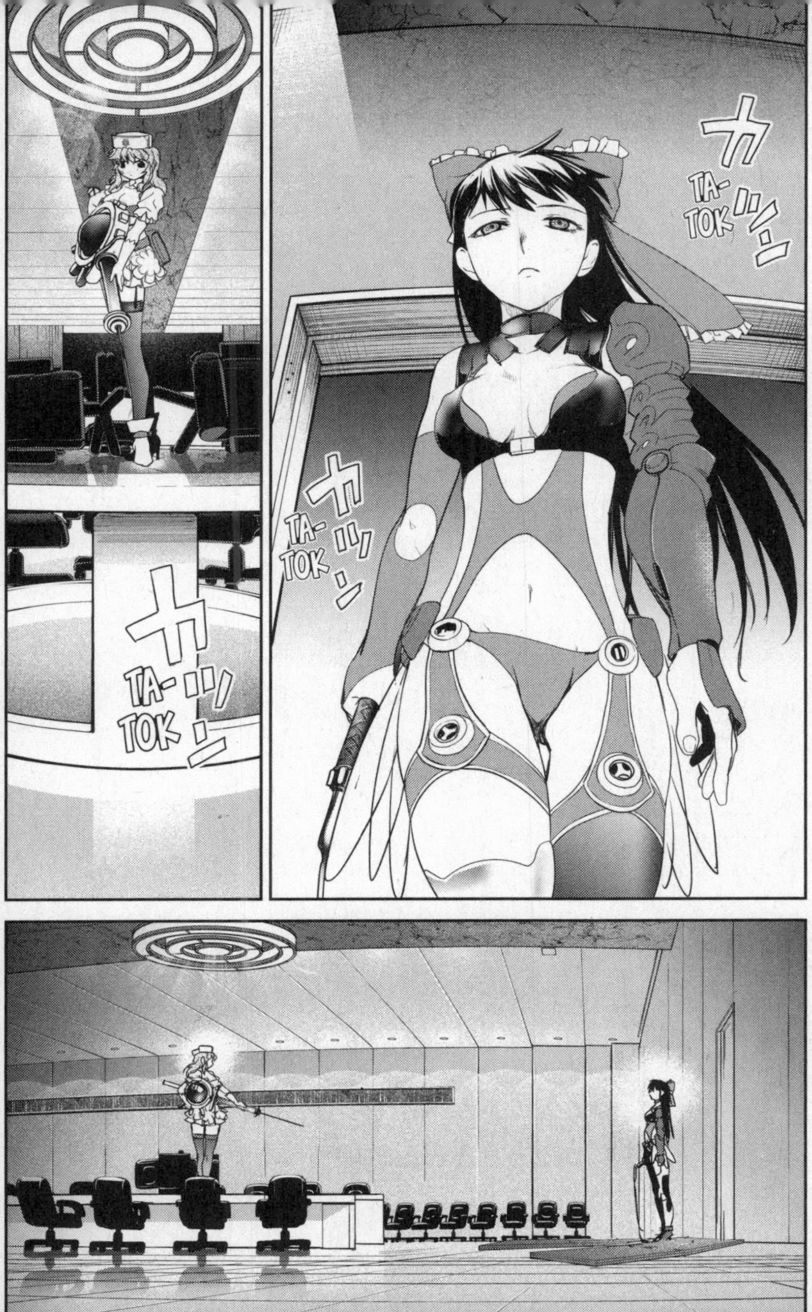
TA-TOK
TA-TOK
TA-TOK

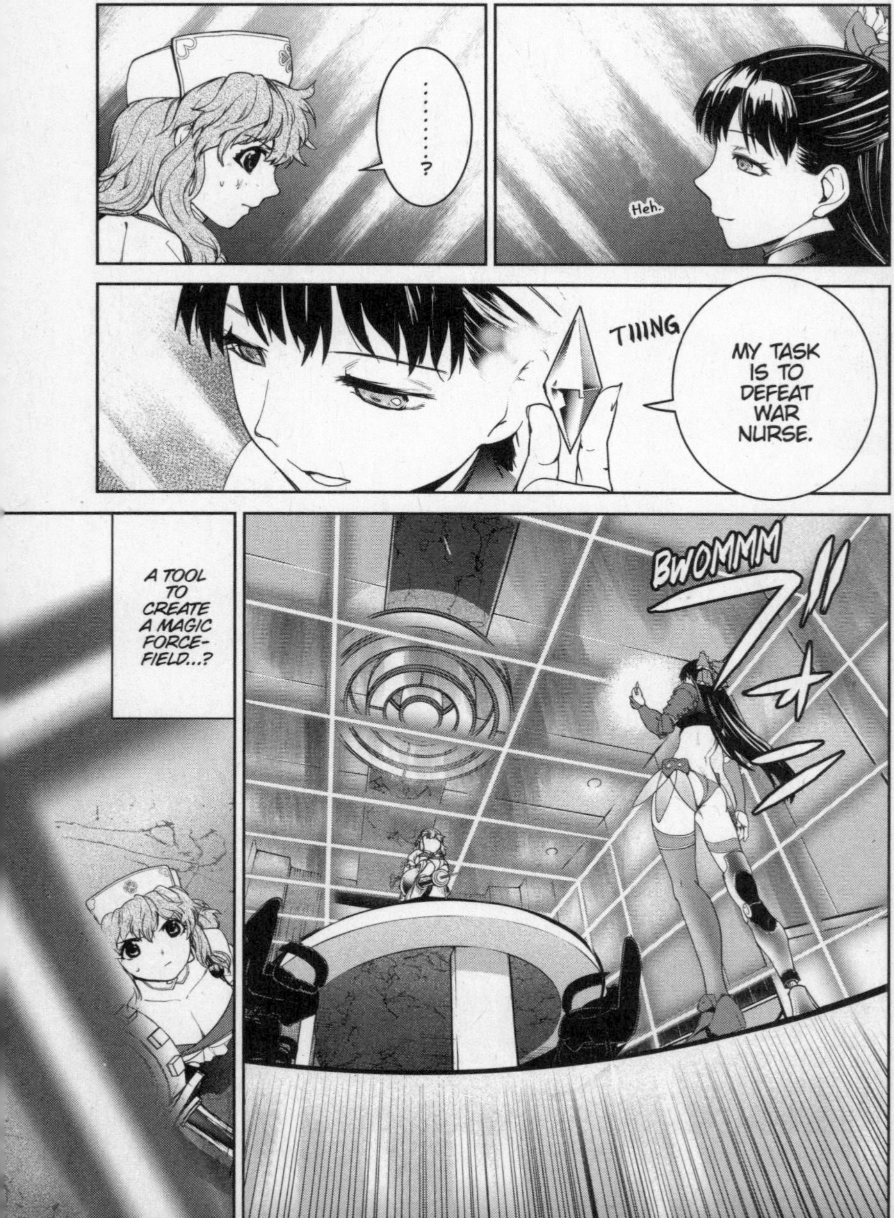
Heh.
......?
TIIING
MY TASK IS TO DEFEAT WAR NURSE.
BWOMMM
A TOOL TO CREATE A MAGIC FORCE-FIELD...?

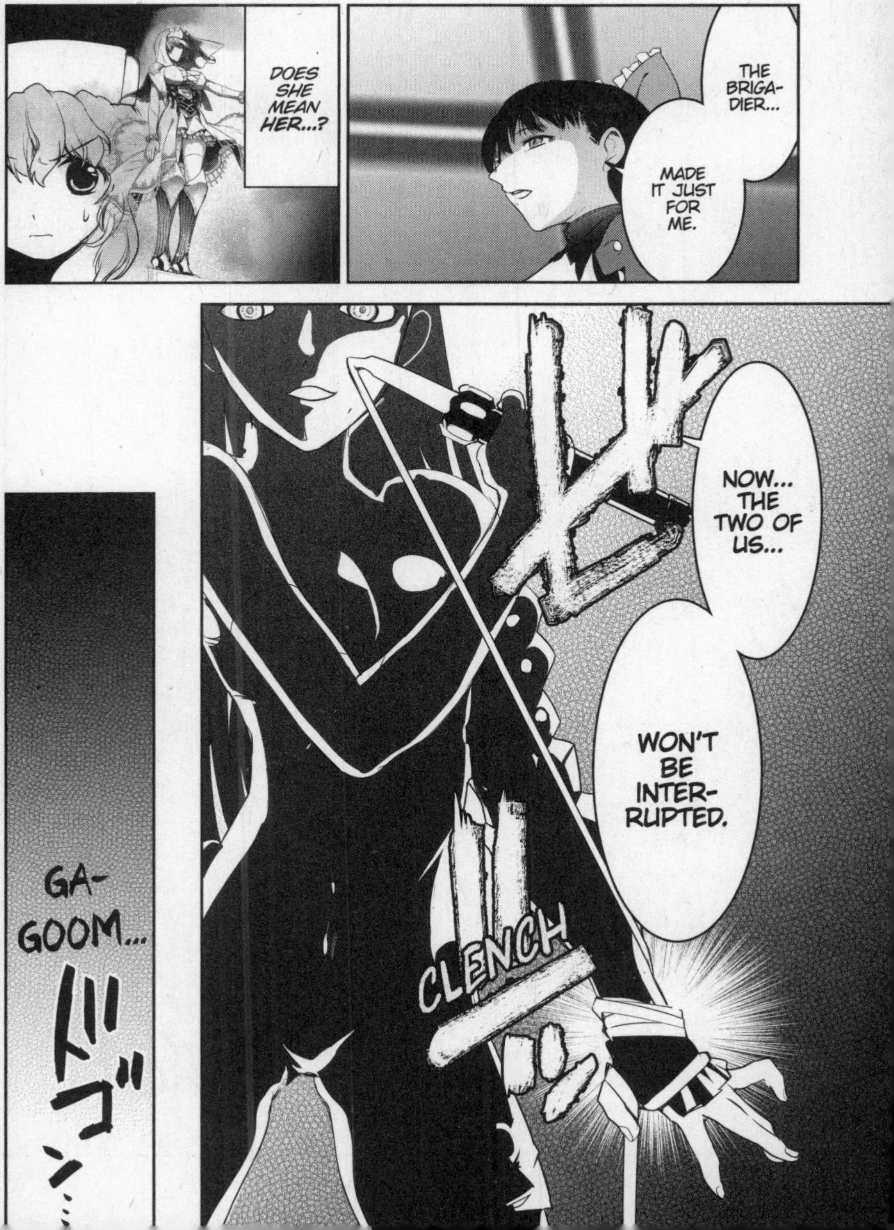
THE BRIGA-DIER...
MADE IT JUST FOR ME.
DOES SHE MEAN HER...?
NOW... THE TWO OF US...
WON'T BE INTER-RUPTED.
CLENCH
GA-GOOM...
ドゴン...

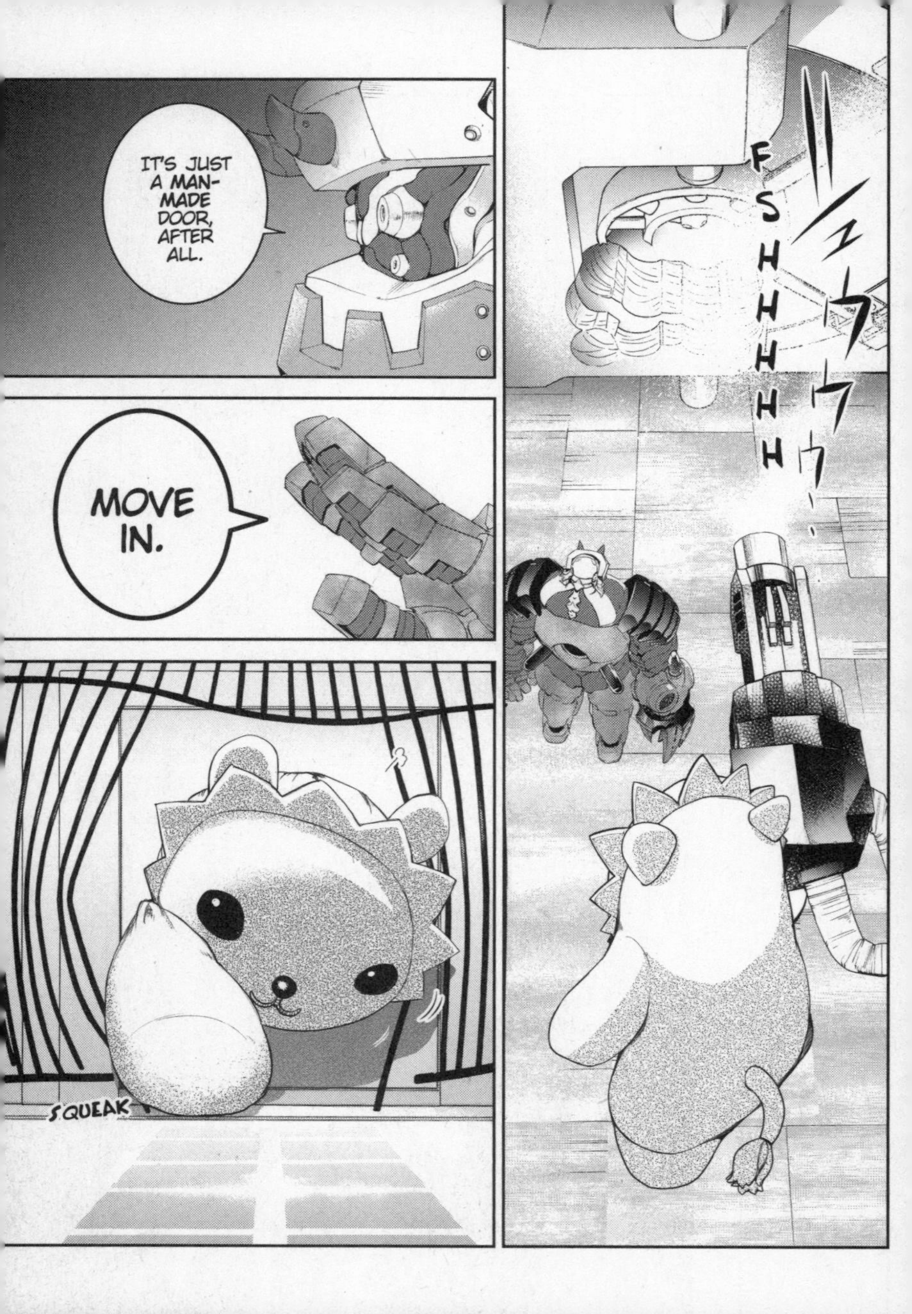
FSHHHHHH
IT'S JUST A MAN-MADE DOOR, AFTER ALL.
MOVE IN.
SQUEAK

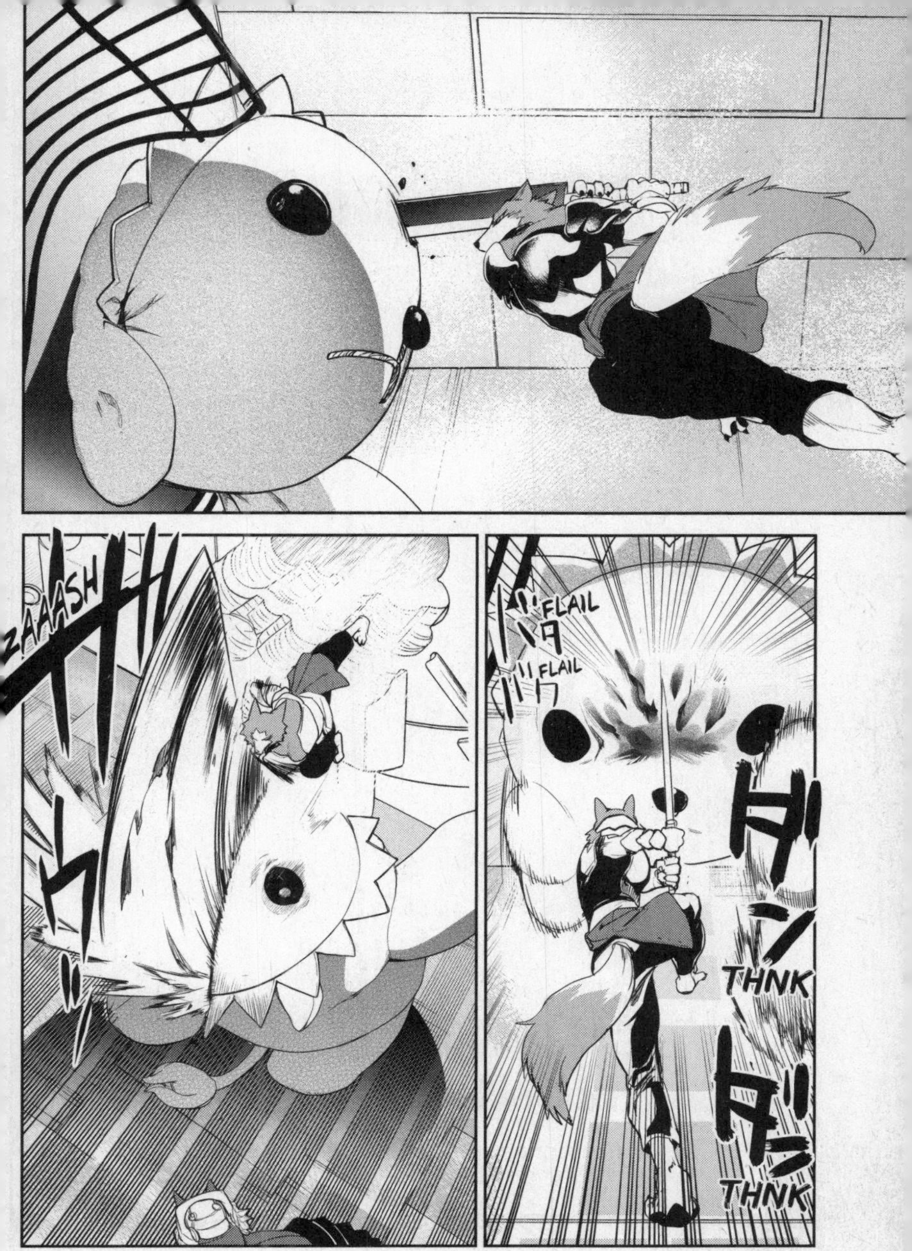
FLAIL
FLAIL
THNK
THNK
ZAAASH

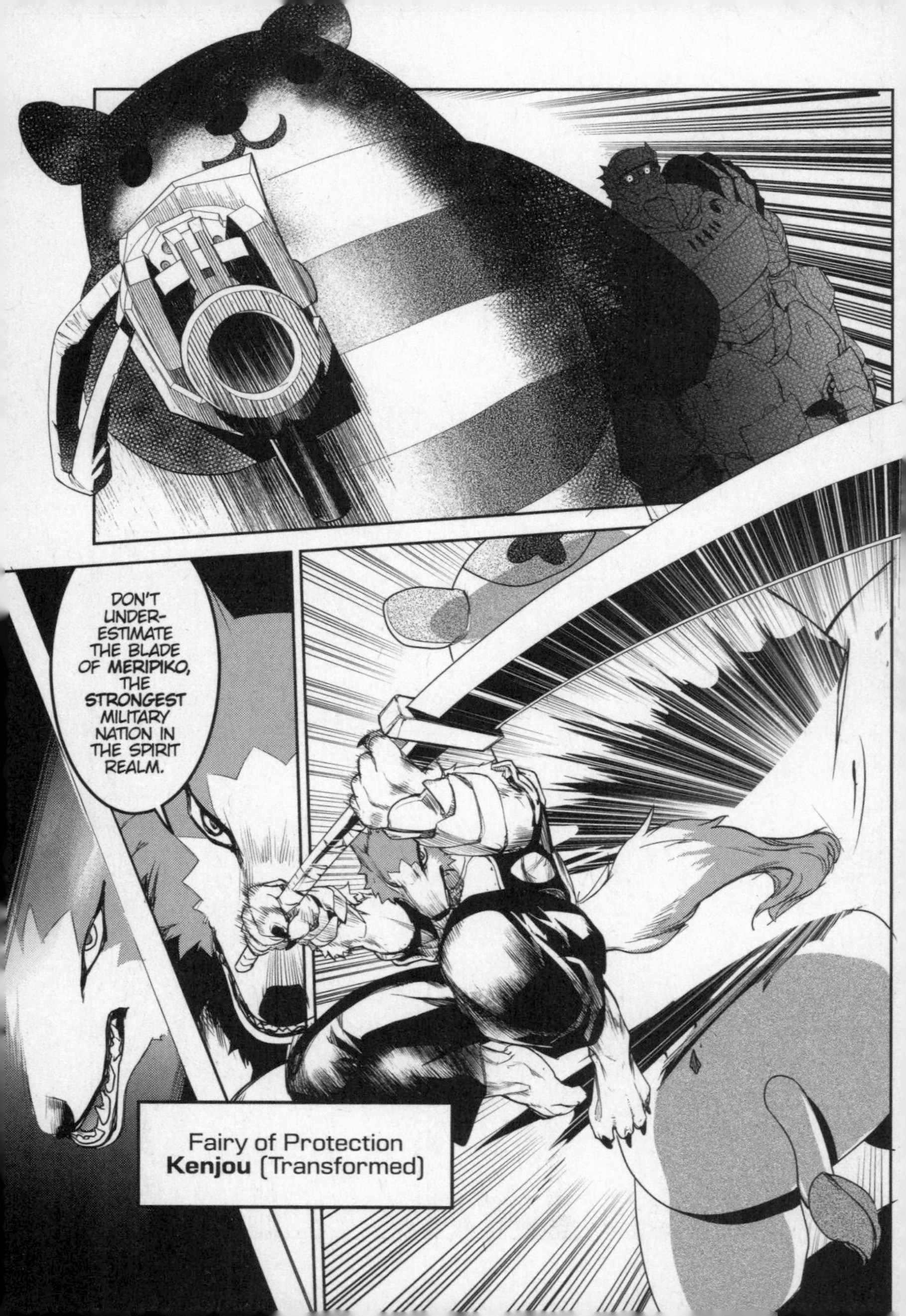
DON'T UNDER-ESTIMATE THE BLADE OF MERIPIKO, THE STRONGEST MILITARY NATION IN THE SPIRIT REALM.
Fairy of Protection
Kenjou (Transformed)

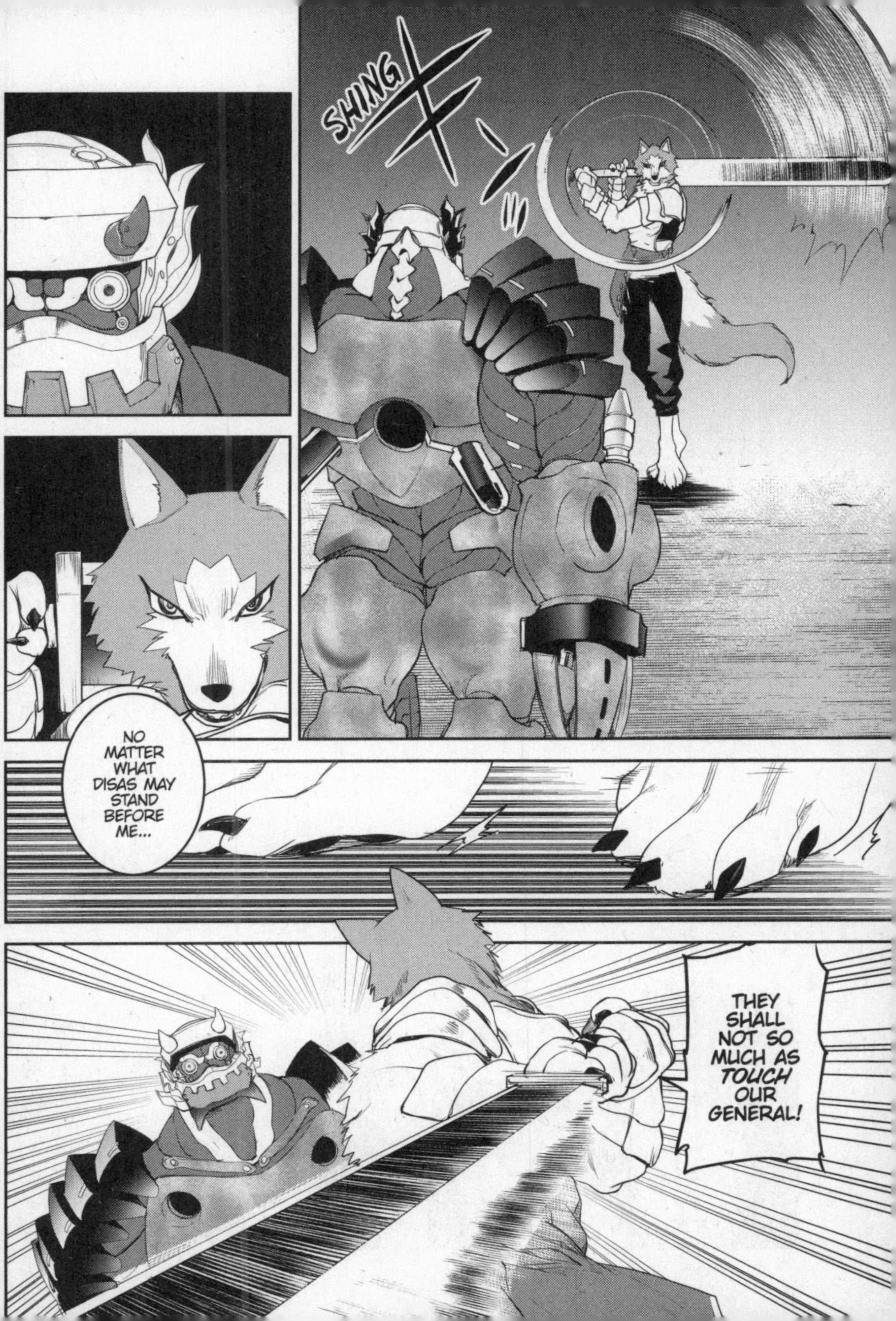
SHING
NO MATTER WHAT DISAS MAY STAND BEFORE ME...
THEY SHALL NOT SO MUCH AS *TOUCH* OUR GENERAL!

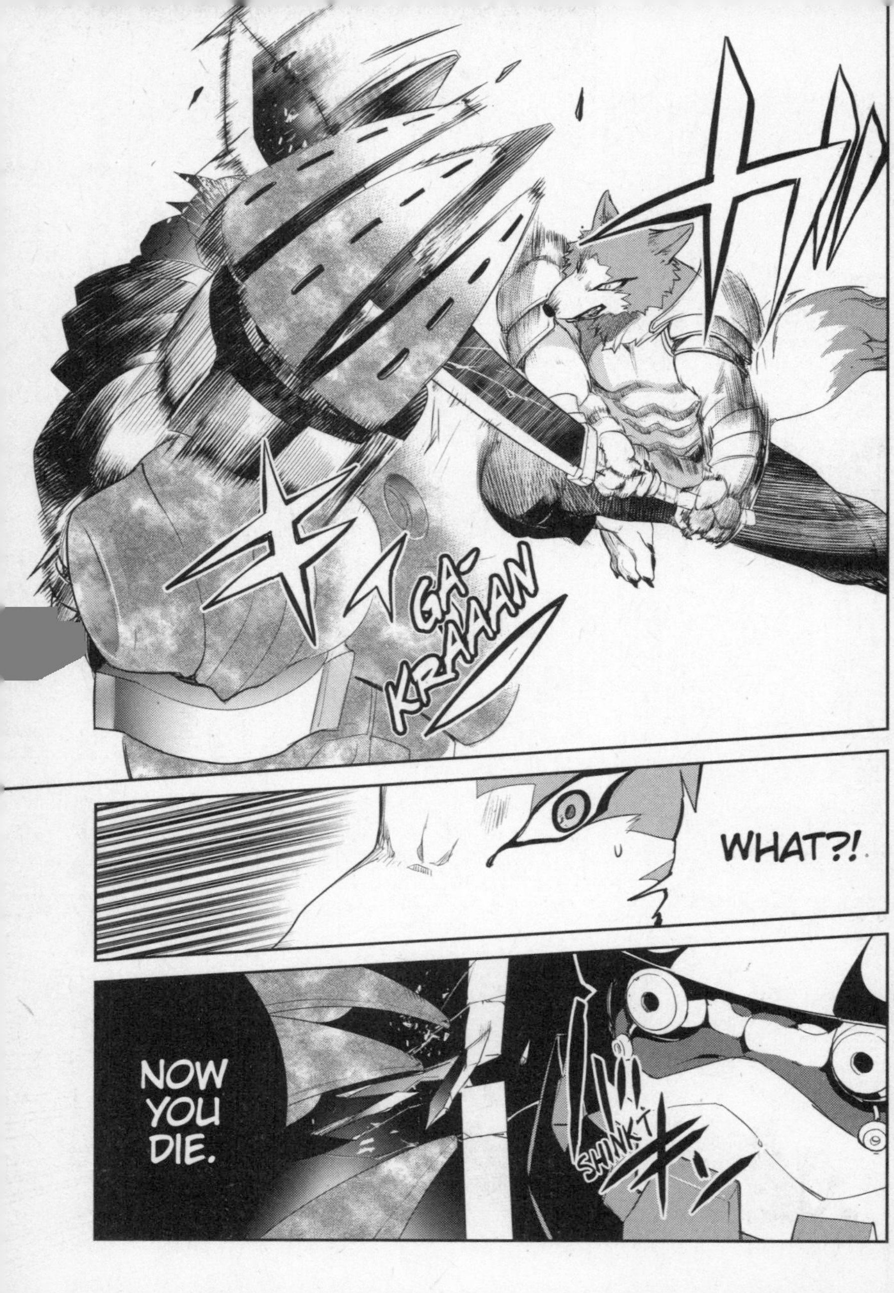
GA-KRAAAN
WHAT?!
NOW YOU DIE.
SHINK

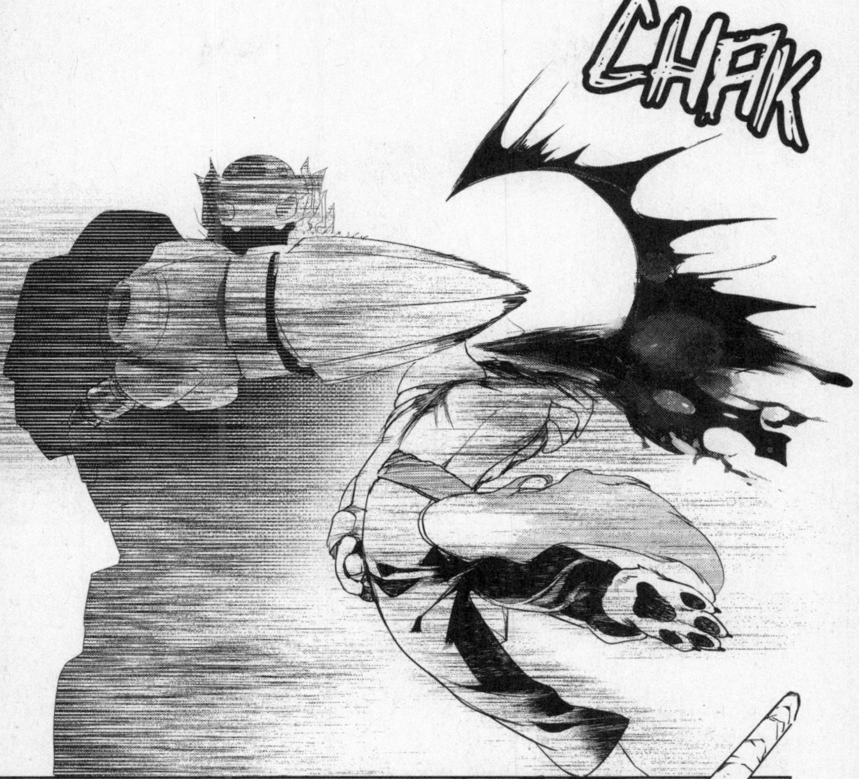
CHAK

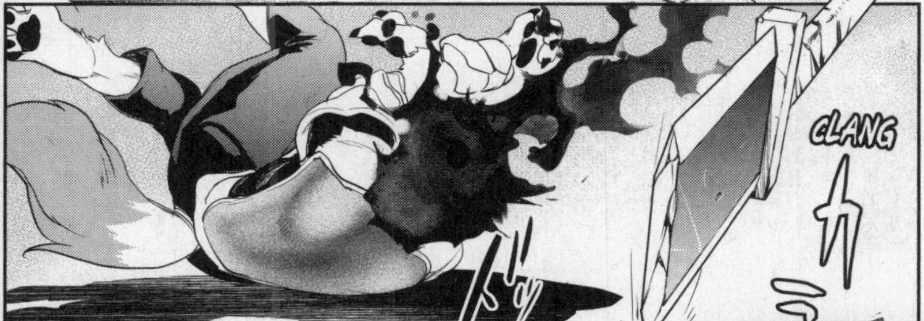
CLANG
THNK

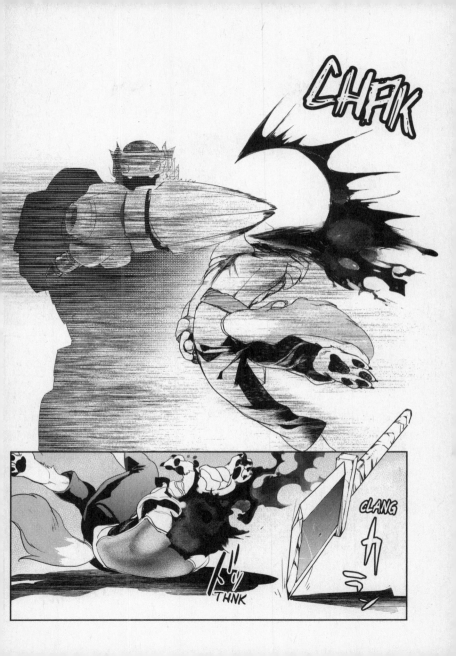

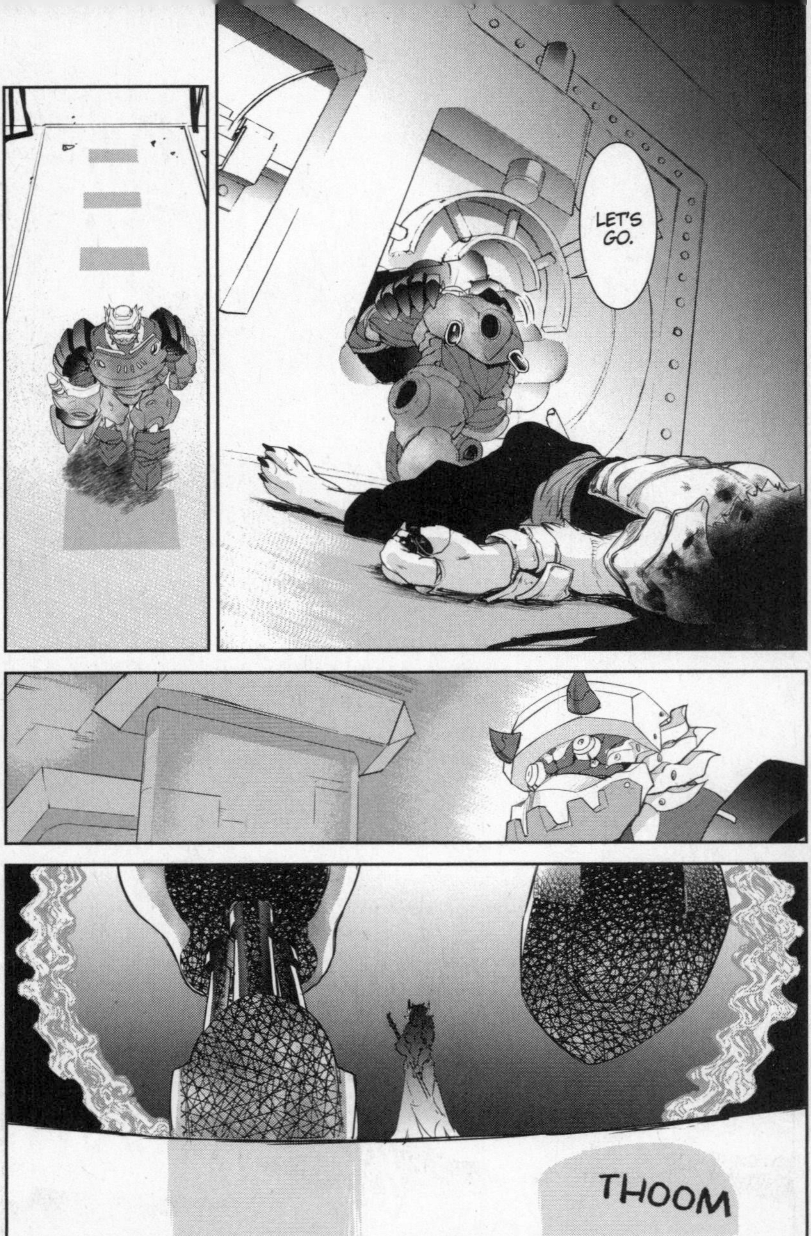
LET'S GO.
THOOM

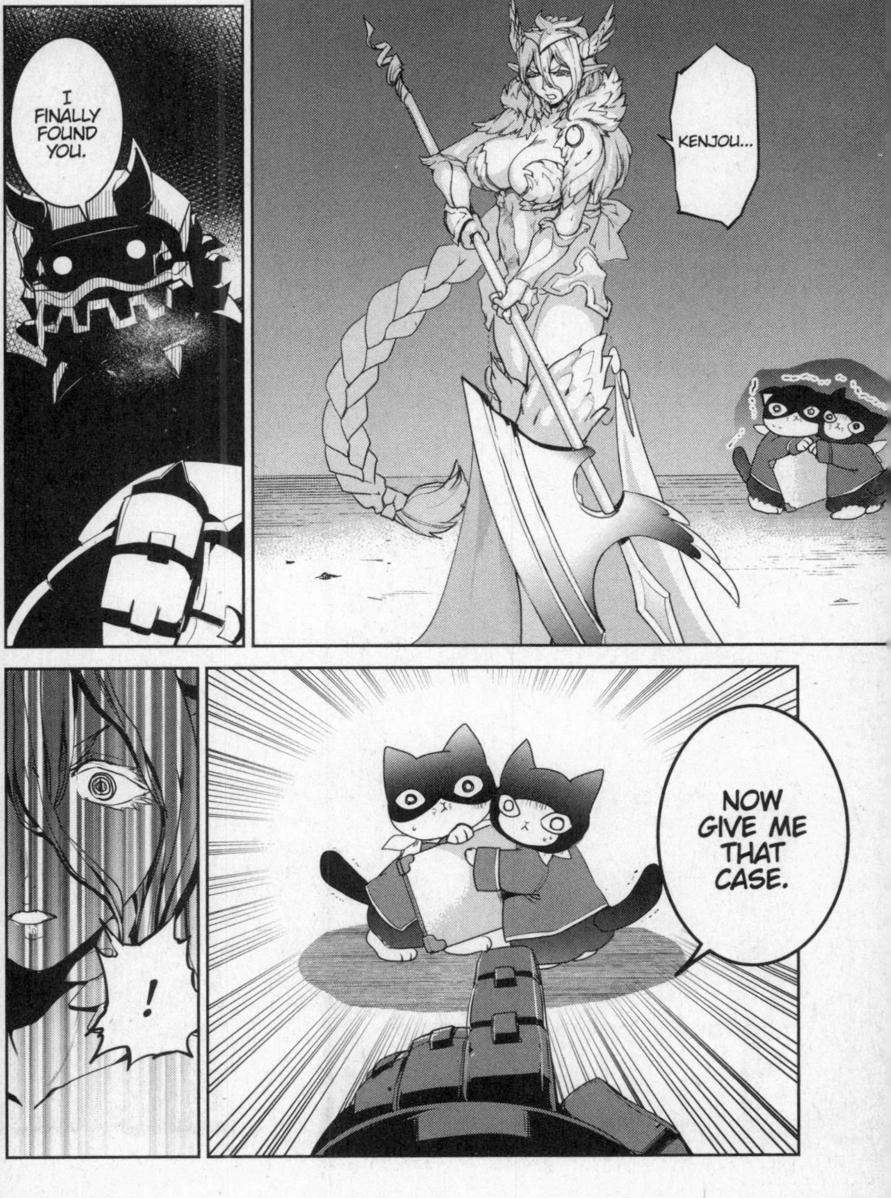
KENJOU...
I FINALLY FOUND YOU.
NOW GIVE ME THAT CASE.
!

MAGICAL GIRL
SPEC-OPS
ASUKA

魔法少女特殊戦
あすか

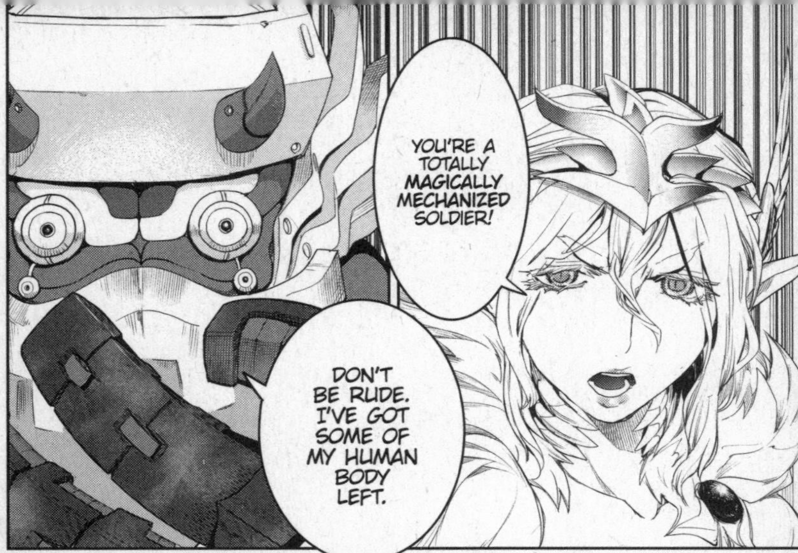
YOU'RE A TOTALLY MAGICALLY MECHANIZED SOLDIER!
DON'T BE RUDE. I'VE GOT SOME OF MY HUMAN BODY LEFT.

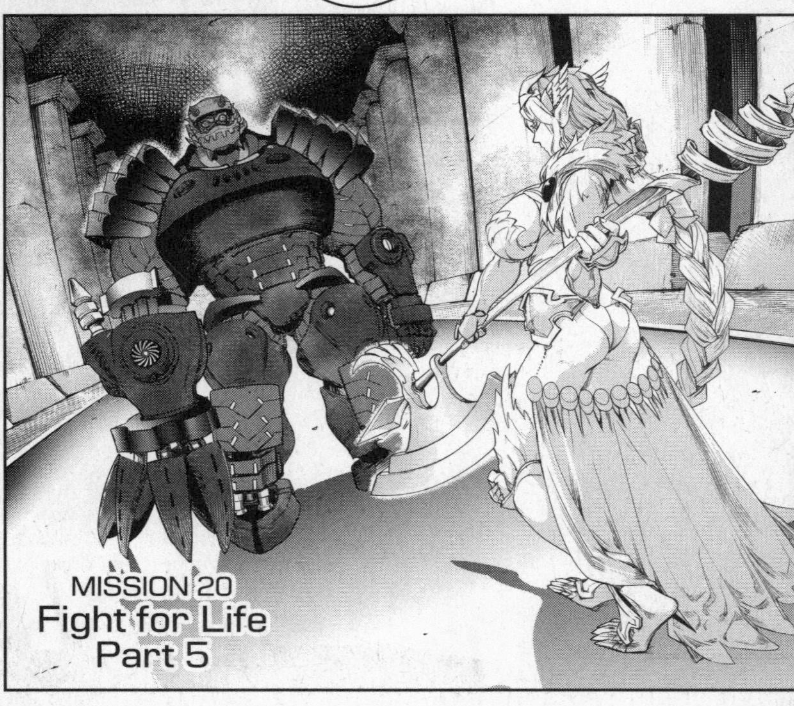
MISSION 20
Fight for Life Part 5

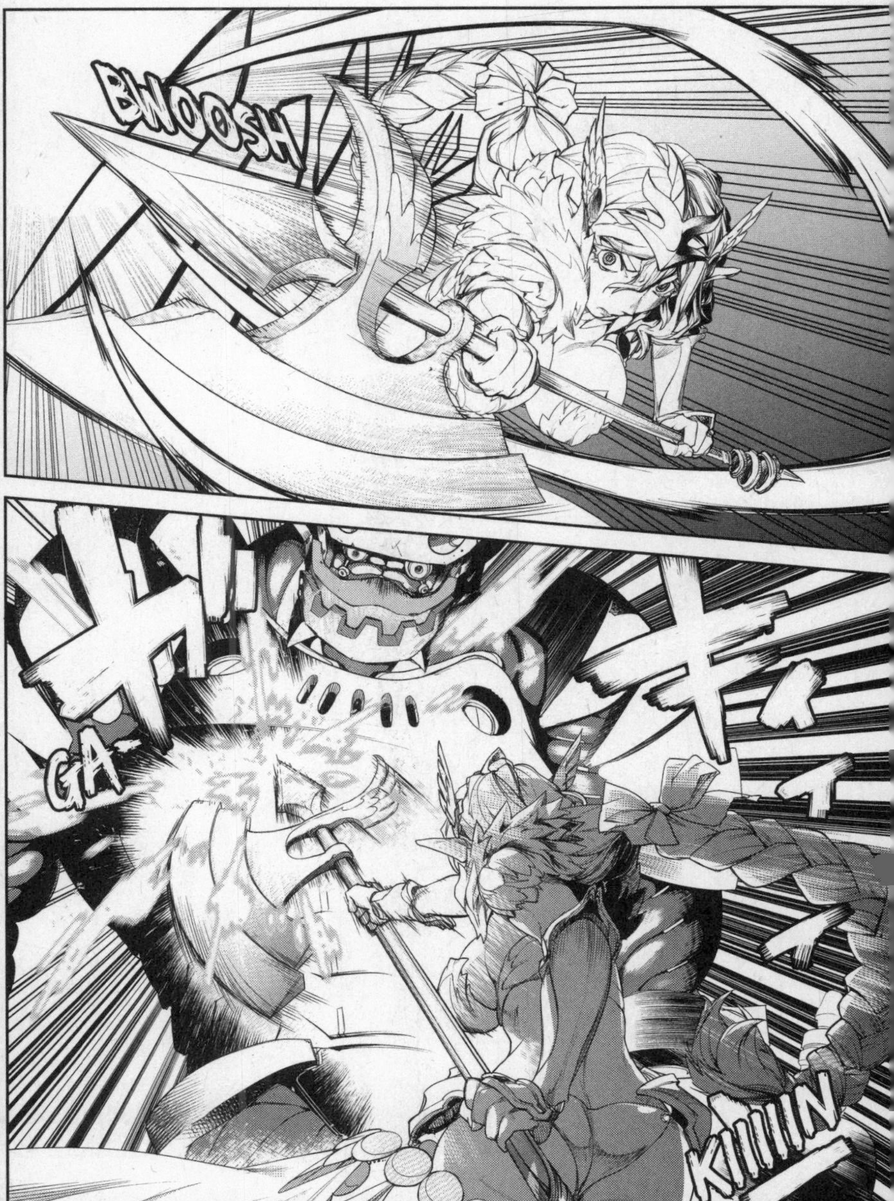
BWOOSH
GA-
KIIIIN

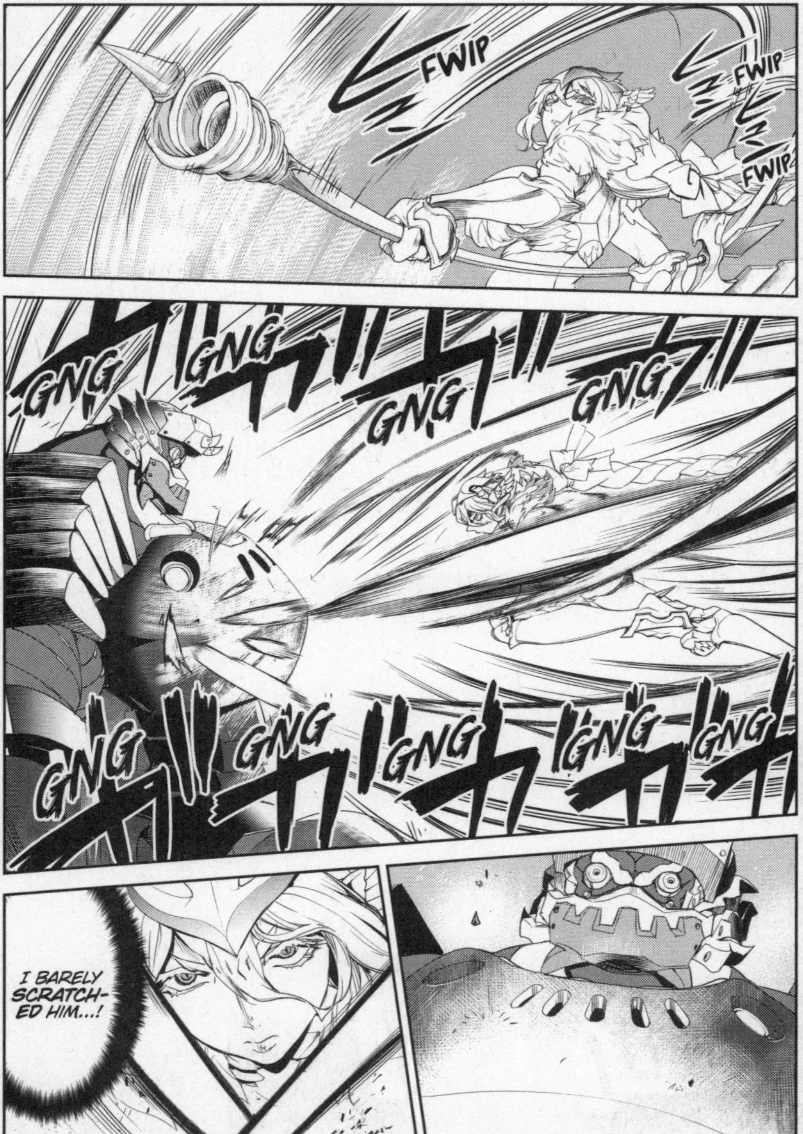
FWIP
FWIP
FWIP
GNG
GNG
GNG
GNG
GNG
GNG
GNG
GNG
GNG
GNG
I BARELY SCRATCH-ED HIM...!

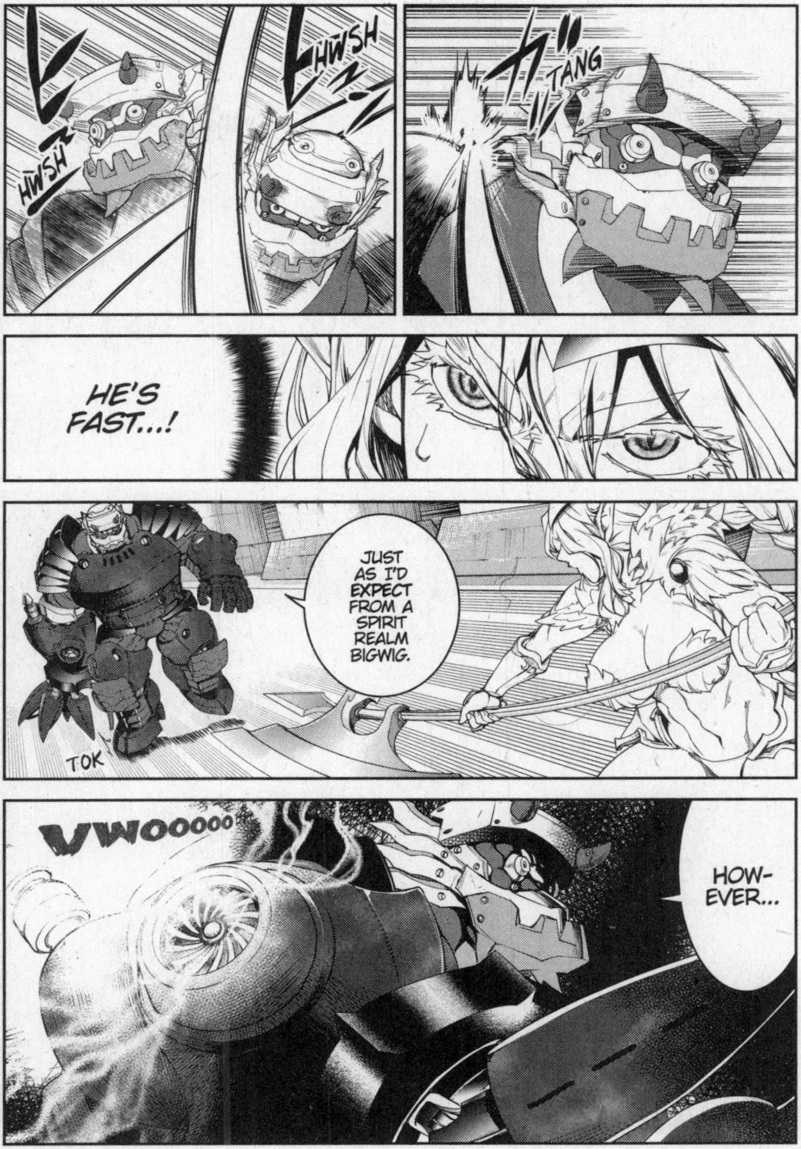
TANG
HWSH
HWSH
HE'S FAST...!
JUST AS I'D EXPECT FROM A SPIRIT REALM BIGWIG.
T.OK
VWOOOOO
HOW-EVER...

CHANK
SHUNK
SHUNK
VRM
VRM
VRM
VRMMM...
VREEEEEEEEE

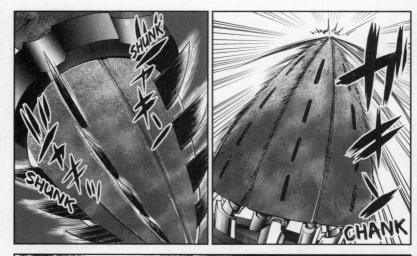

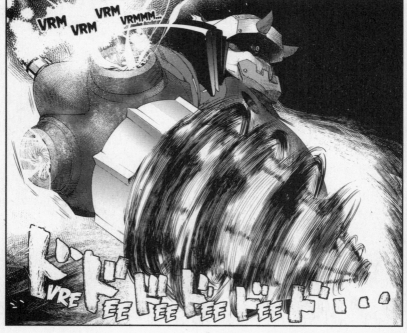

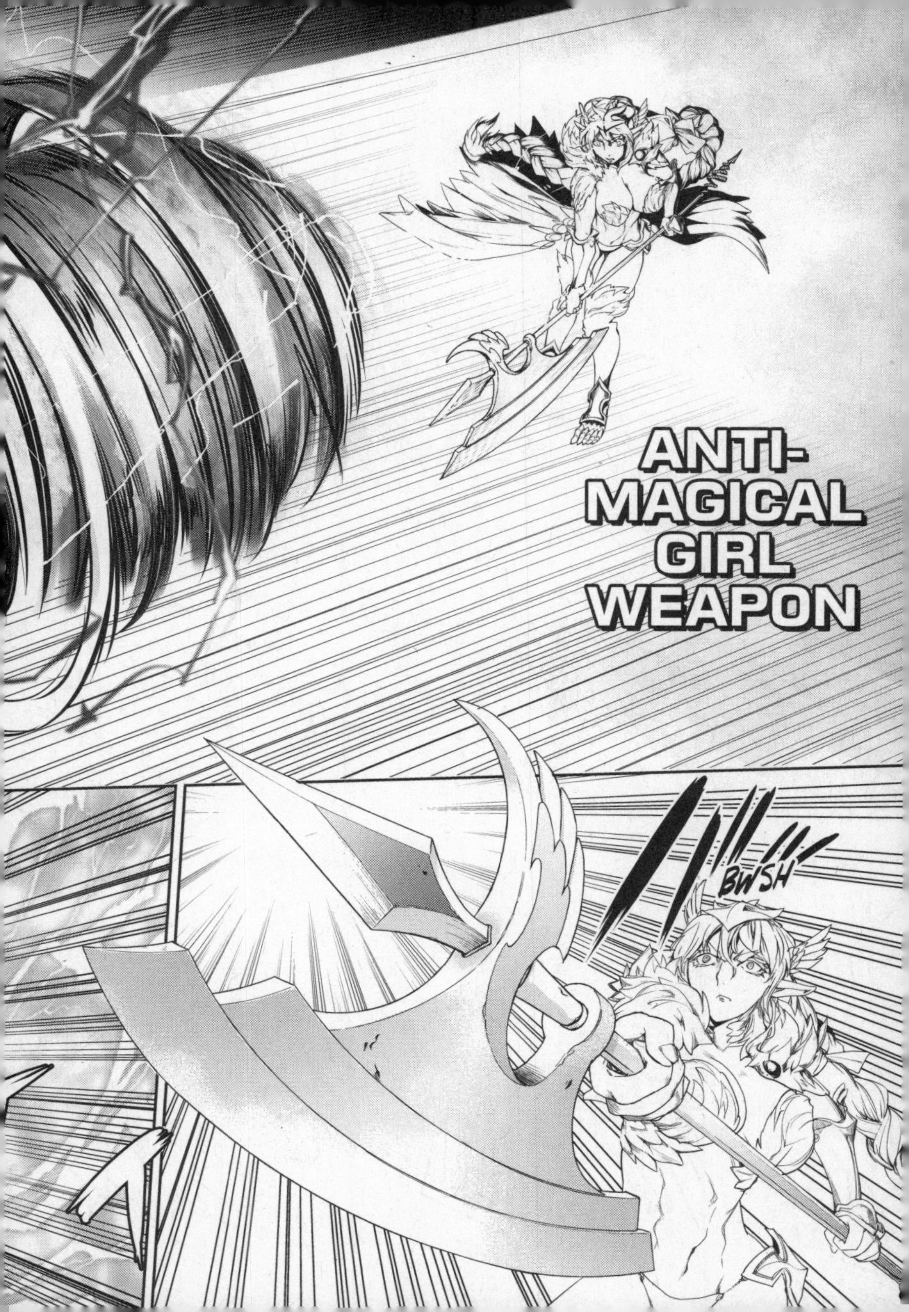
ANTI-
MAGICAL
GIRL
WEAPON
BWSH

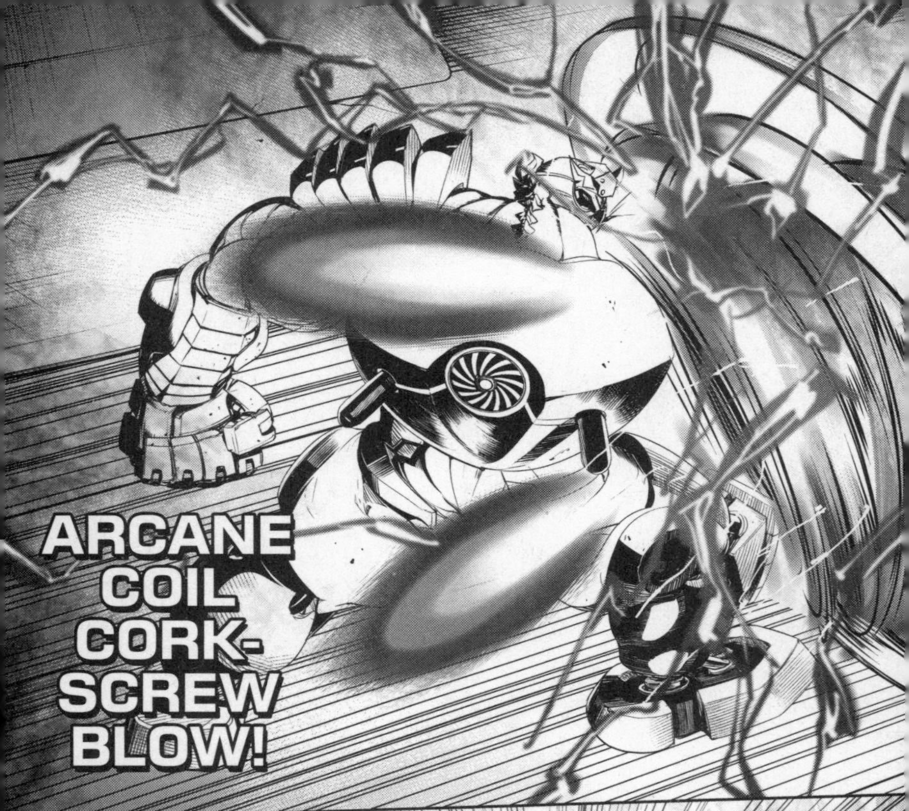
ARCANE COIL CORK-SCREW BLOW!
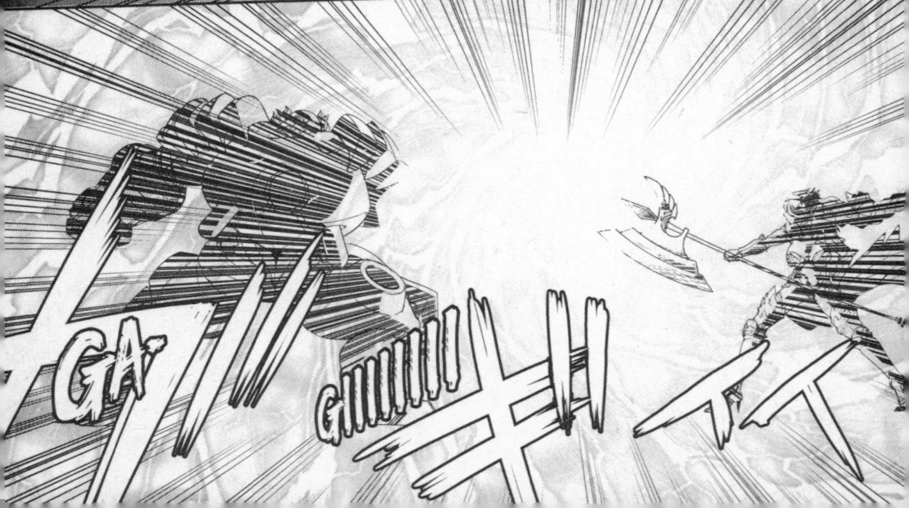
GA
GIIIIIII

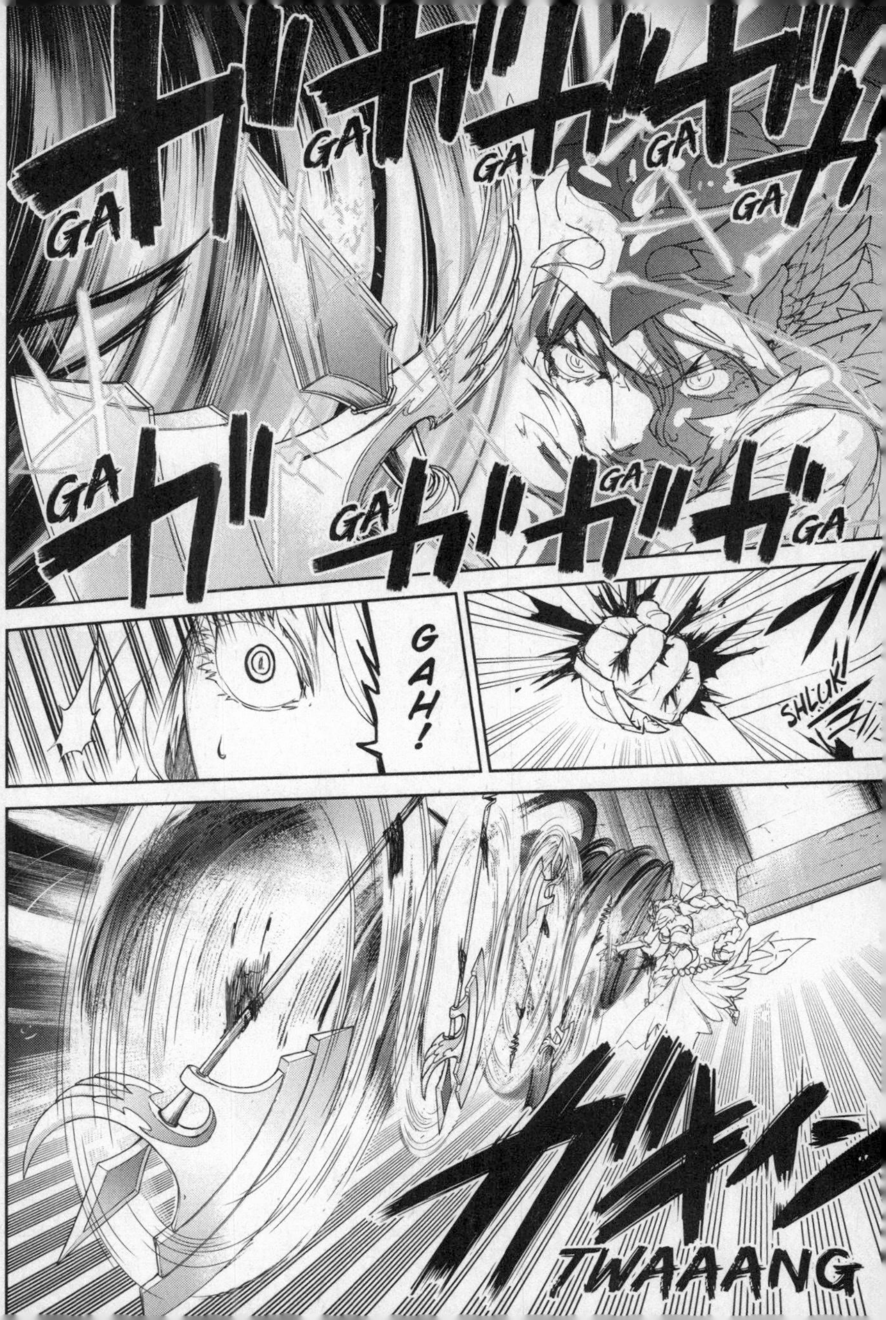
GA
GA
GA
GA
GA
GA
GA
GA
GA
SHLUK!
GAH!
TWAAANG

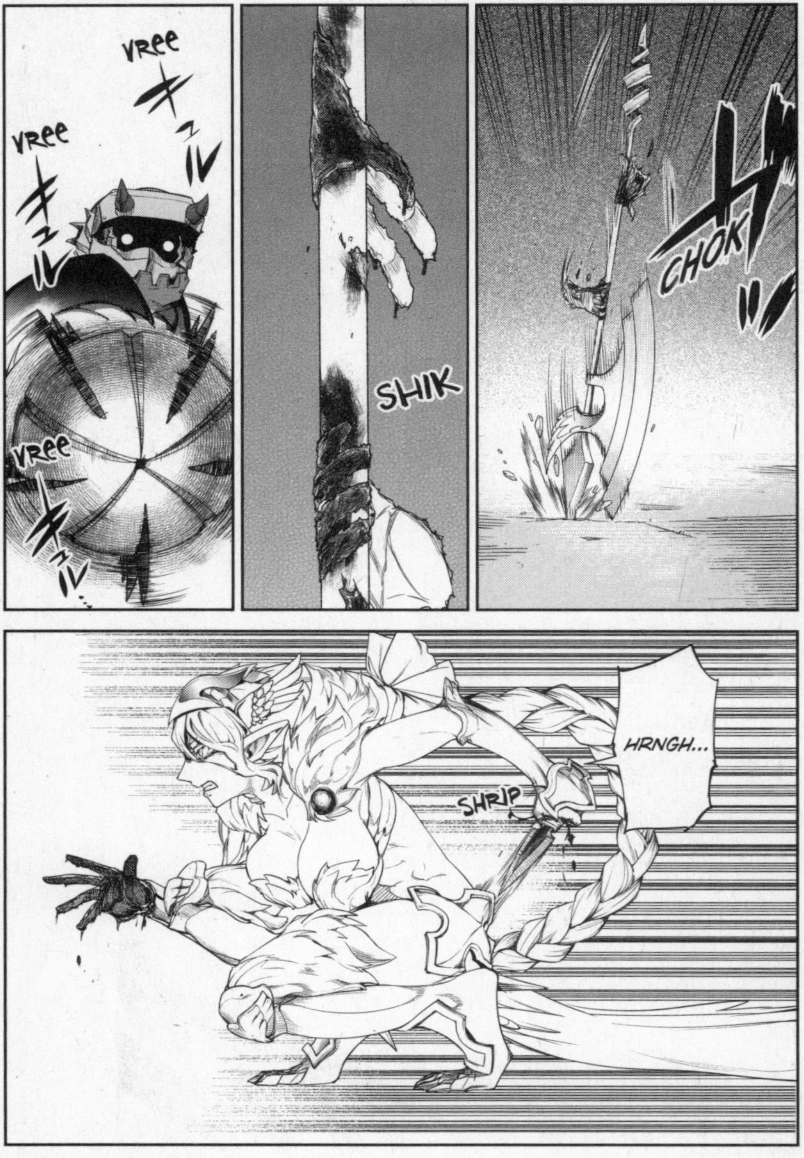
CHOK
SHIK
vRee
vRee
vRee
HRNGH...
SHRIP

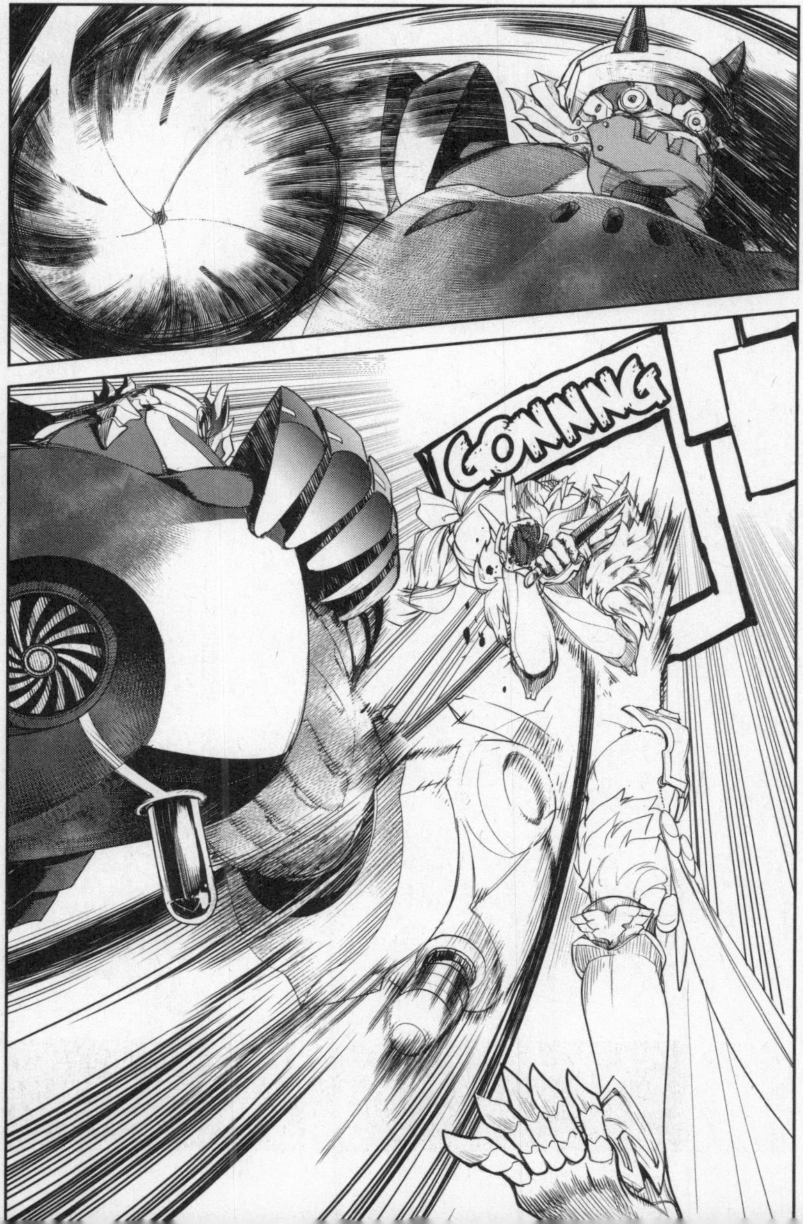
GONNNG

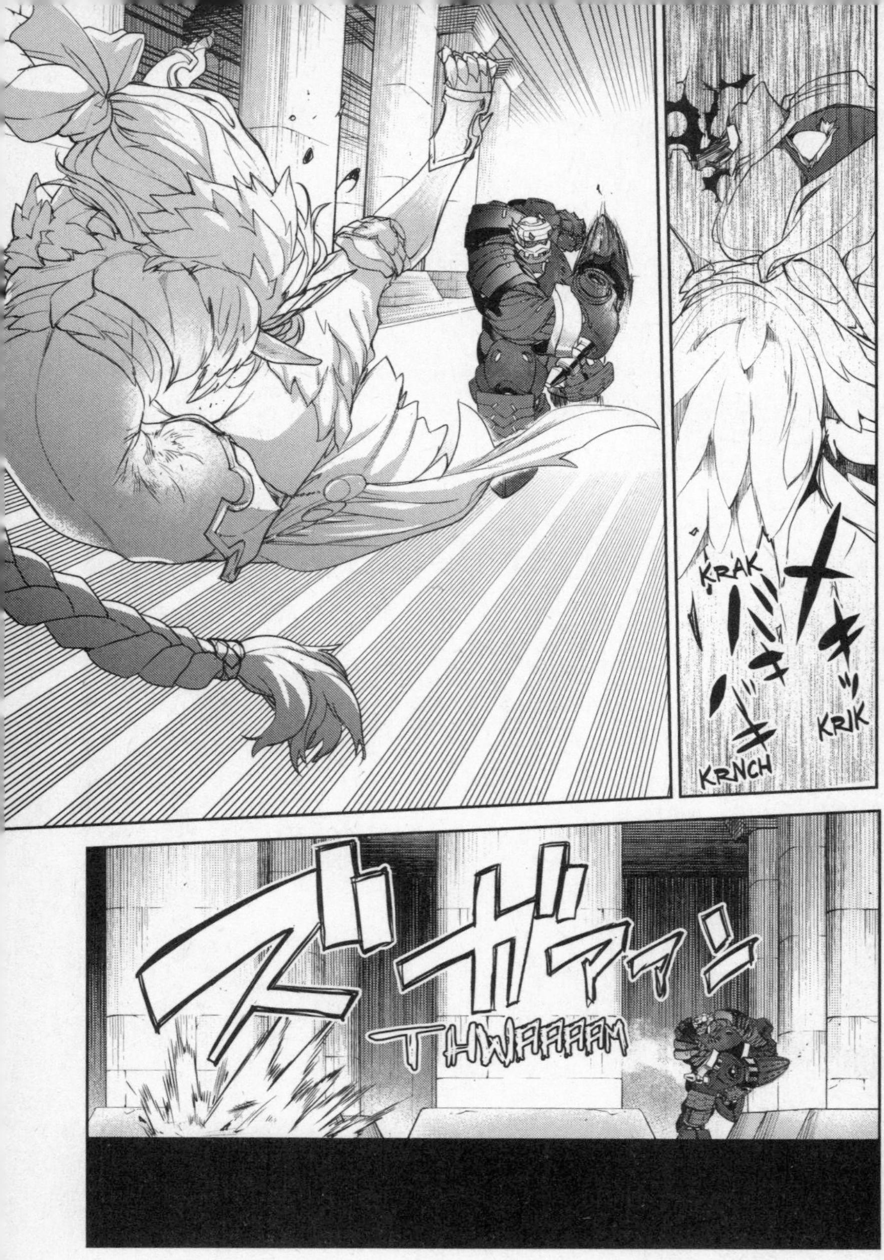
メキッ
KRIK
バキバキ
KRAK
KRNCH
ズガァァン
THWAAAAM

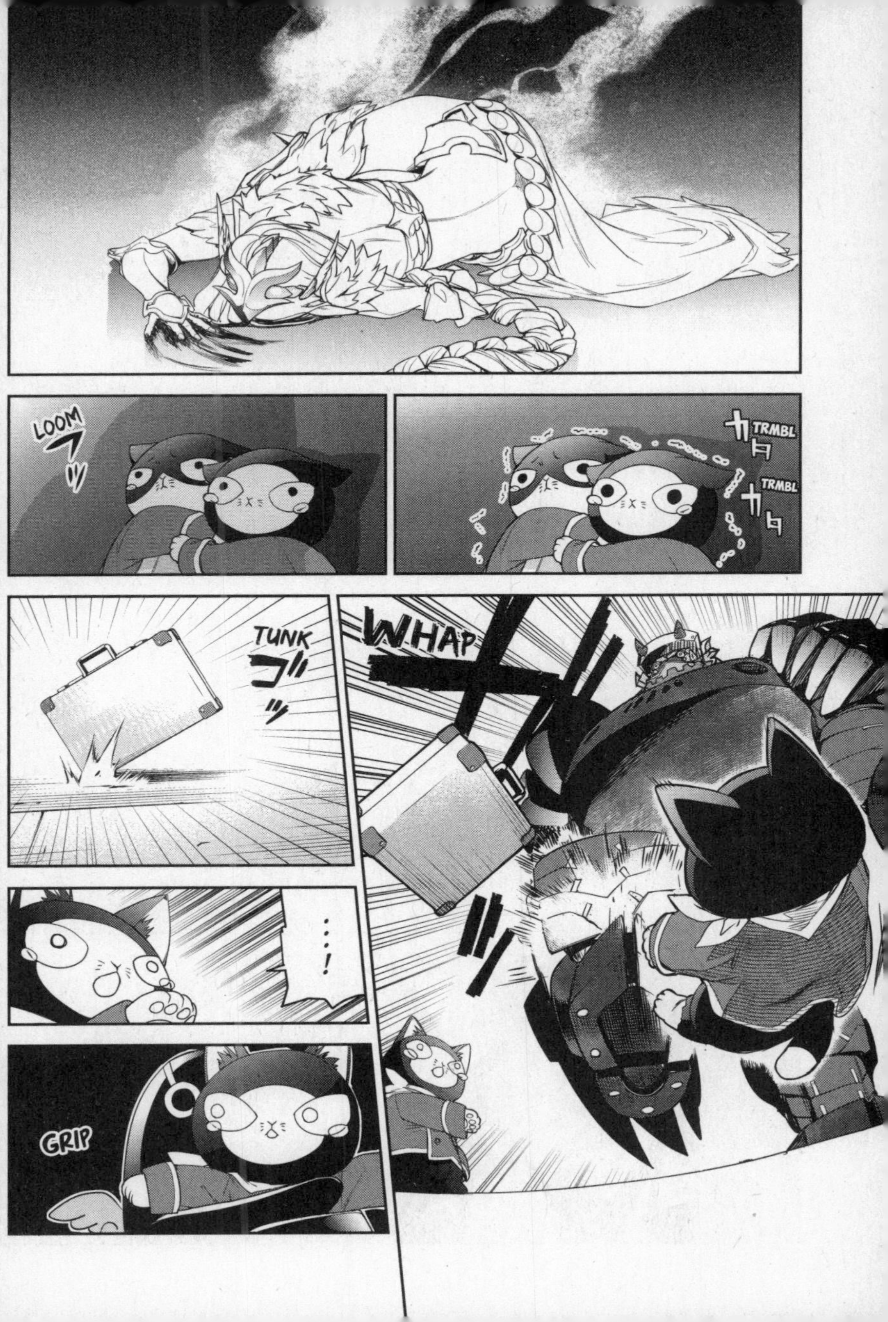
TRMBL
TRMBL
LOOM
WHAP
TUNK
...!
GRIP

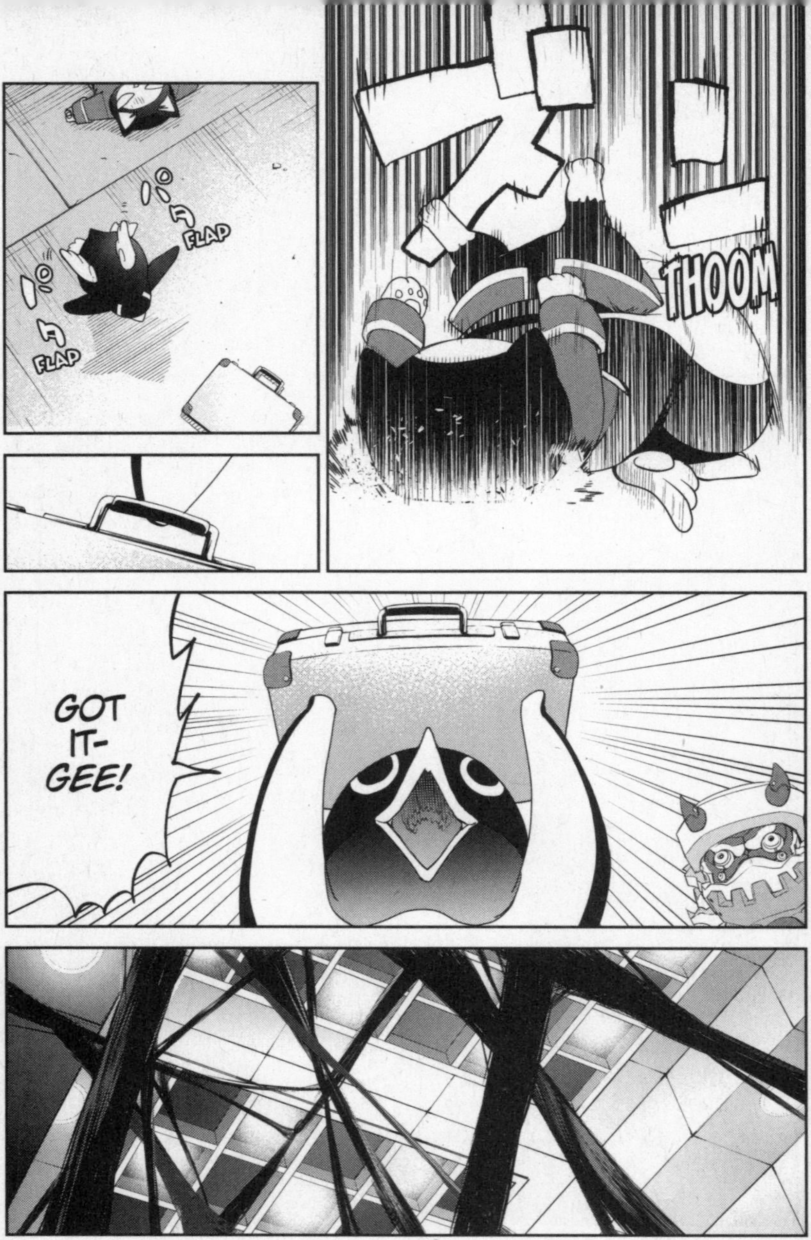
THOOM
FLAP
FLAP
GOT IT-GEE!

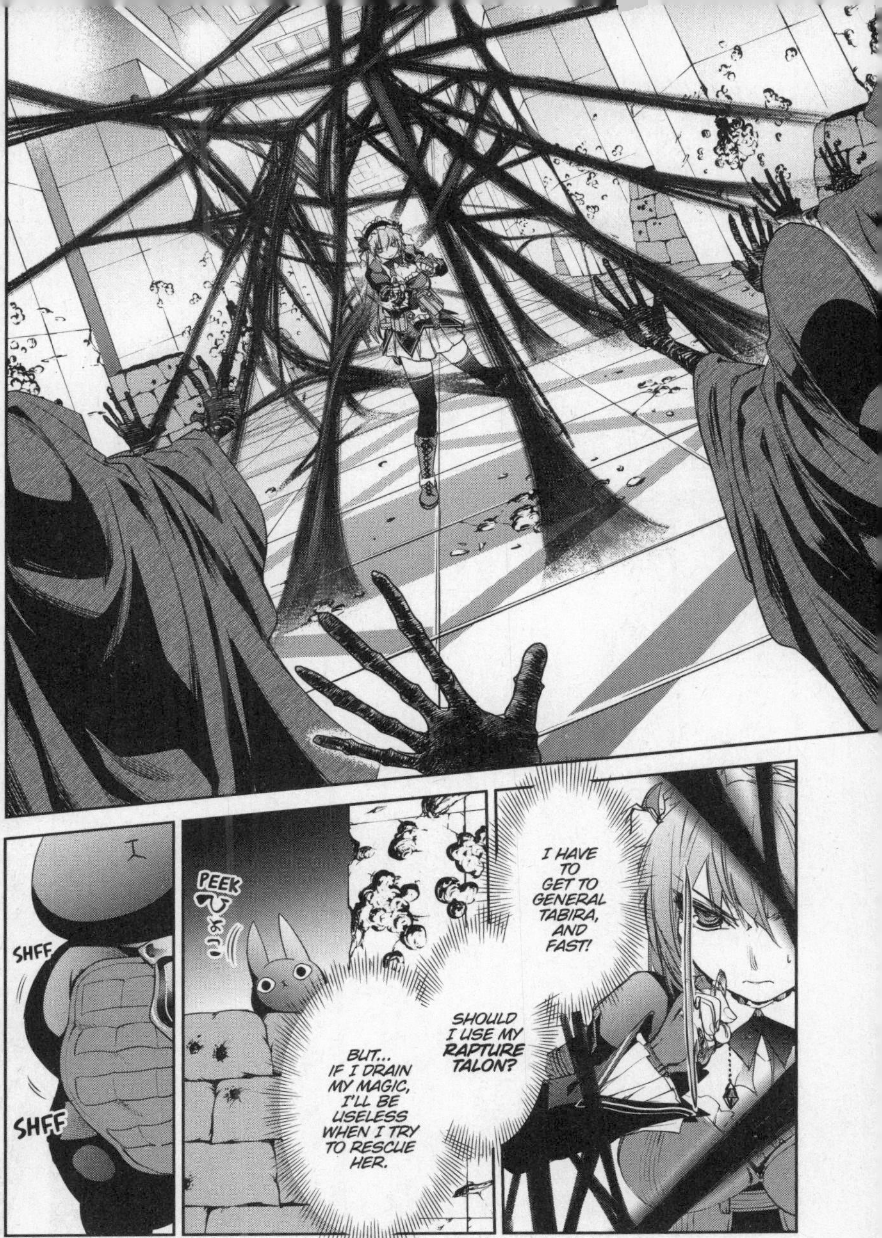
I HAVE TO GET TO GENERAL TABIRA, AND FAST!
SHOULD I USE MY RAPTURE TALON?
BUT... IF I DRAIN MY MAGIC, I'LL BE USELESS WHEN I TRY TO RESCUE HER.
PEEK
SHFF
SHFF

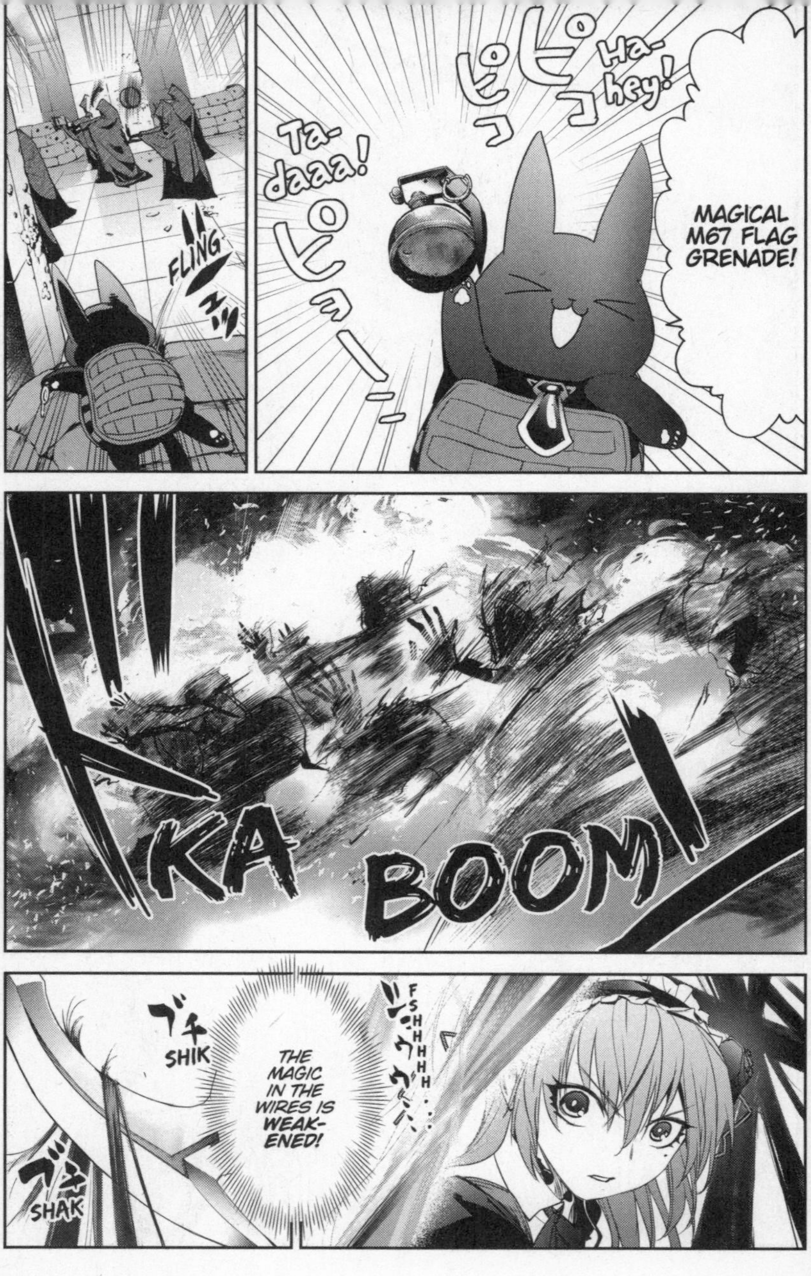

Ha-hey!
MAGICAL M67 FLAG GRENADE!
Ta-daaa!
FLING
KA BOOM
FSHHHHH...
THE MAGIC IN THE WIRES IS WEAK-ENED!
SHIK
SHAK

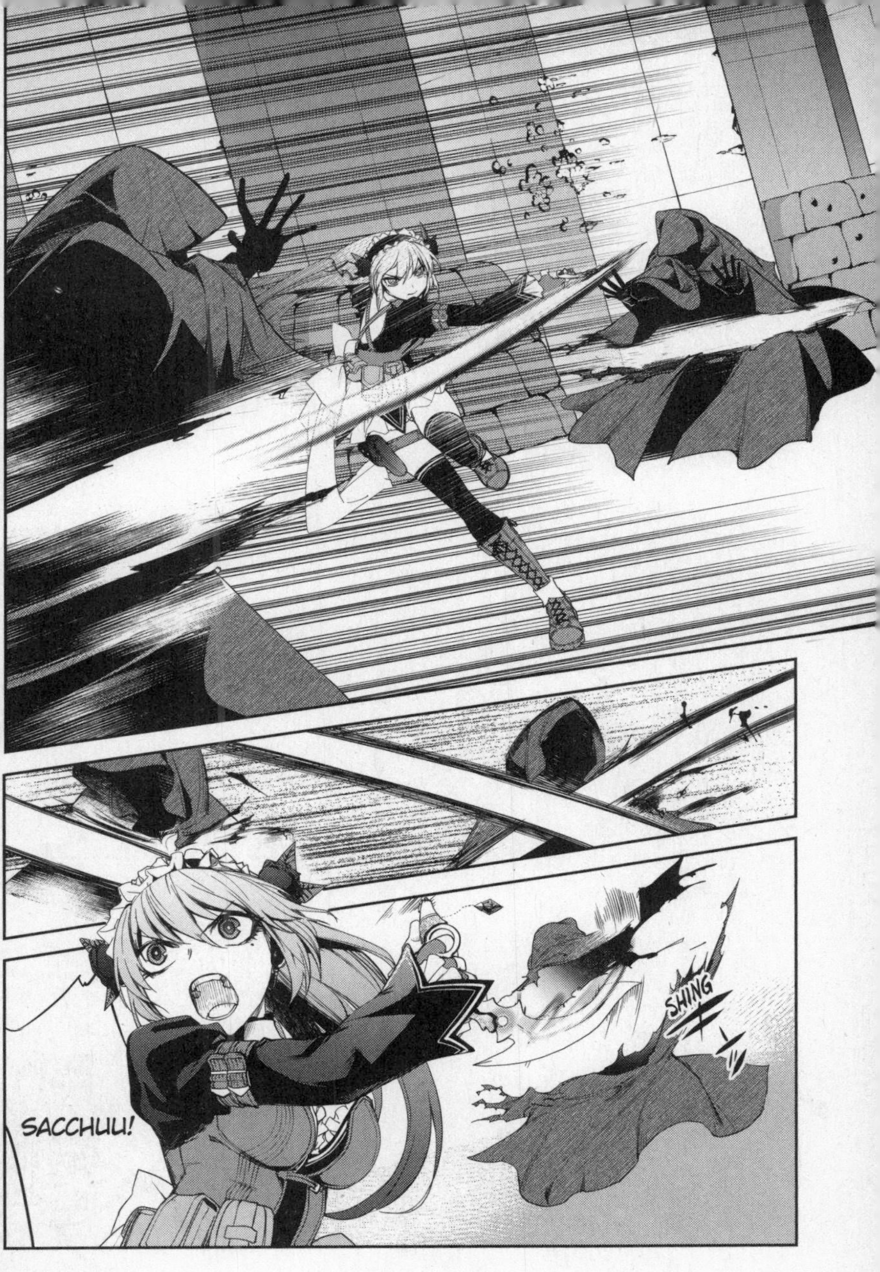
SHING
SACCHUU!

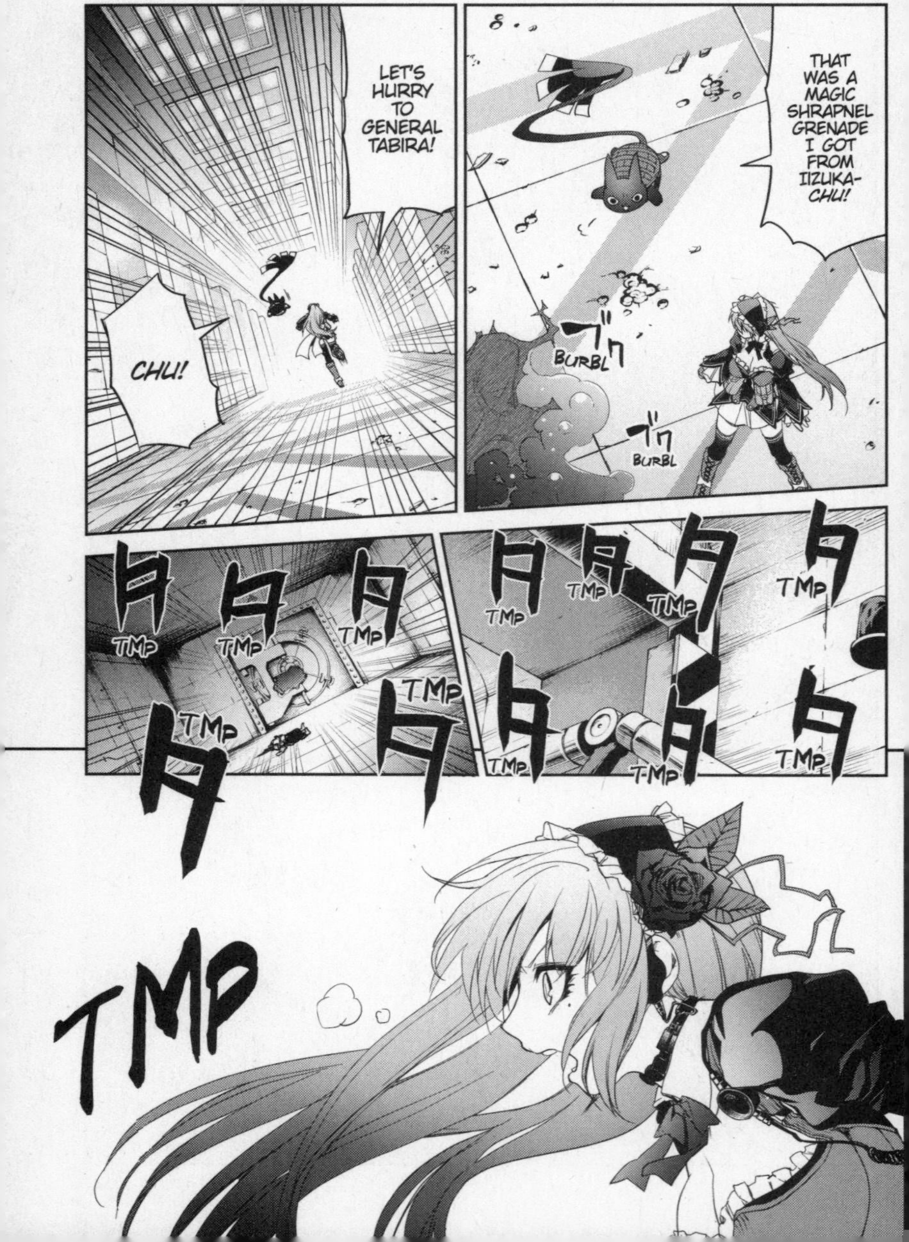
THAT WAS A MAGIC SHRAPNEL GRENADE I GOT FROM IIZUKA-CHU!
BURBL
BURBL
LET'S HURRY TO GENERAL TABIRA!
CHU!
TMP
TMP
TMP
TMP
TMP
TMP
TMP
TMP
TMP
TMP
TMP
TMP
TMP

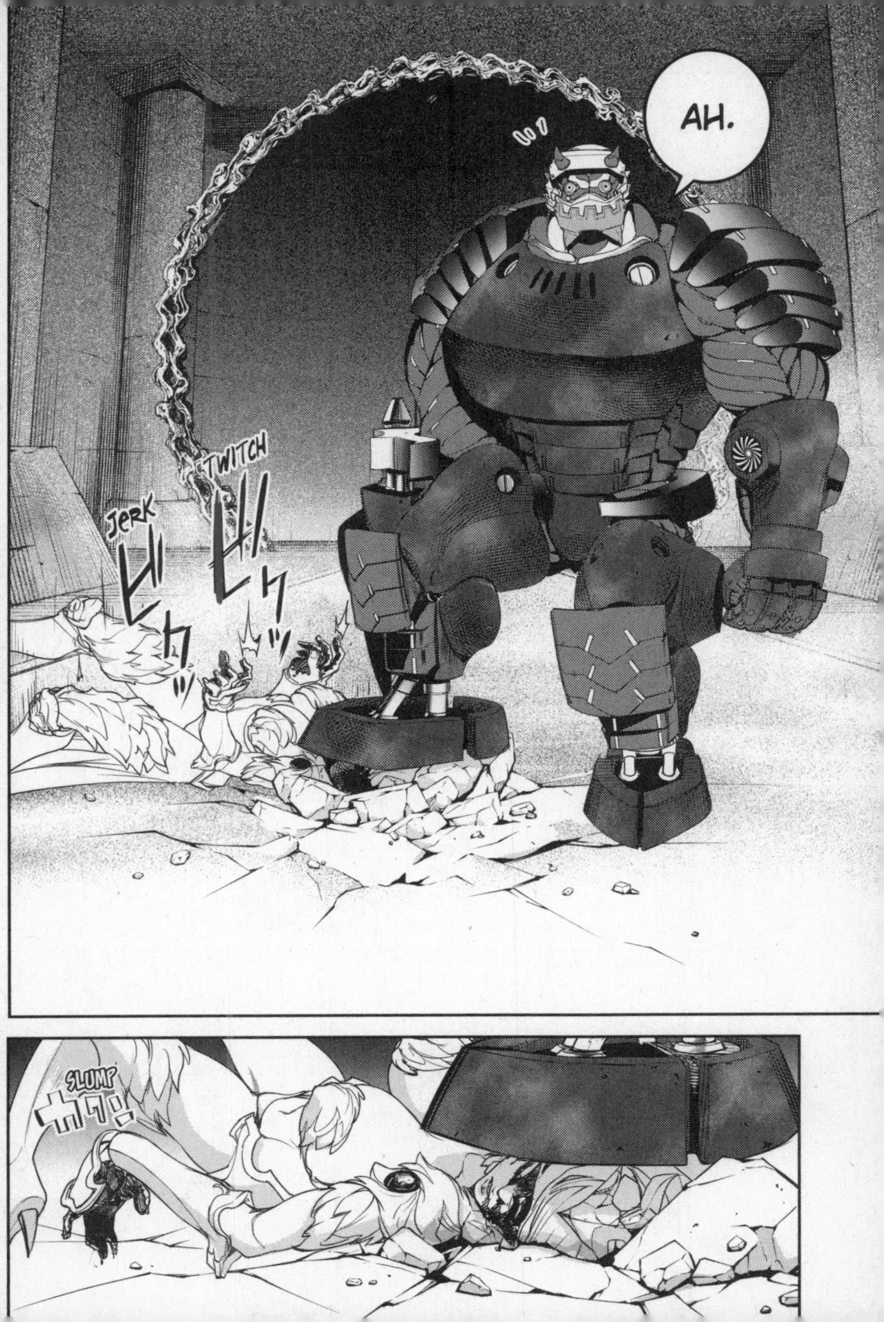
AH.
TWITCH
JERK
SLUMP

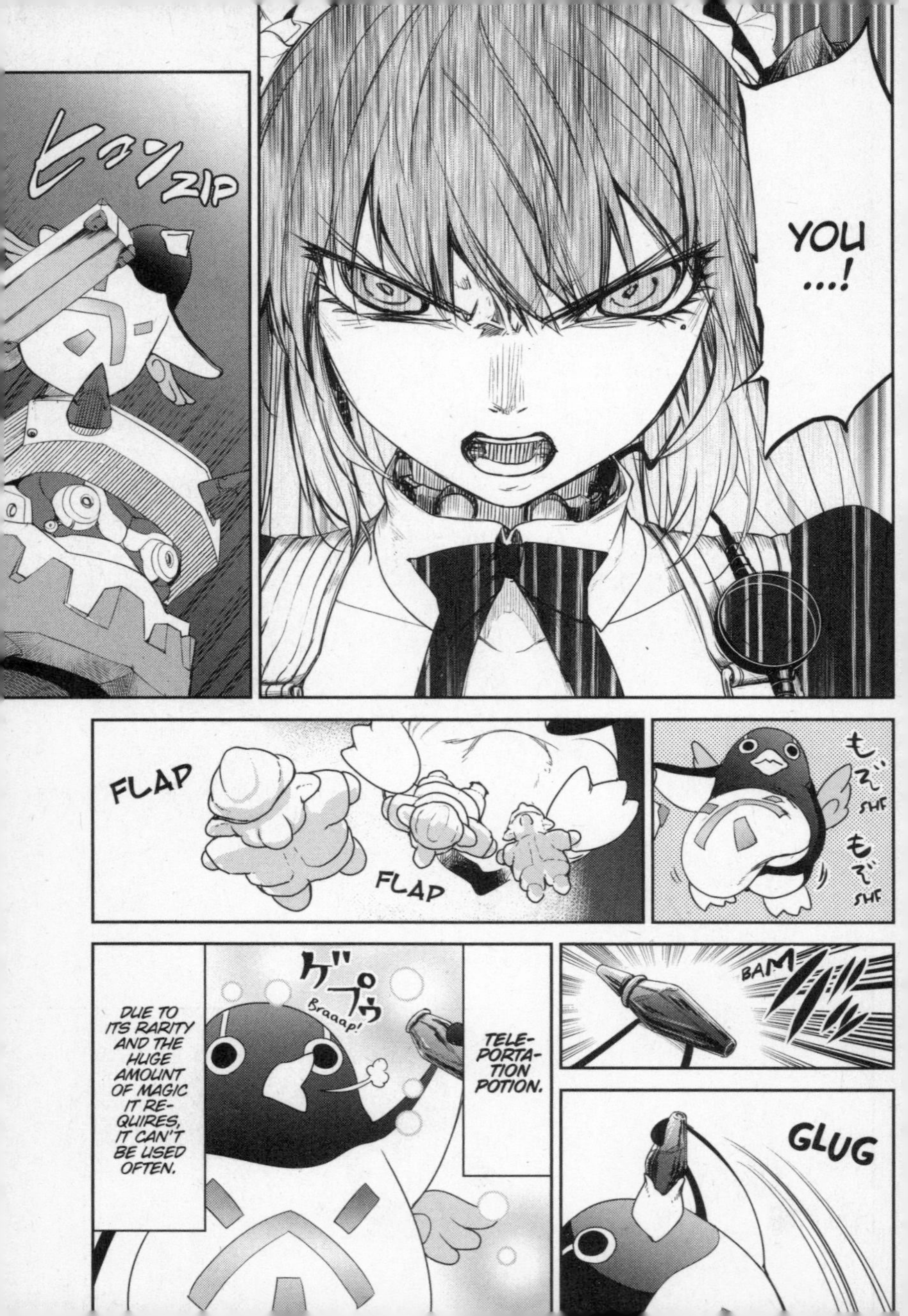
YOU ...!
ヒュン
ZIP
もぞ
SHF
もぞ
SHF
FLAP
FLAP
BAM
GLUG
TELE-PORTA-TION POTION.
ゲプゥ
Braaaap!
DUE TO ITS RARITY AND THE HUGE AMOUNT OF MAGIC IT RE-QUIRES, IT CAN'T BE USED OFTEN.

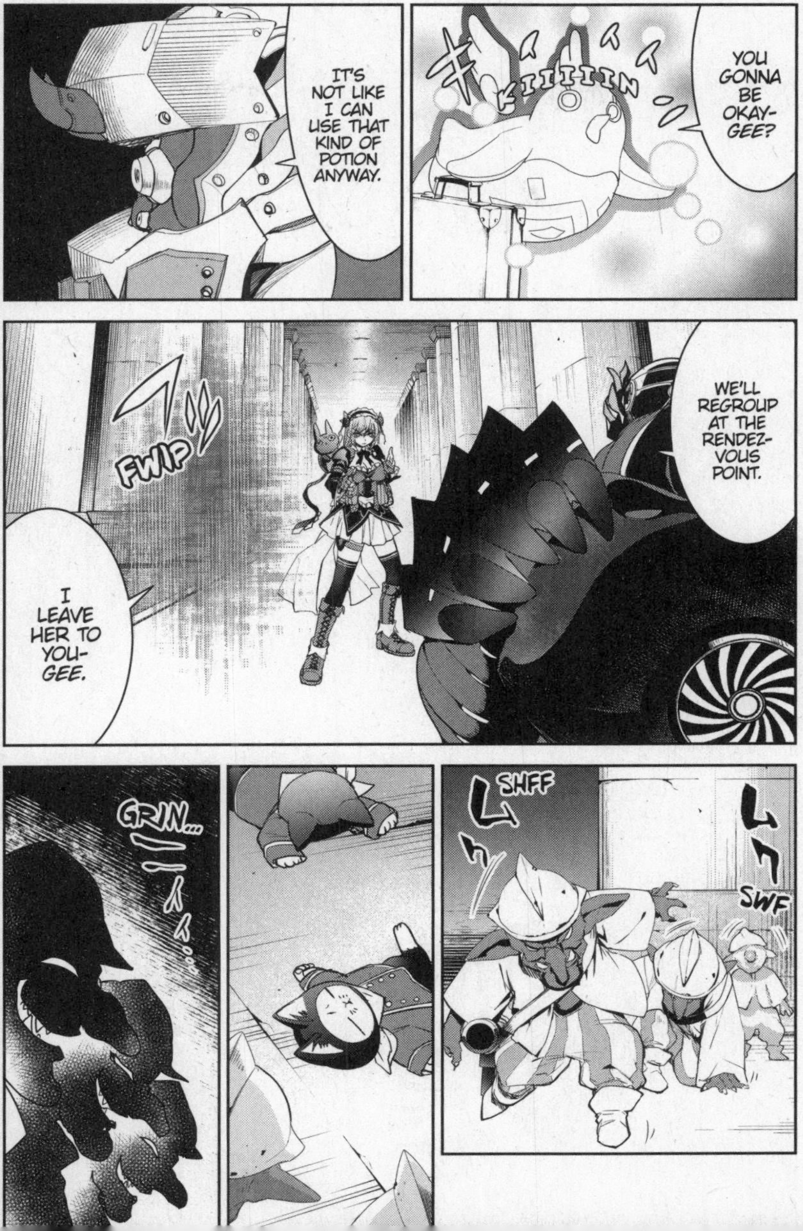
YOU GONNA BE OKAY-GEE?
KIIIIIIN
IT'S NOT LIKE I CAN USE THAT KIND OF POTION ANYWAY.
WE'LL REGROUP AT THE RENDEZ-VOUS POINT.
FWIP
I LEAVE HER TO YOU-GEE.
SHFF
SWF
GRIN...

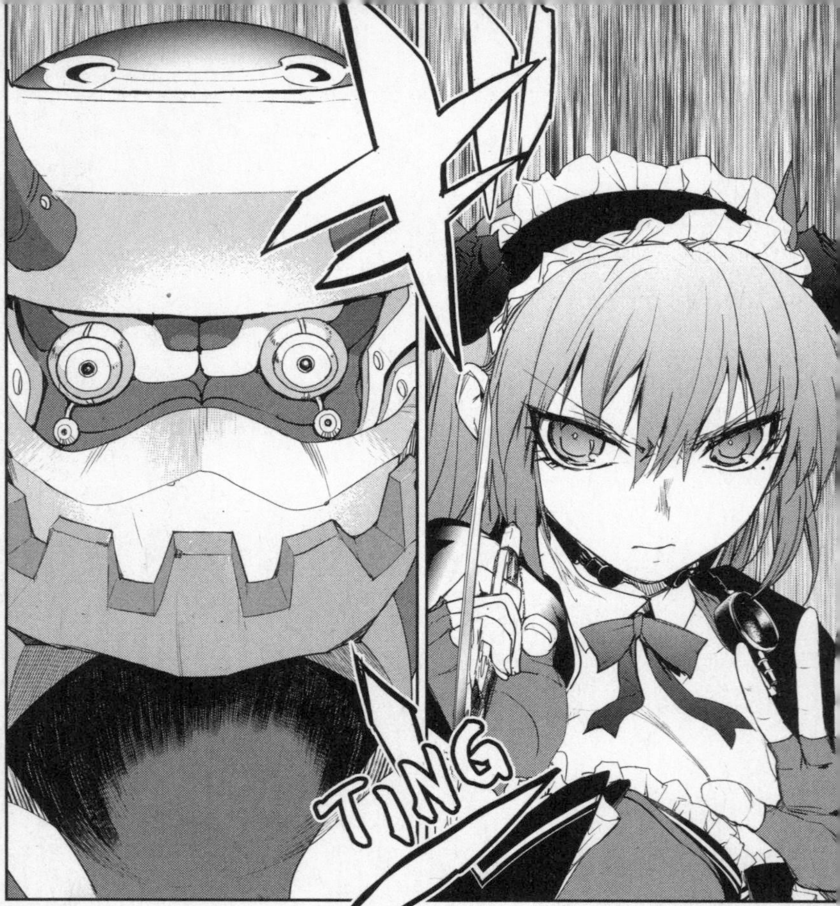
TING
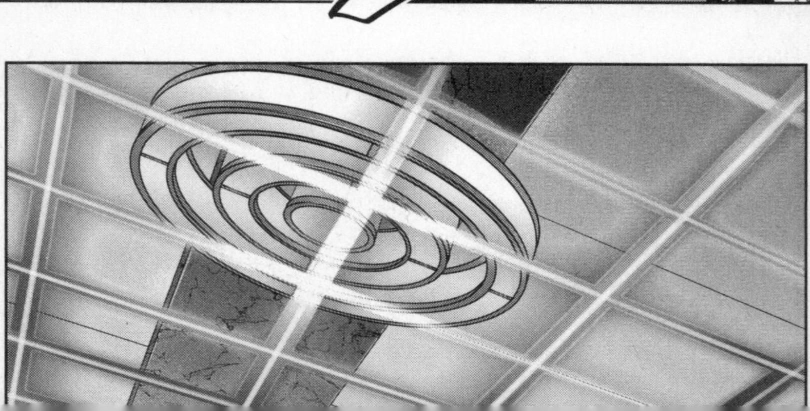

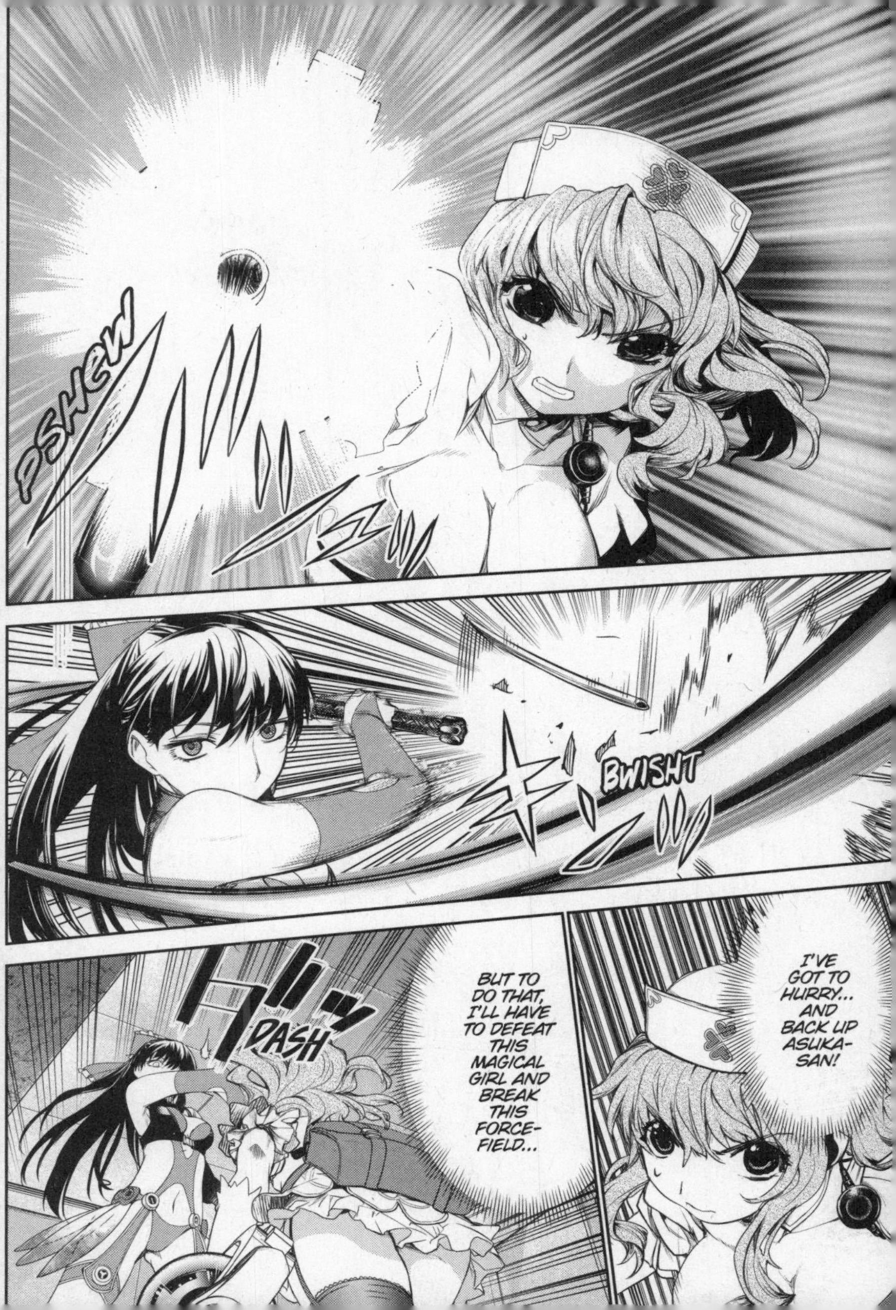
PSHEW
BWISHT
I'VE GOT TO HURRY... AND BACK UP ASUKA-SAN!
BUT TO DO THAT, I'LL HAVE TO DEFEAT THIS MAGICAL GIRL AND BREAK THIS FORCE-FIELD...
DASH

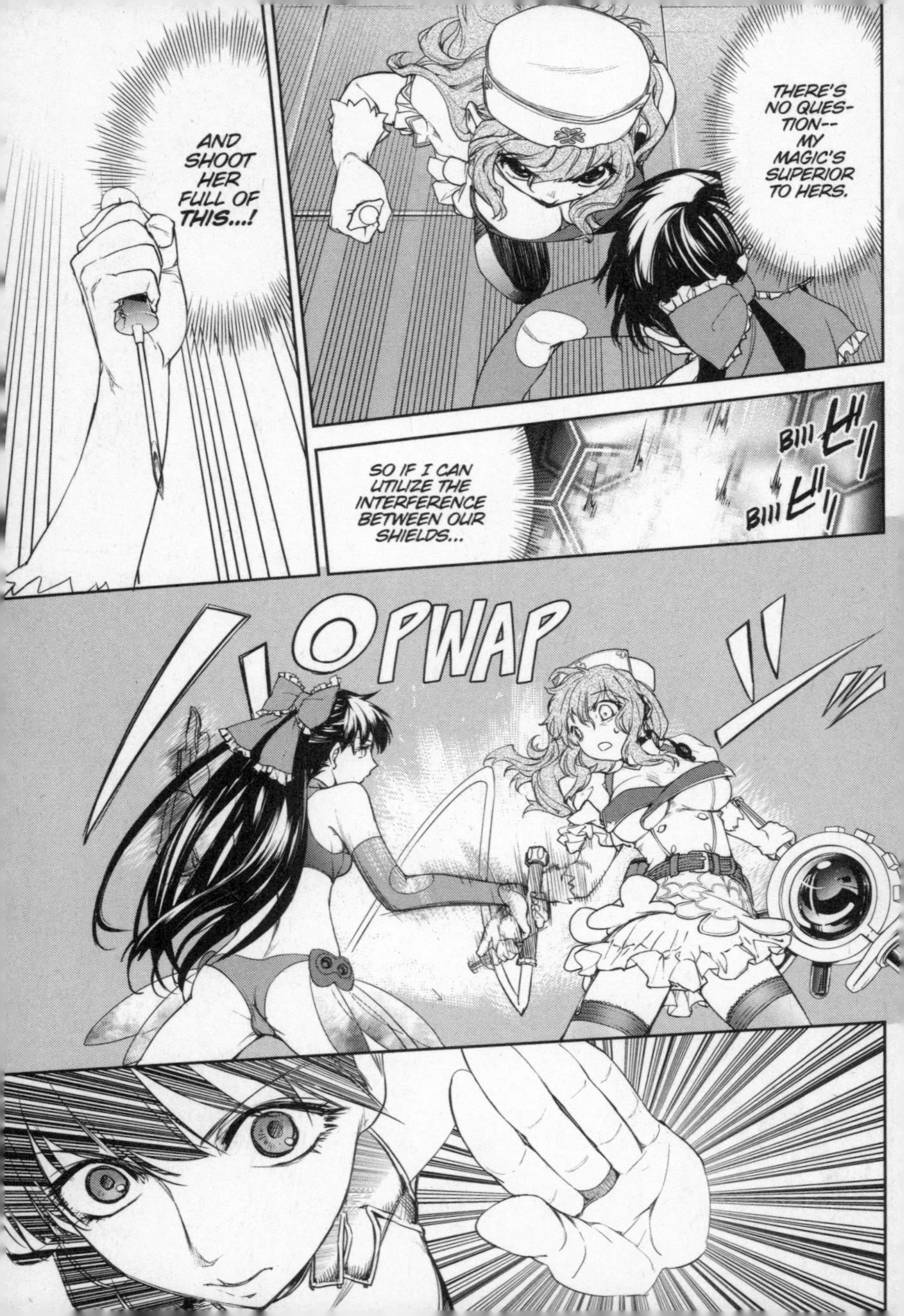
THERE'S NO QUESTION-- MY MAGIC'S SUPERIOR TO HERS.
SO IF I CAN UTILIZE THE INTERFERENCE BETWEEN OUR SHIELDS...
BIII
BIII
AND SHOOT HER FULL OF THIS...!
OPWAP

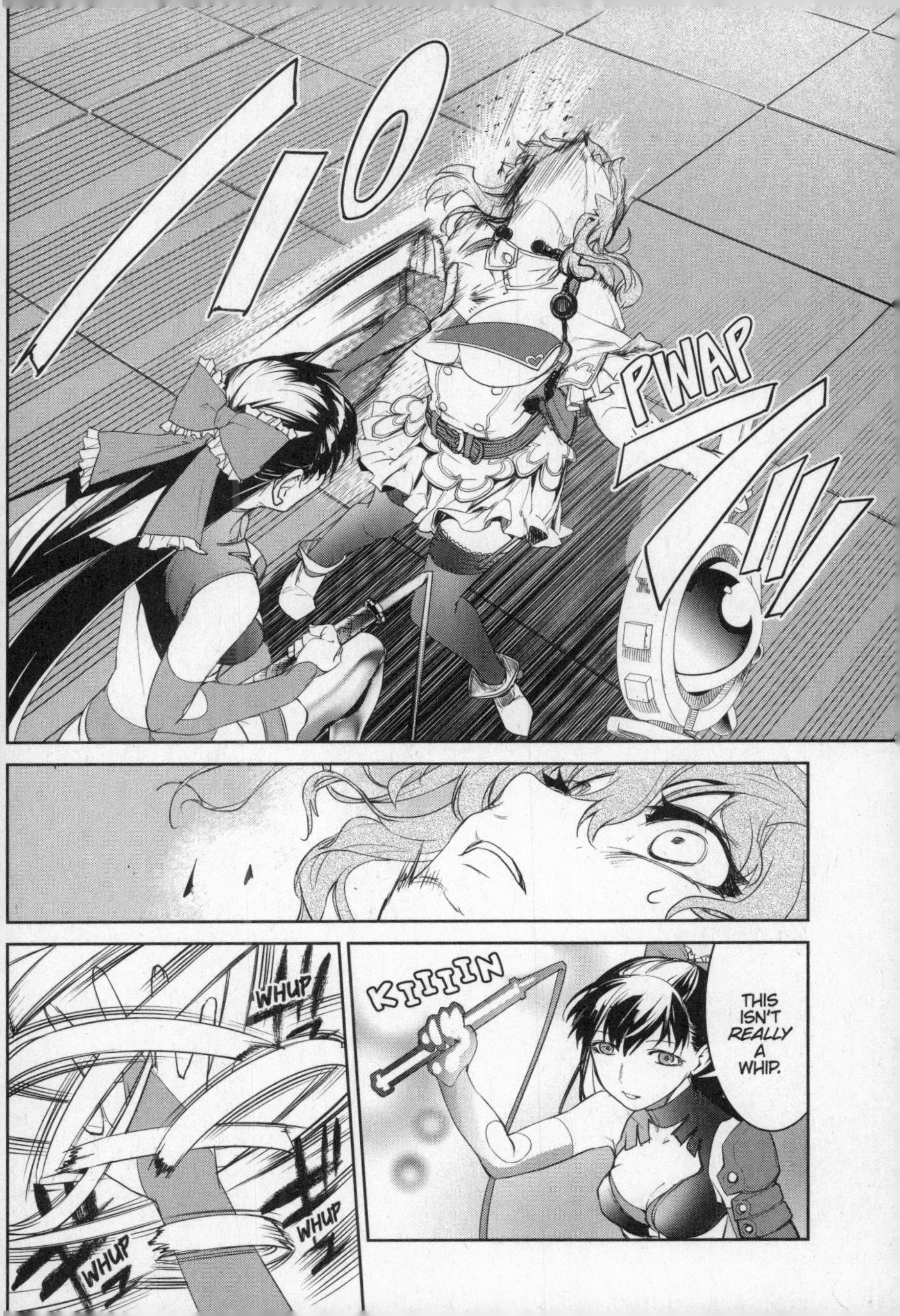
PWAP
KIIIIN
THIS ISN'T *REALLY* A WHIP.
WHUP
WHUP
WHUP

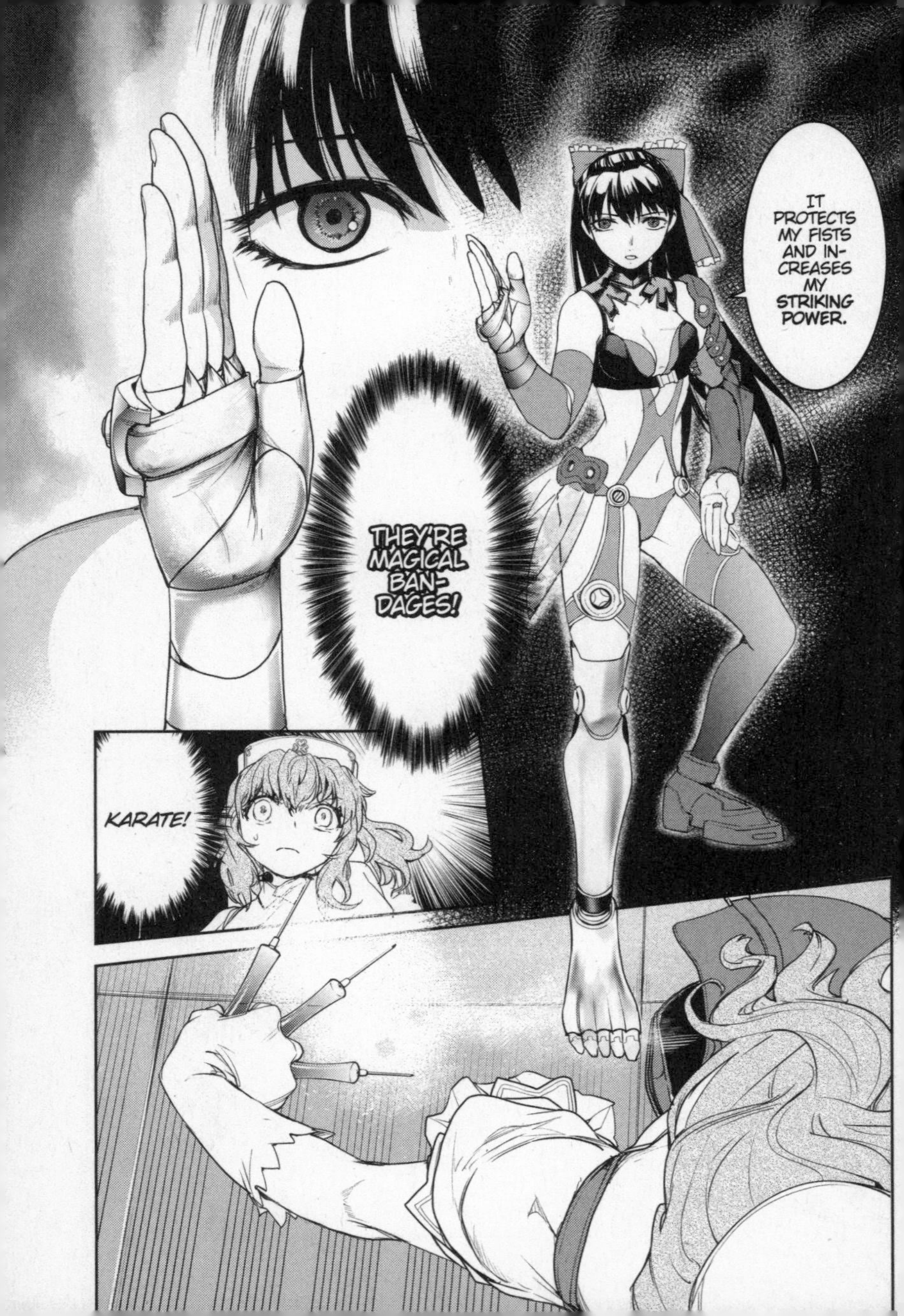
IT PROTECTS MY FISTS AND IN-CREASES MY STRIKING POWER.
THEY'RE MAGICAL BAN-DAGES!
KARATE!

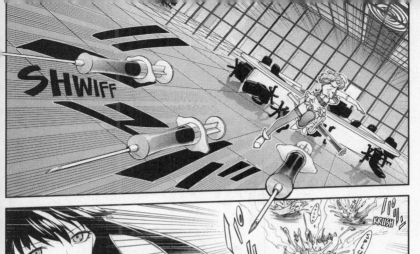

SHWIFF

KRIISH

KRIISH

DMM

SPIN
SPIN
SPIN

MY CALL SIGN... WHIP-LASH...

ISN'T BECAUSE I USE A WHIP.

BZZT

BZZT

BZZT

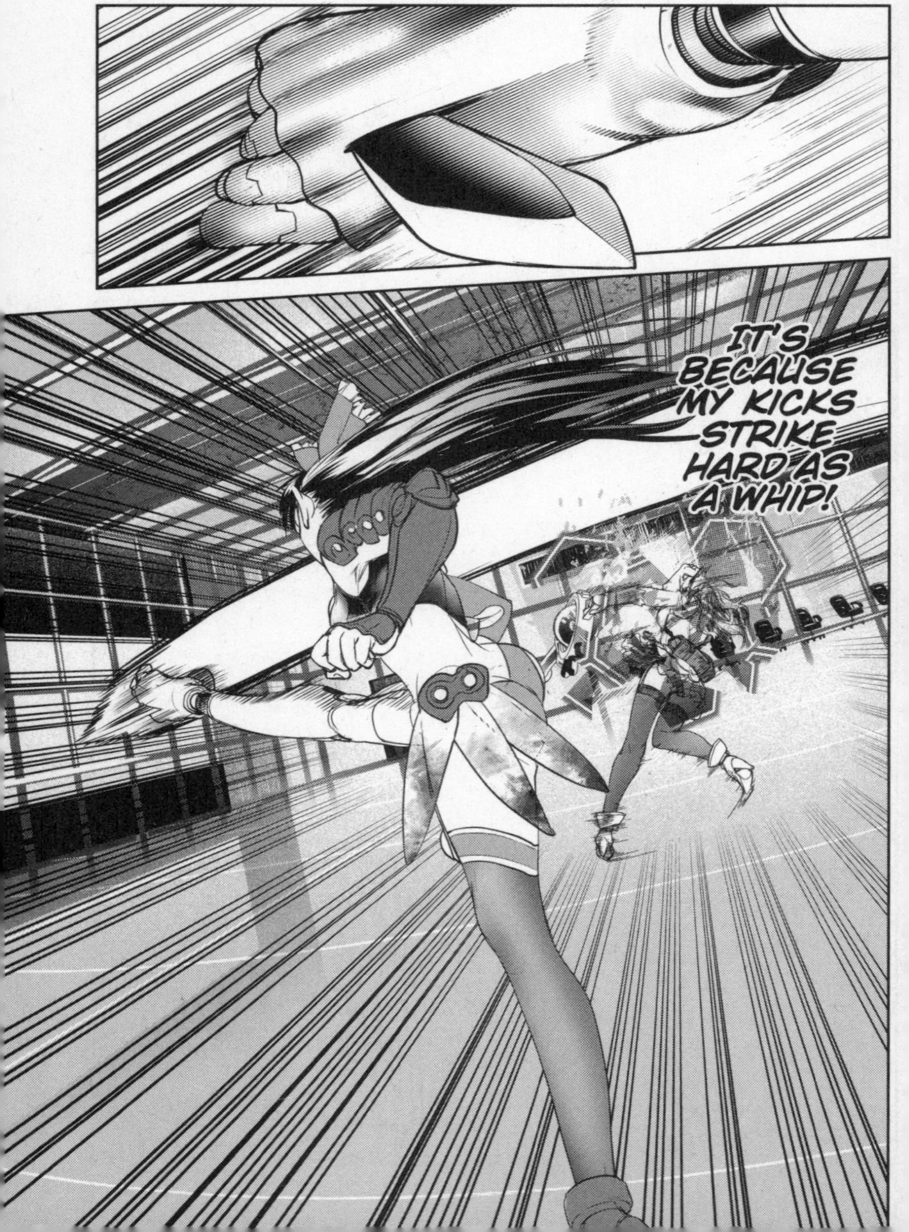
IT'S BECAUSE MY KICKS STRIKE HARD AS A WHIP!

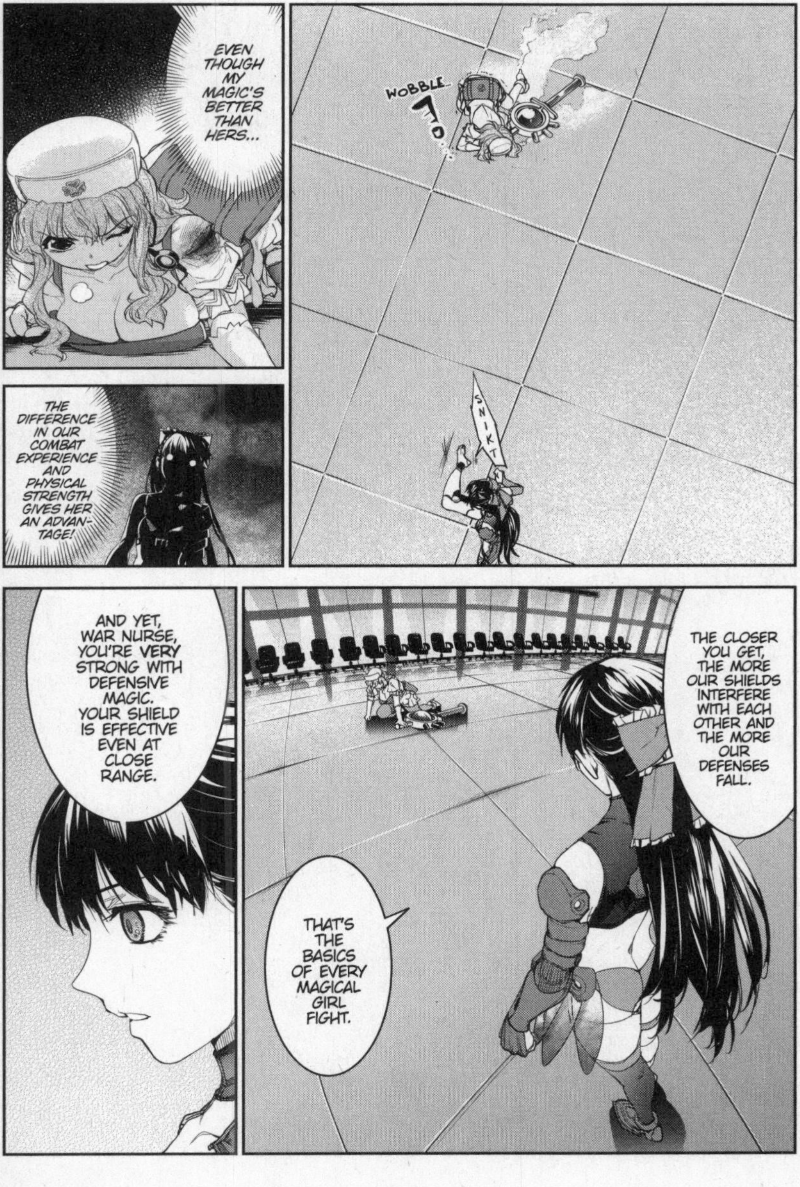
WOBBLE
SNIKT
EVEN THOUGH MY MAGIC'S BETTER THAN HERS...
THE DIFFERENCE IN OUR COMBAT EXPERIENCE AND PHYSICAL STRENGTH GIVES HER AN ADVAN-TAGE!
THE CLOSER YOU GET, THE MORE OUR SHIELDS INTERFERE WITH EACH OTHER AND THE MORE OUR DEFENSES FALL.
THAT'S THE BASICS OF EVERY MAGICAL GIRL FIGHT.
AND YET, WAR NURSE, YOU'RE VERY STRONG WITH DEFENSIVE MAGIC. YOUR SHIELD IS EFFECTIVE EVEN AT CLOSE RANGE.

HOW-EVER... I CAN'T LET IT END LIKE THAT.

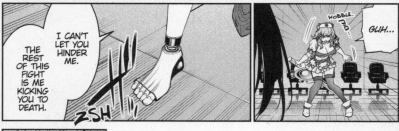

I CAN'T LET YOU HINDER ME.

THE REST OF THIS FIGHT IS ME KICKING YOU TO DEATH.

ZSH

WOBBLE

GUH...

YOU'RE GONNA BE MY OWN PERSONAL SANDBAG.

YOUR SAND-BAG?

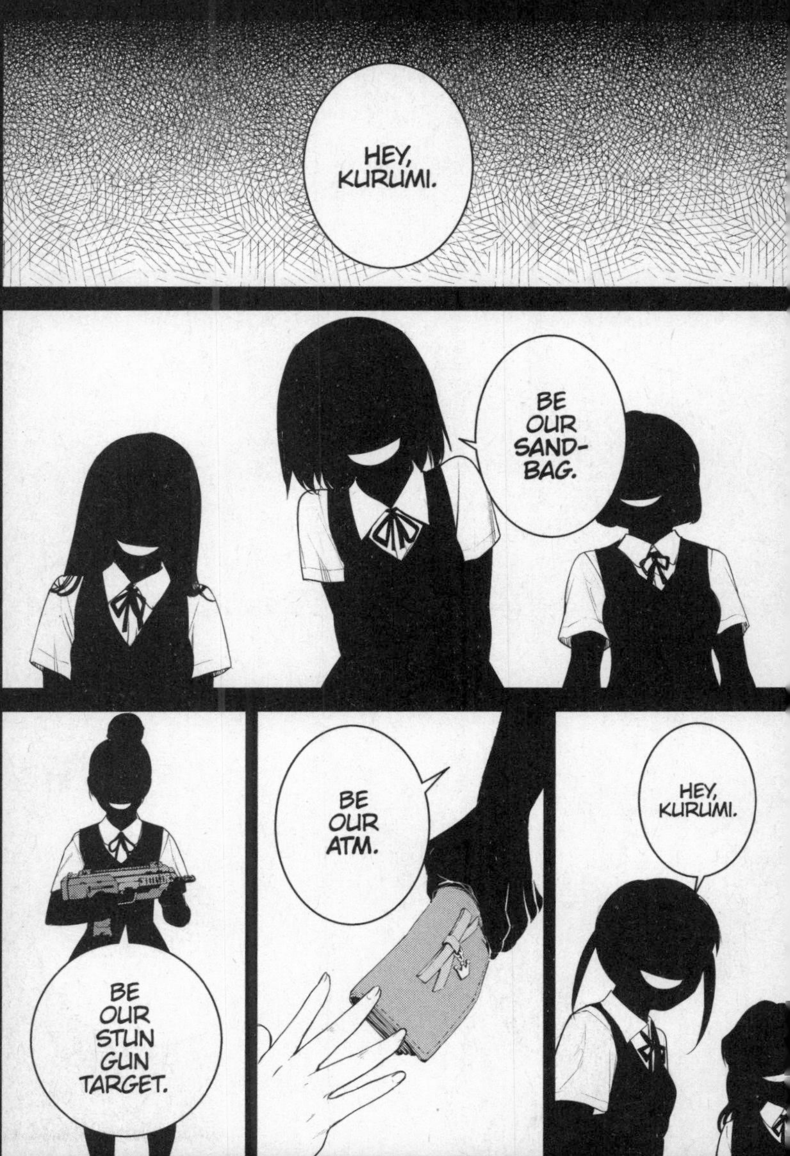
HEY, KURUMI.
BE OUR SANDBAG.
HEY, KURUMI.
BE OUR ATM.
BE OUR STUN GUN TARGET.

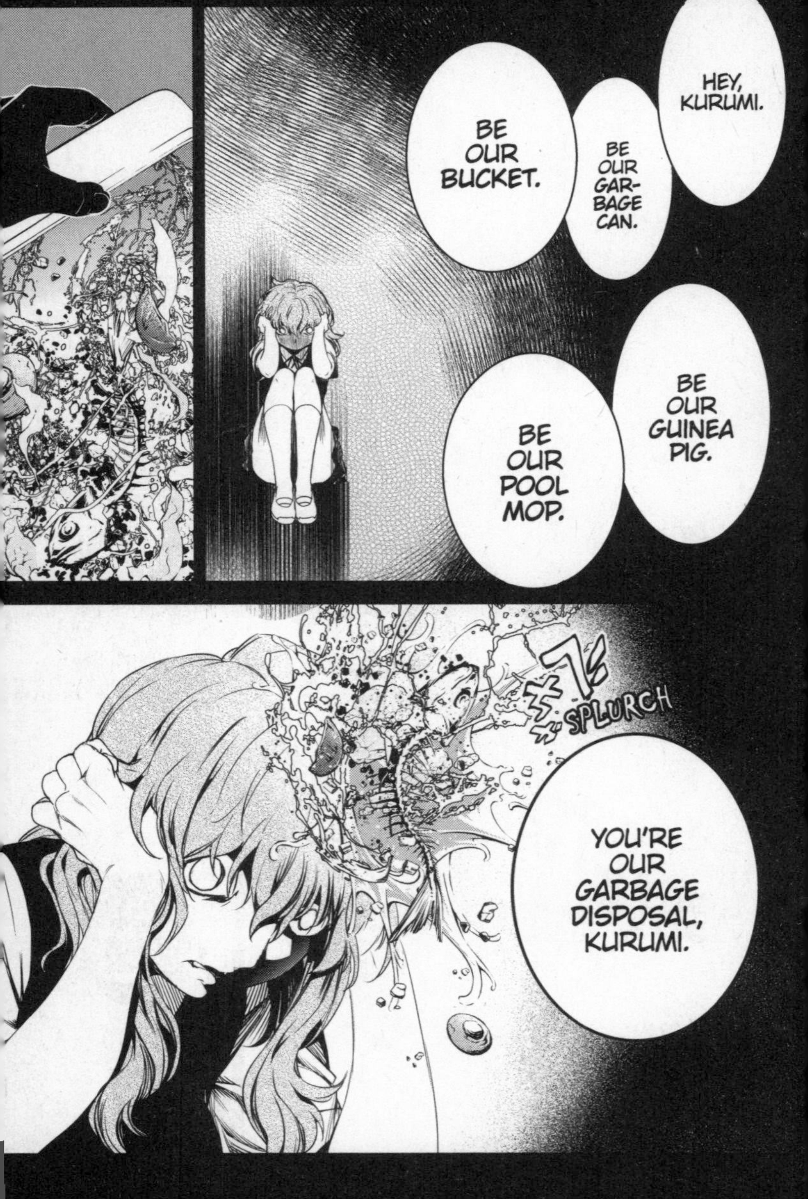
HEY, KURUMI.
BE OUR GAR-BAGE CAN.
BE OUR BUCKET.
BE OUR GUINEA PIG.
BE OUR POOL MOP.
SPLURCH
YOU'RE OUR GARBAGE DISPOSAL, KURUMI.

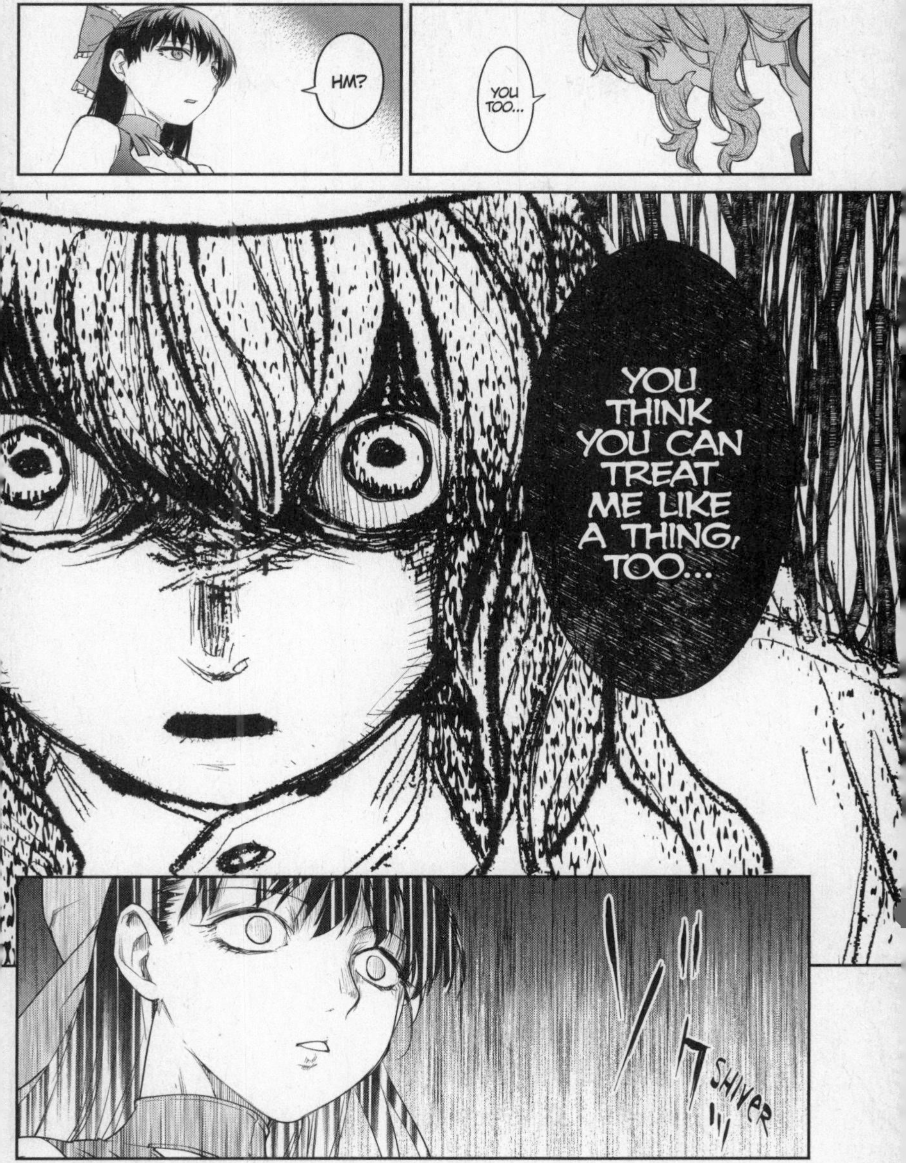
YOU TOO...
HM?
YOU THINK YOU CAN TREAT ME LIKE A THING, TOO...
SHIVER

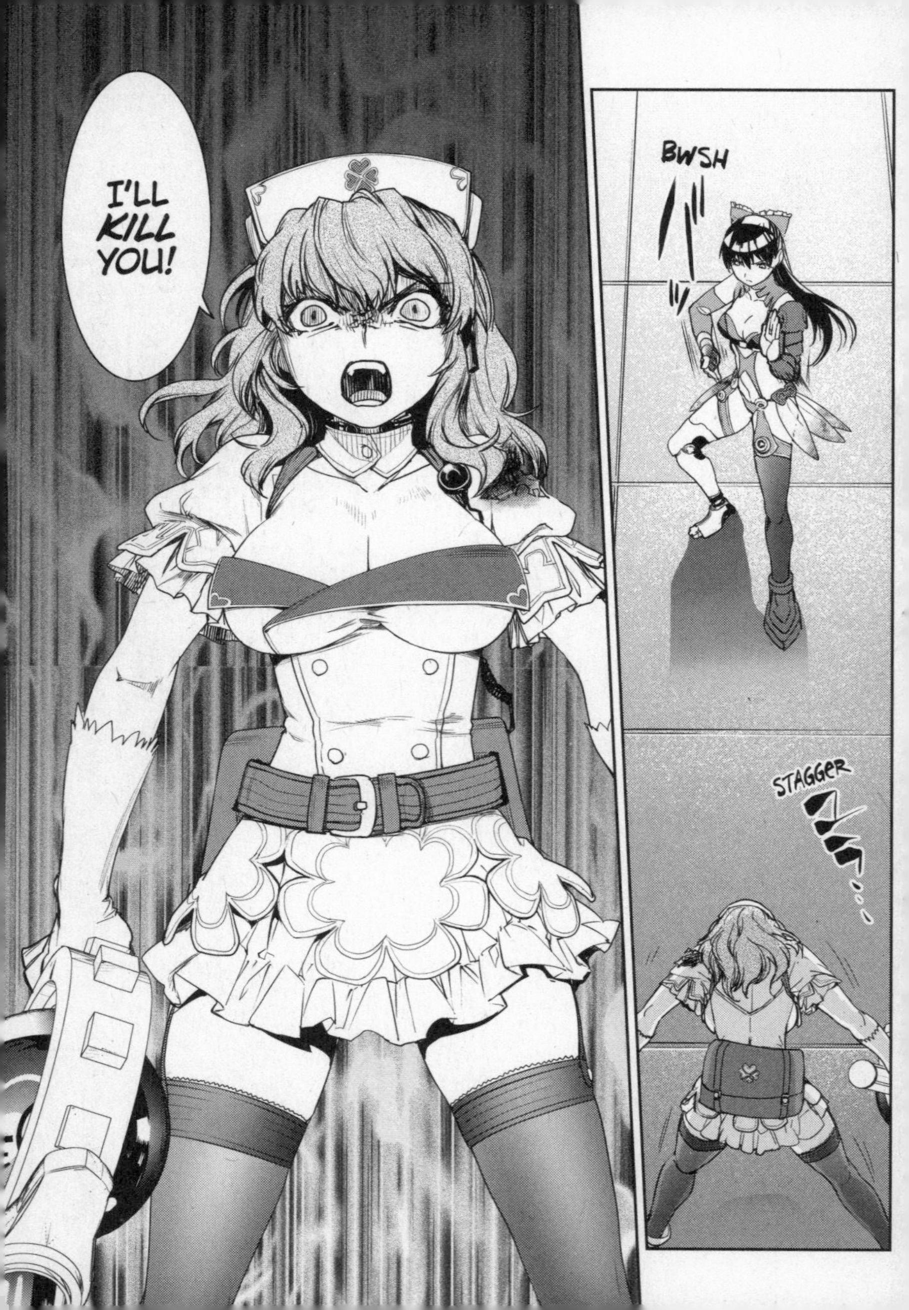
BWSH
STAGGER
I'LL KILL YOU!

魔法少女特殊戦
あすか

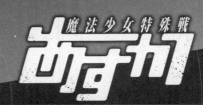

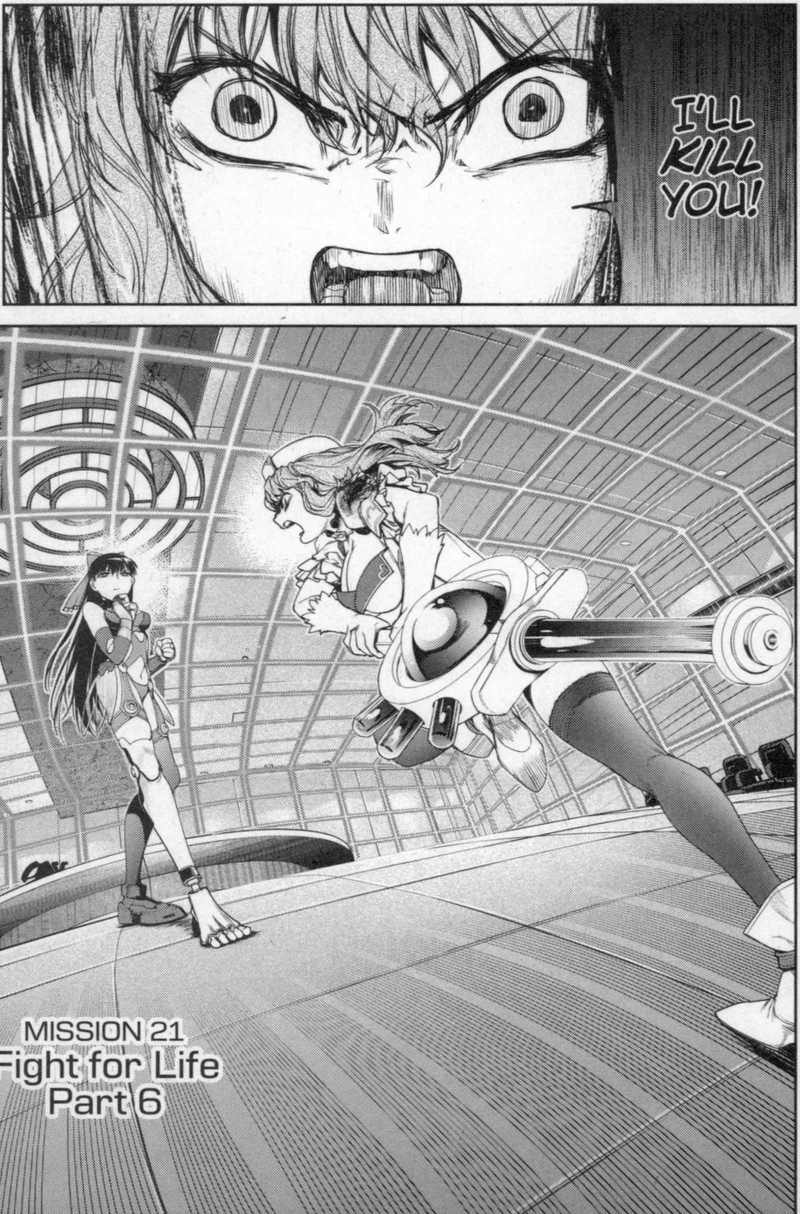
I'LL KILL YOU!
MISSION 21
Fight for Life
Part 6

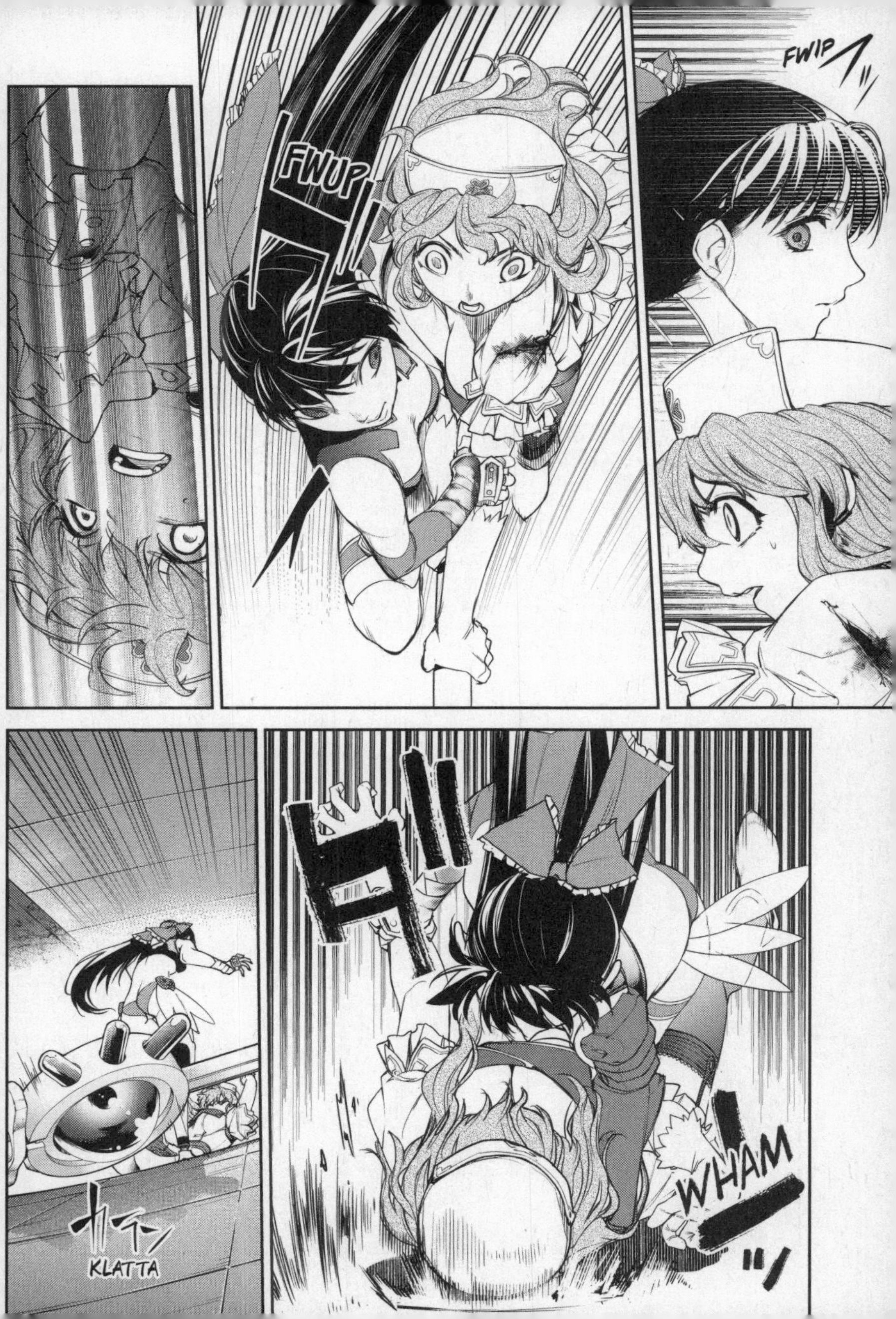
FWIP
FWUP
WHAM
KLATTA

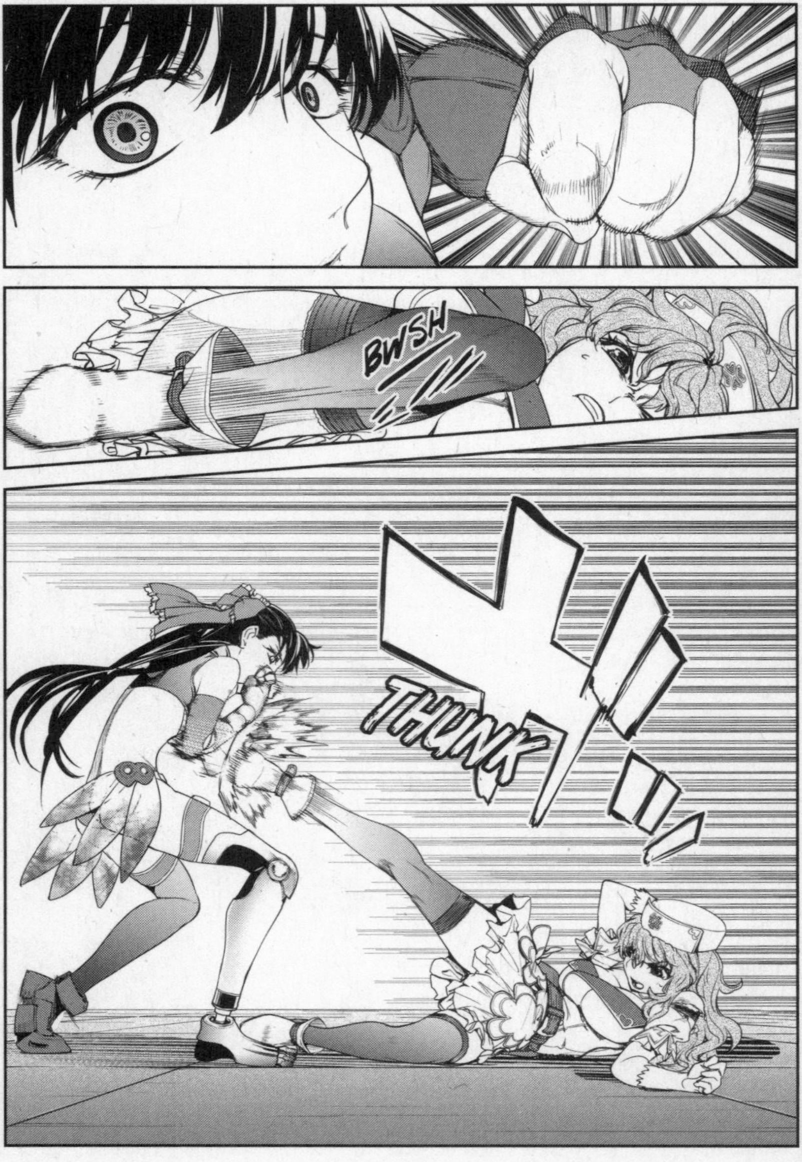
BWSH
THUNK

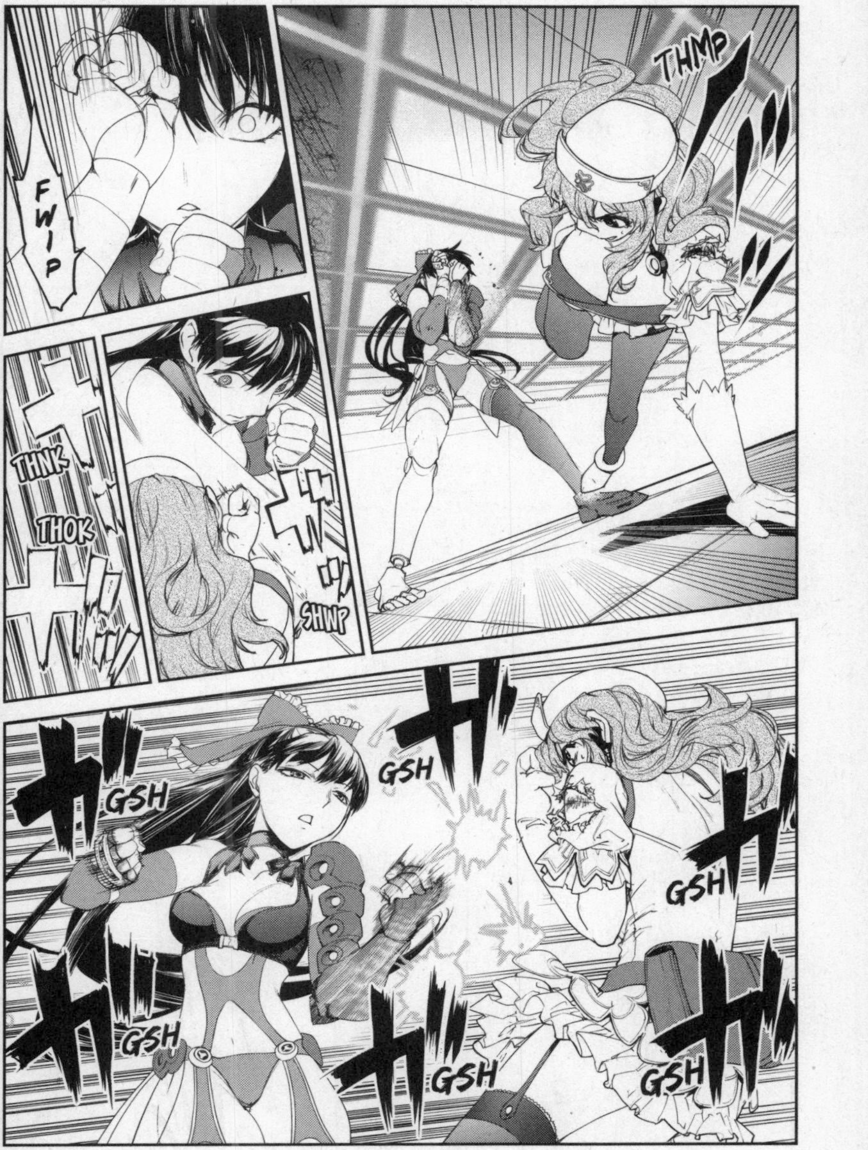
THMP
FWIP
SHWP
THNK
THOK
GSH
GSH
GSH
GSH
GSH
GSH

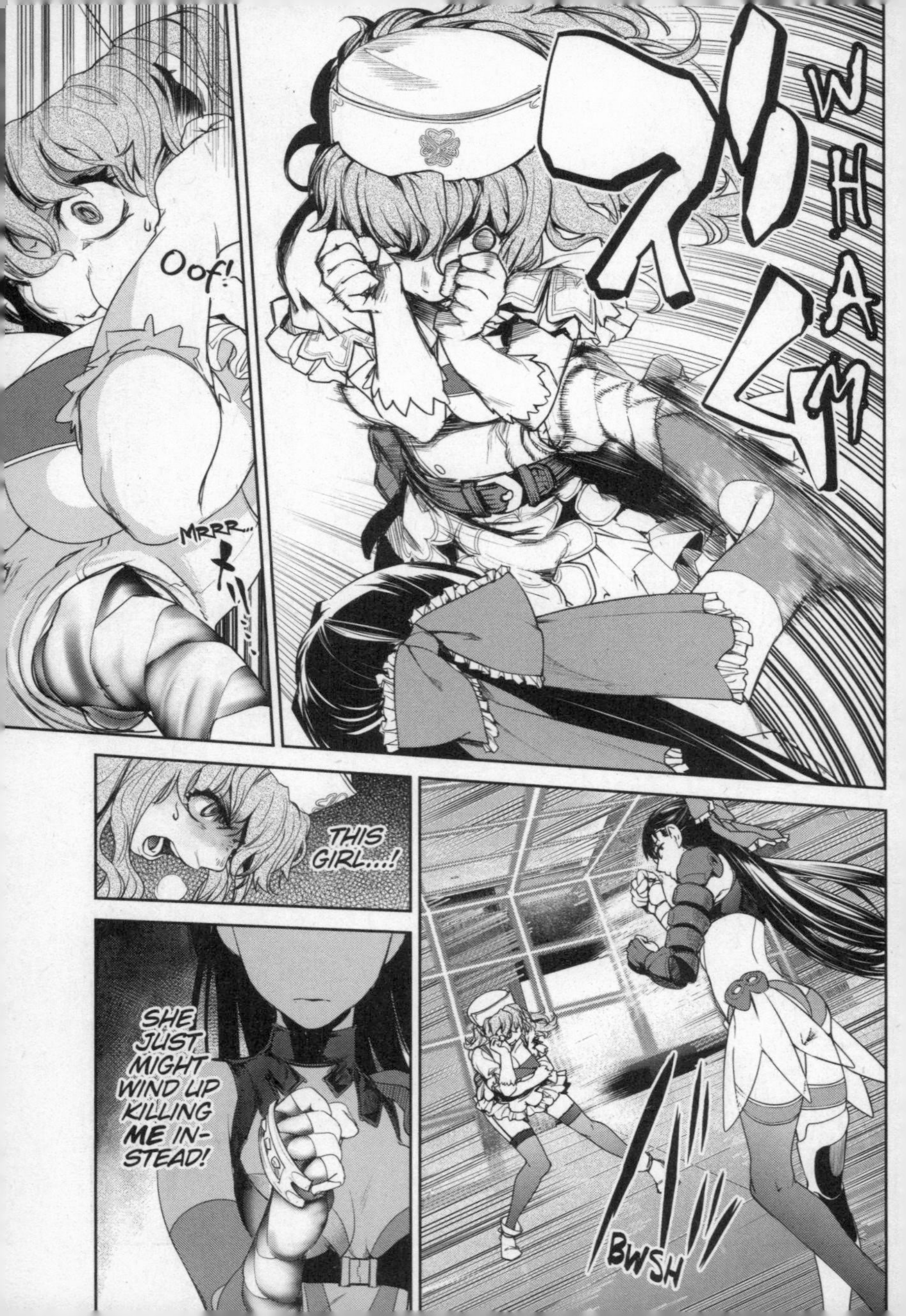
WHAM
Oof!
MRRR...
BWSH
THIS GIRL...!
SHE JUST MIGHT WIND UP KILLING ME IN-STEAD!

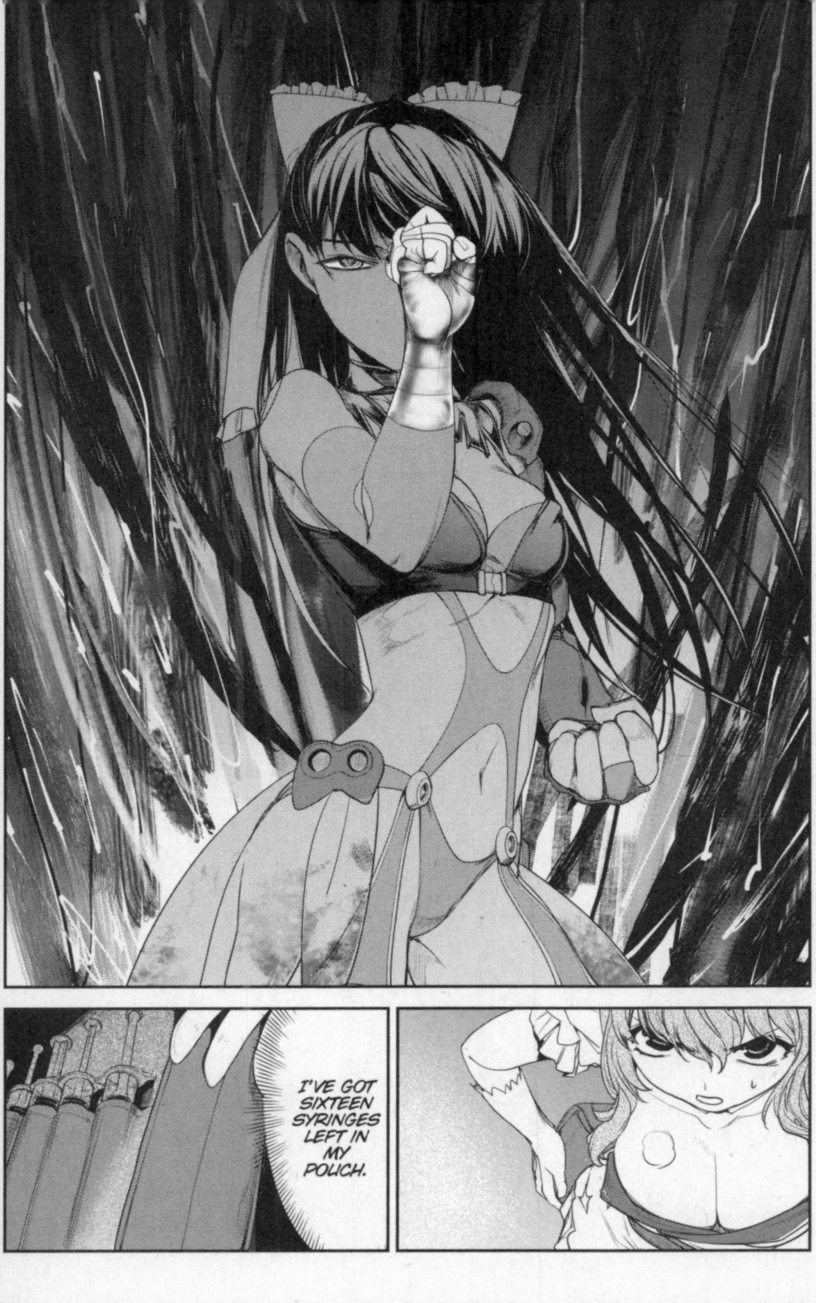
I'VE GOT SIXTEEN SYRINGES LEFT IN MY POUCH.

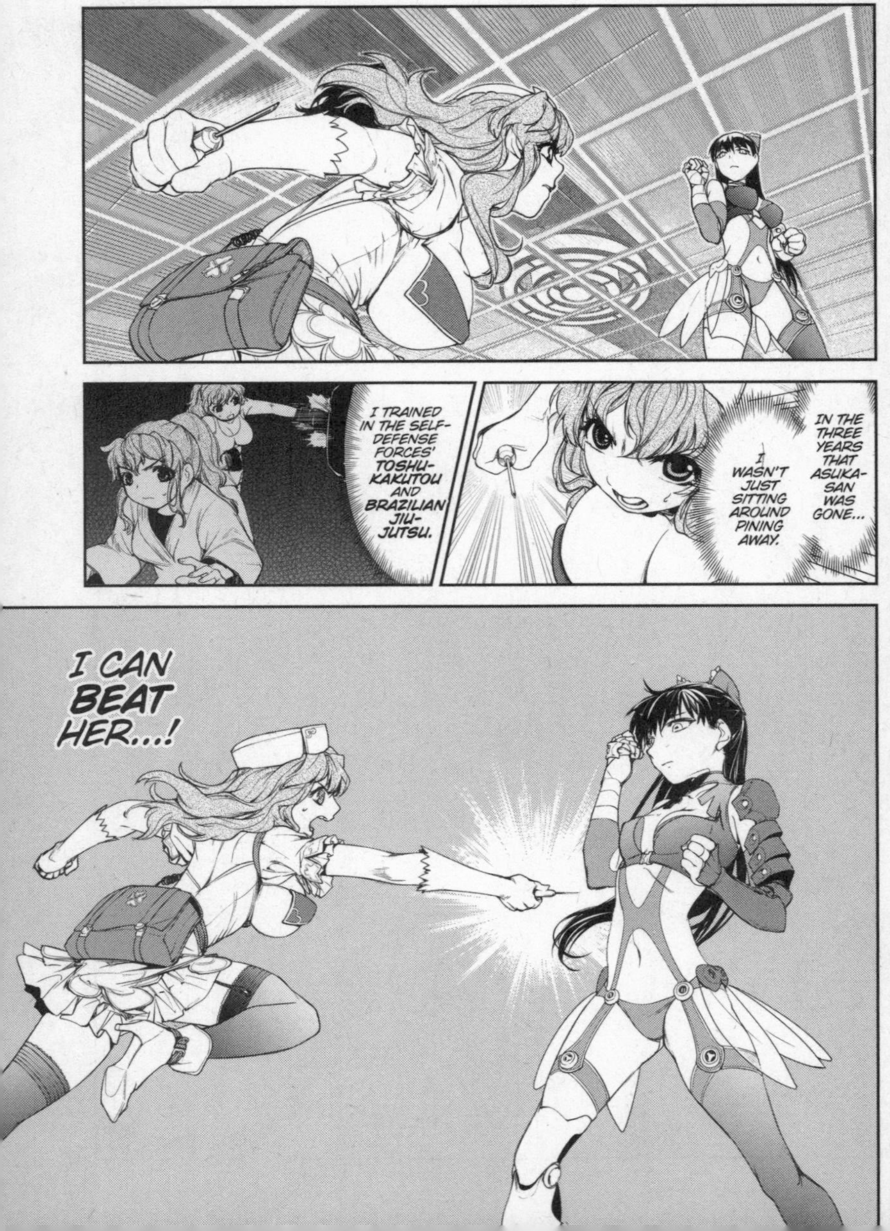
IN THE THREE YEARS THAT ASUKA-SAN WAS GONE...
I WASN'T JUST SITTING AROUND PINING AWAY.
I TRAINED IN THE SELF-DEFENSE FORCES' TOSHU-KAKUTOU AND BRAZILIAN JIU-JITSU.
I CAN BEAT HER...!

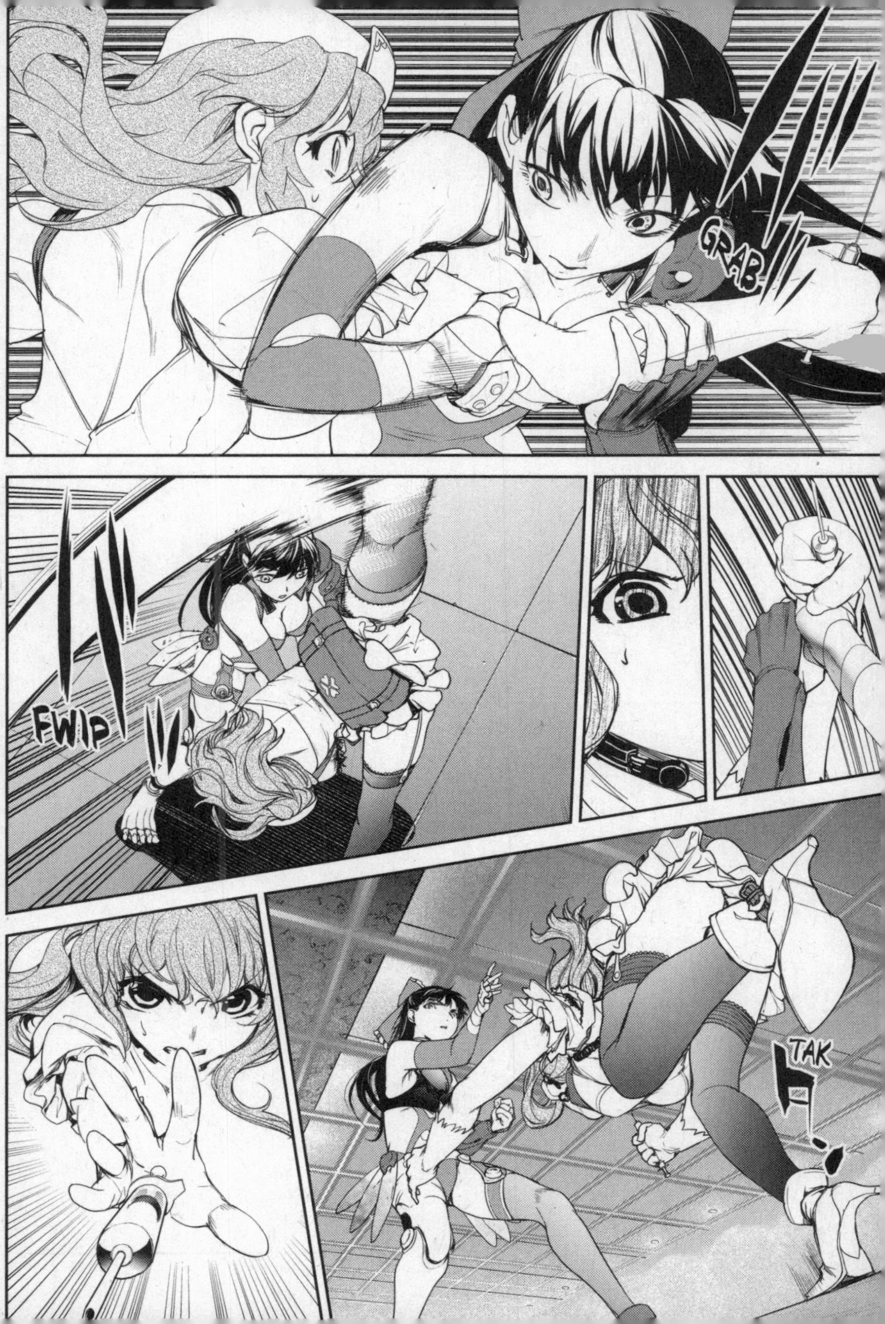
GRAB
FWIP
TAK

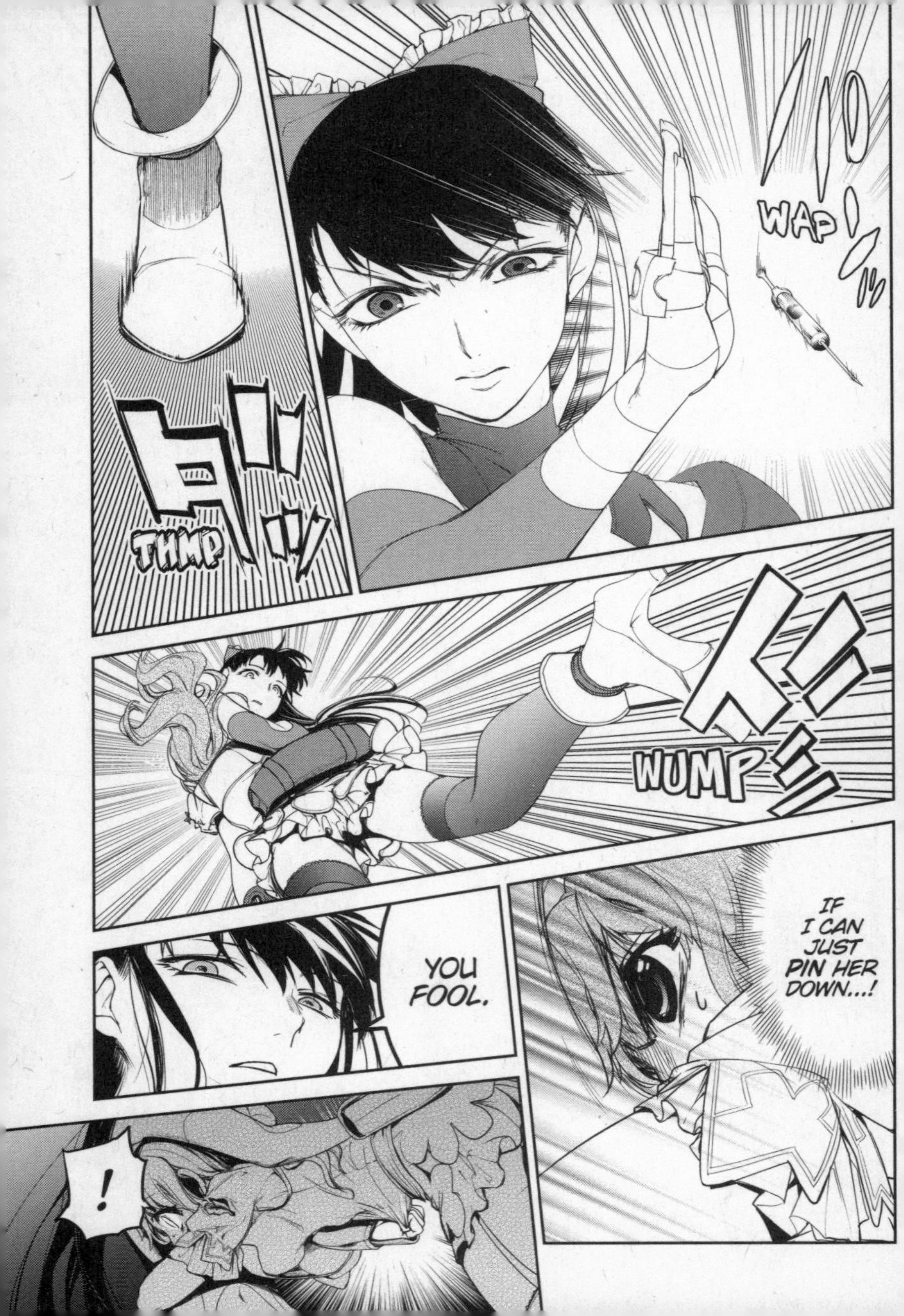
WAP
THMP
WUMP
IF I CAN JUST PIN HER DOWN...!
YOU FOOL.
!

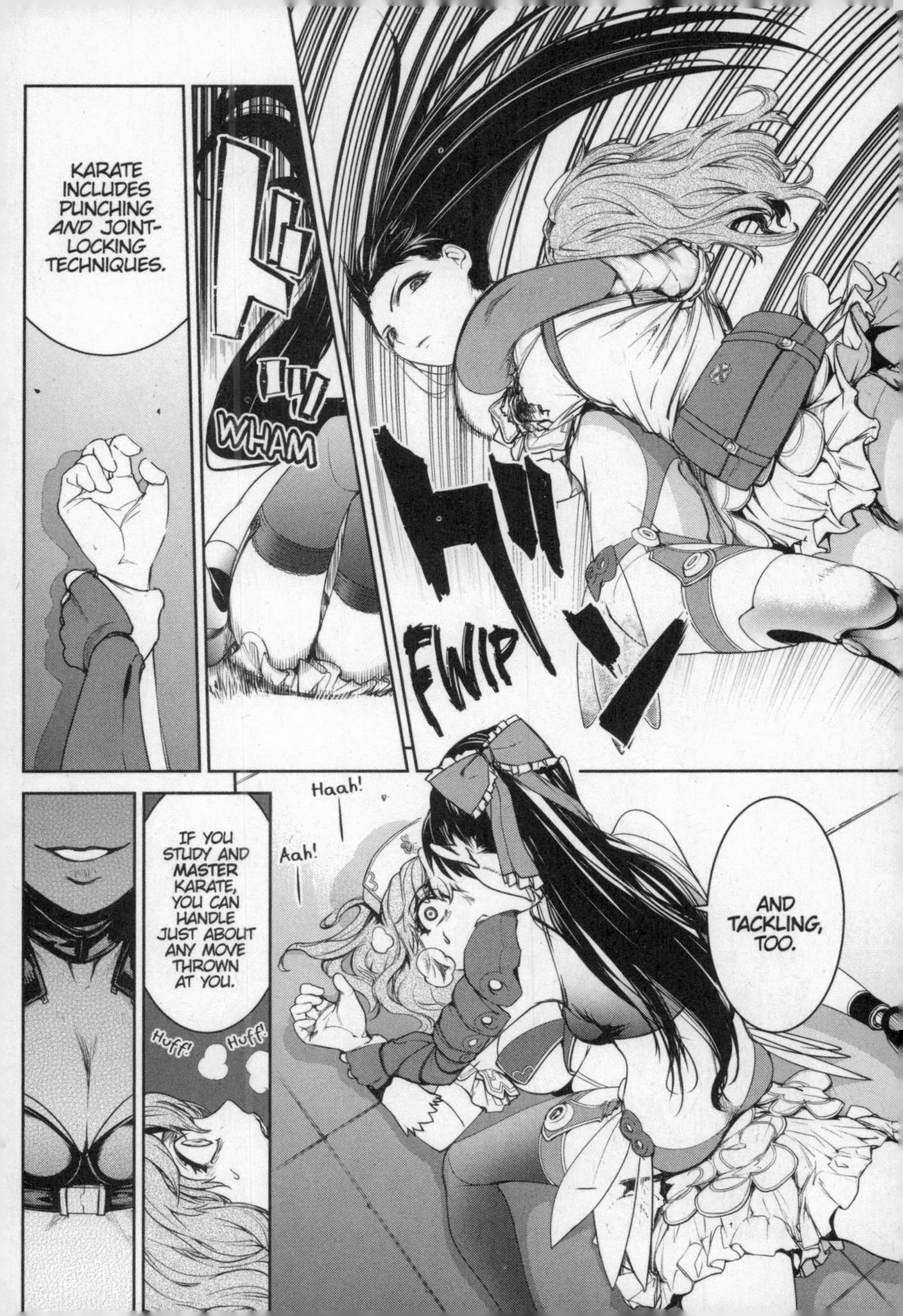
FWIP
WHAM
KARATE INCLUDES PUNCHING AND JOINT-LOCKING TECHNIQUES.
Haah!
Aah!
AND TACKLING, TOO.
IF YOU STUDY AND MASTER KARATE, YOU CAN HANDLE JUST ABOUT ANY MOVE THROWN AT YOU.
Huff! Huff!

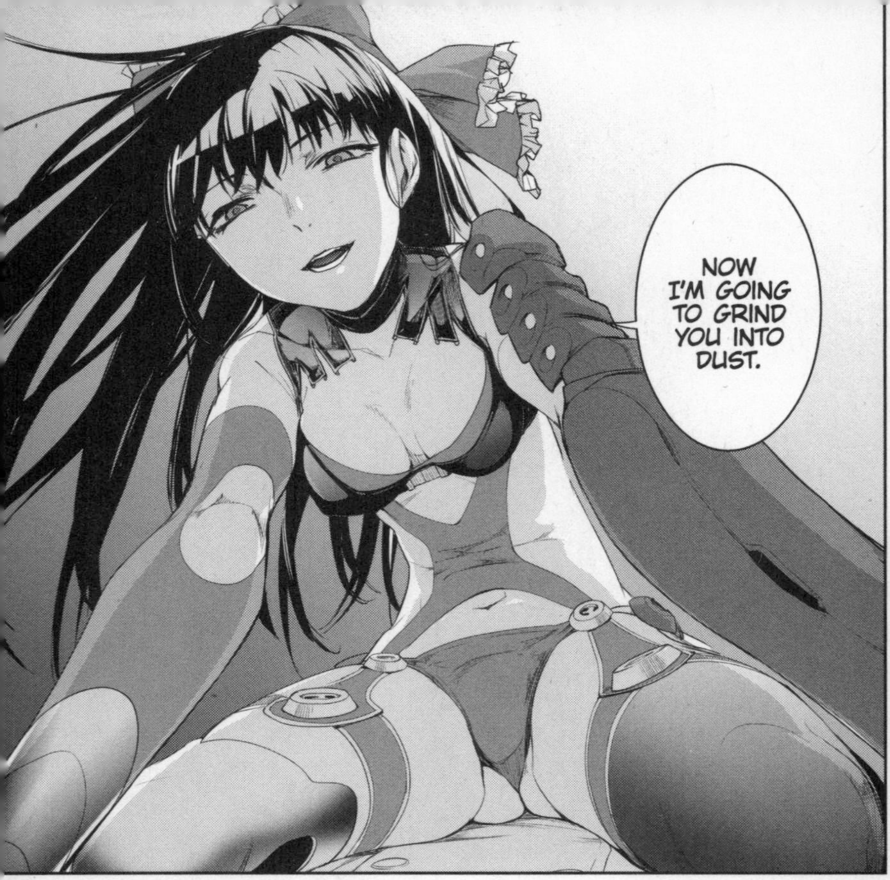
NOW I'M GOING TO GRIND YOU INTO DUST.
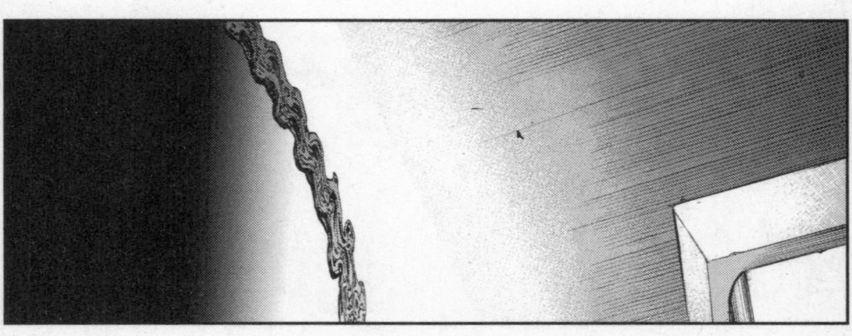

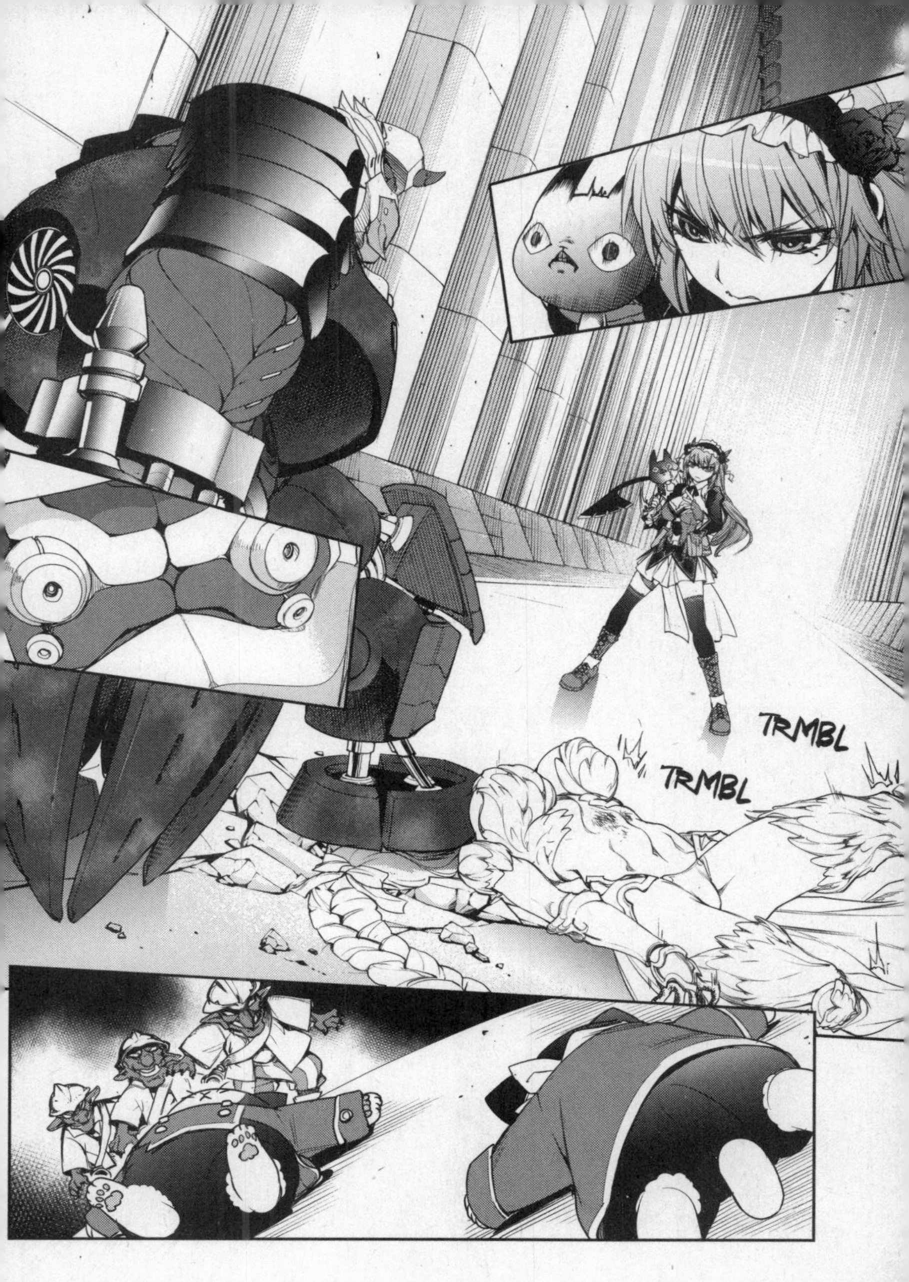
TRMBL
TRMBL

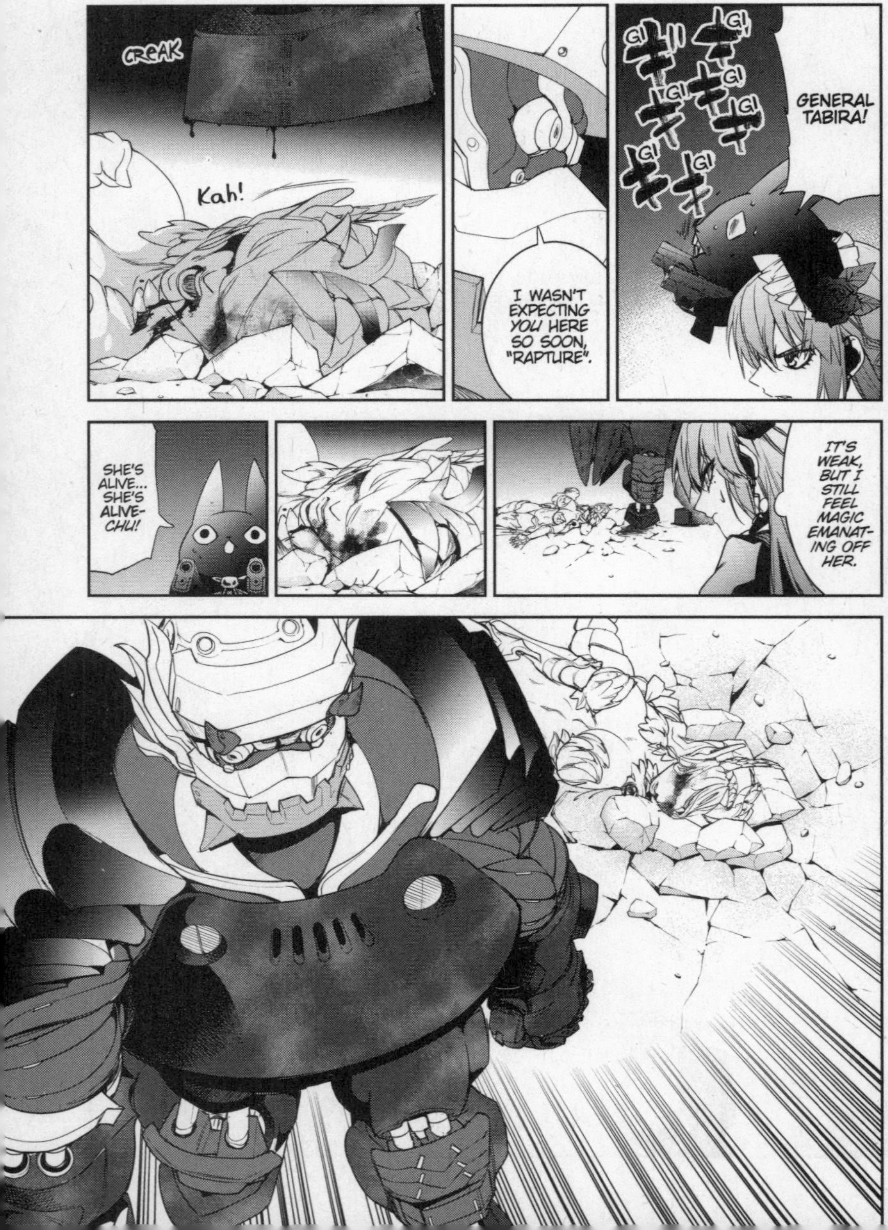
GI GI GI GI GI GI GI
GENERAL TABIRA!
I WASN'T EXPECTING YOU HERE SO SOON, "RAPTURE".
CREAK
Kah!
IT'S WEAK, BUT I STILL FEEL MAGIC EMANATING OFF HER.
SHE'S ALIVE... SHE'S ALIVE-CHU!

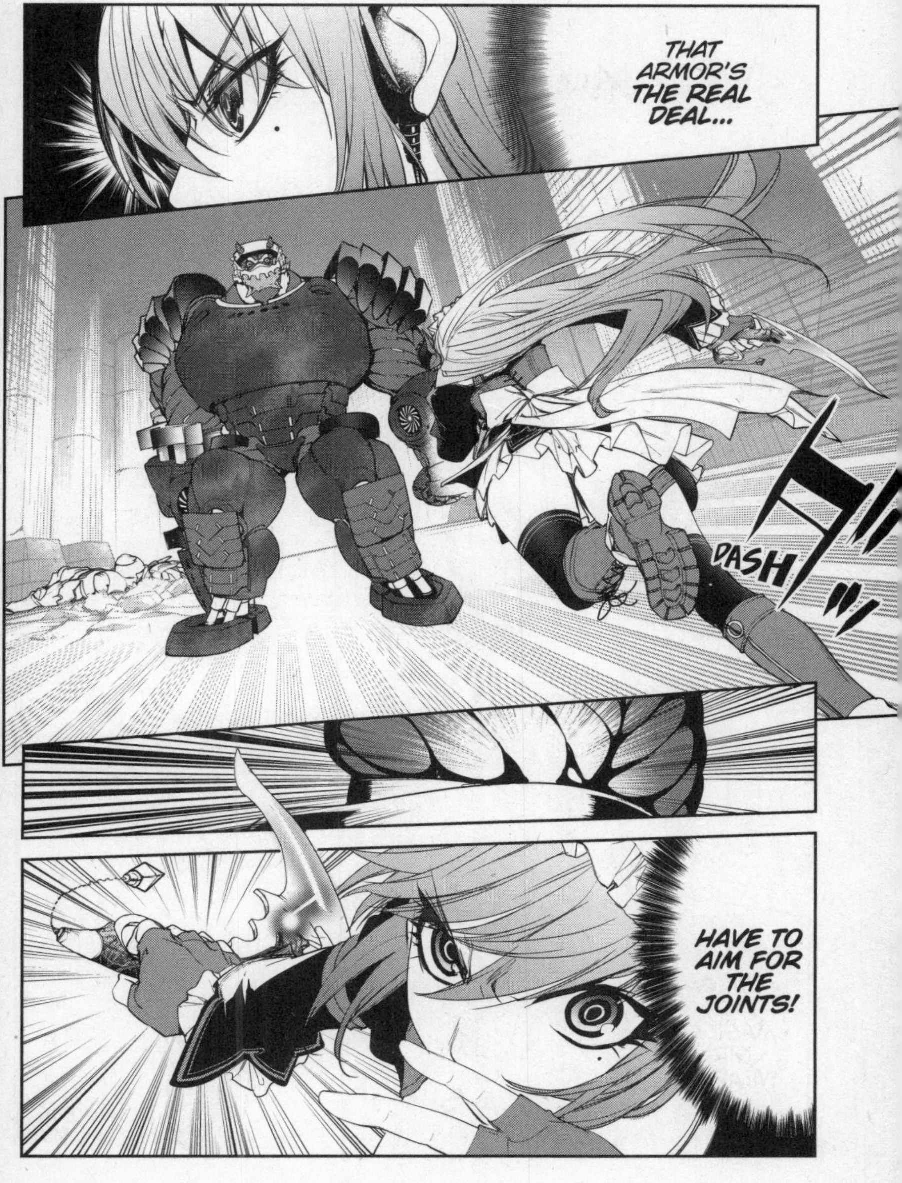
THAT ARMOR'S THE REAL DEAL...
DASH
HAVE TO AIM FOR THE JOINTS!

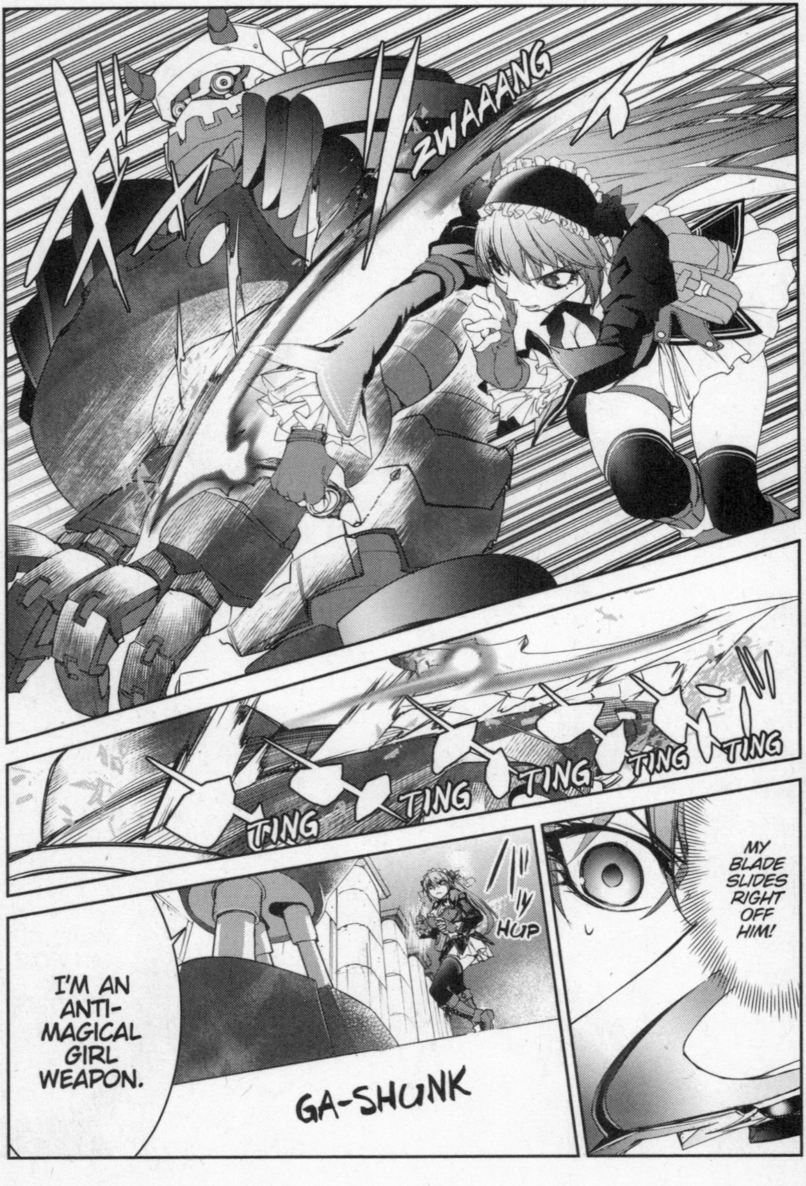
ZWAAANG
TING
TING
TING
TING
TING
MY BLADE SLIDES RIGHT OFF HIM!
HUP
I'M AN ANTI-MAGICAL GIRL WEAPON.
GA-SHUNK

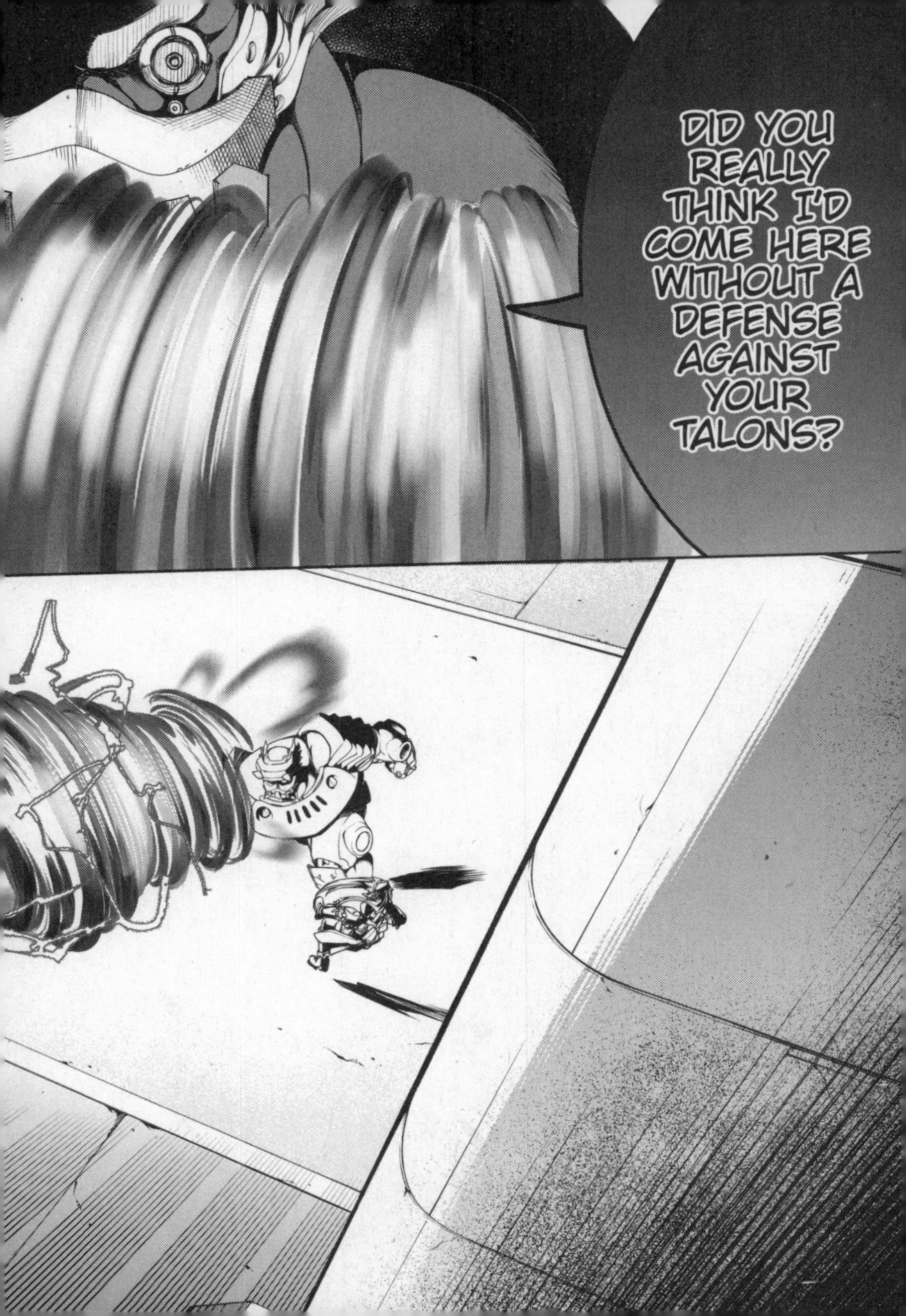
DID YOU REALLY THINK I'D COME HERE WITHOUT A DEFENSE AGAINST YOUR TALONS?

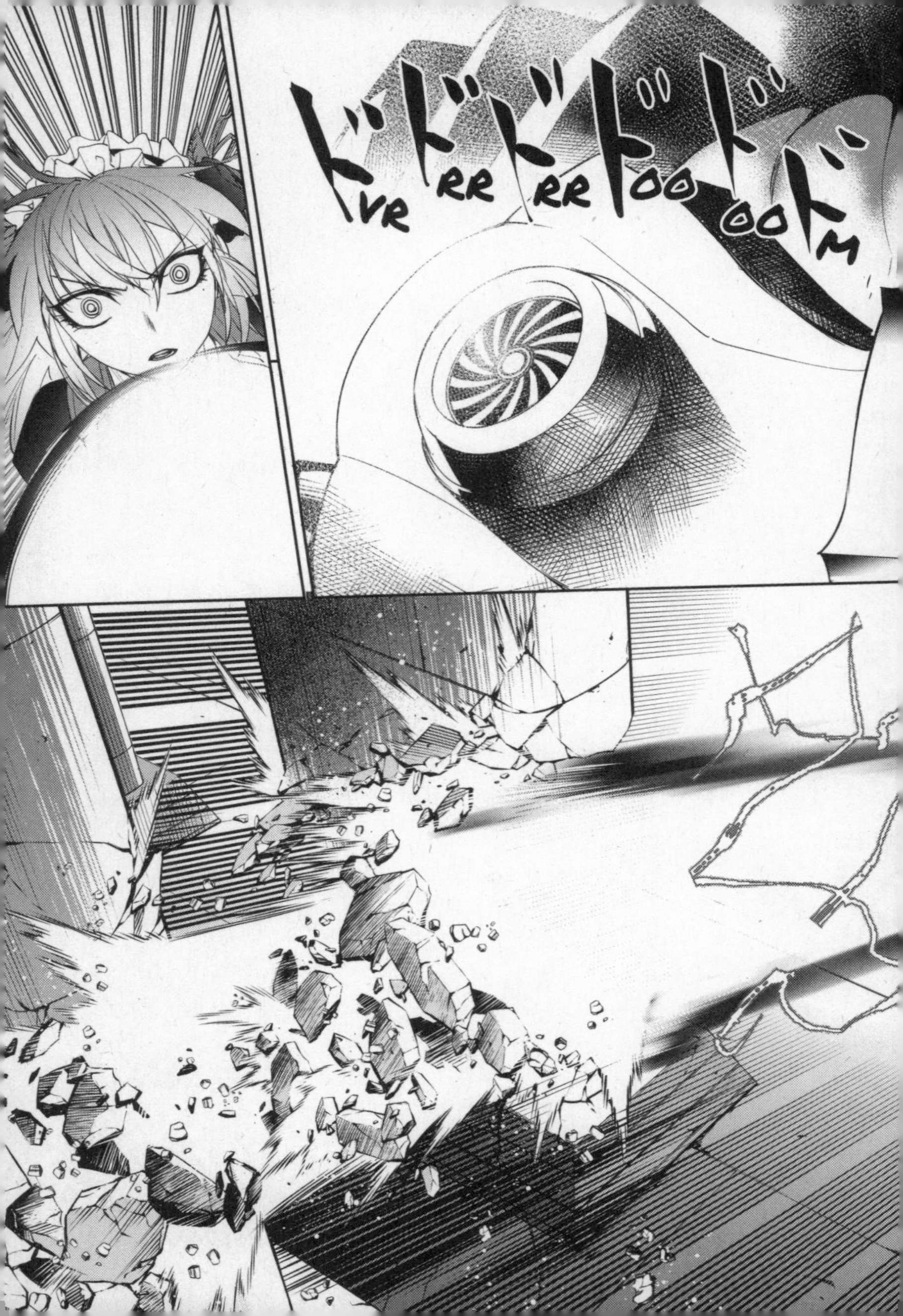
ドドドドドドドド
VRRRRROOOOOM

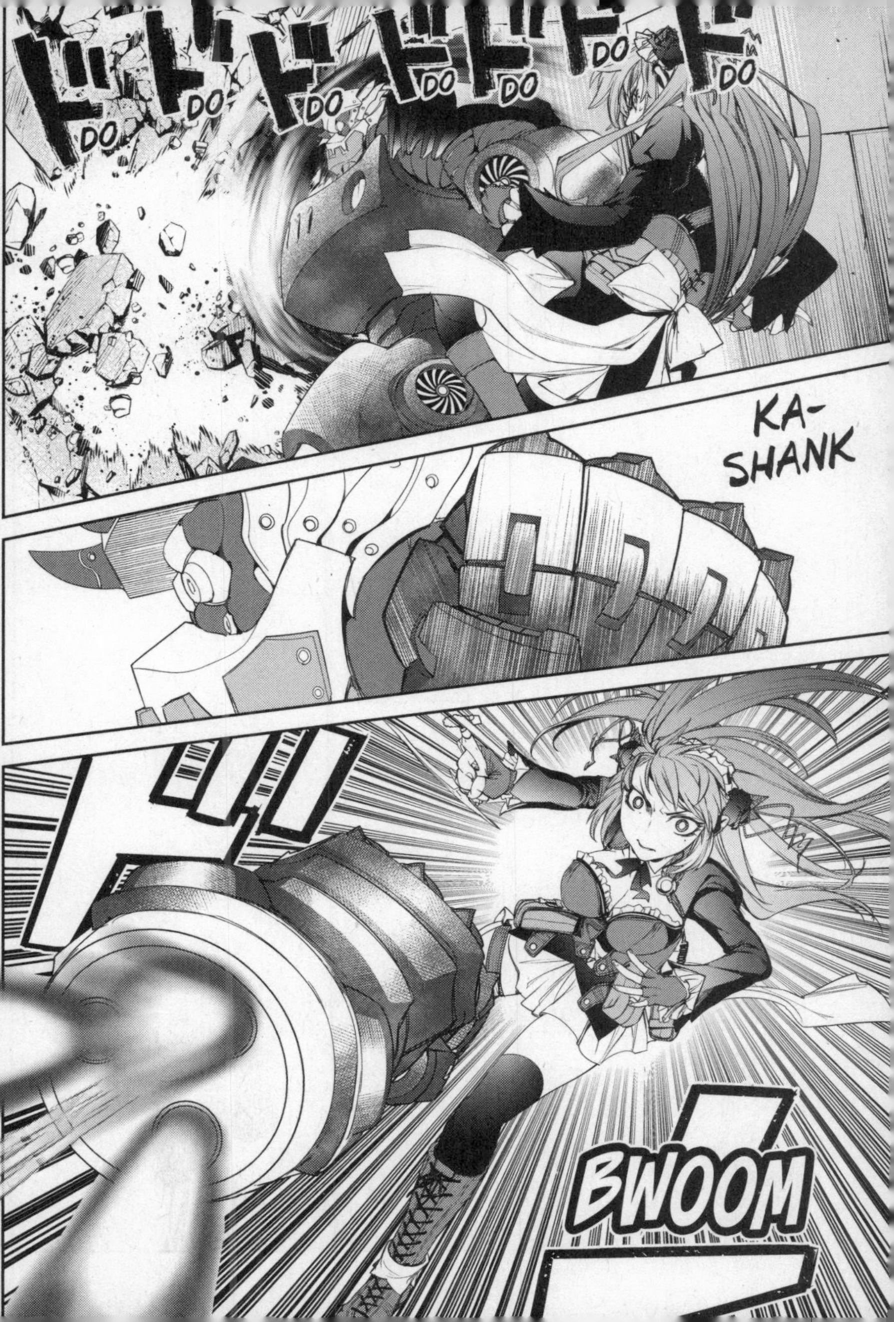
DO
DO
DO
DO
DO
DO
DO
KA-SHANK
BWOOM

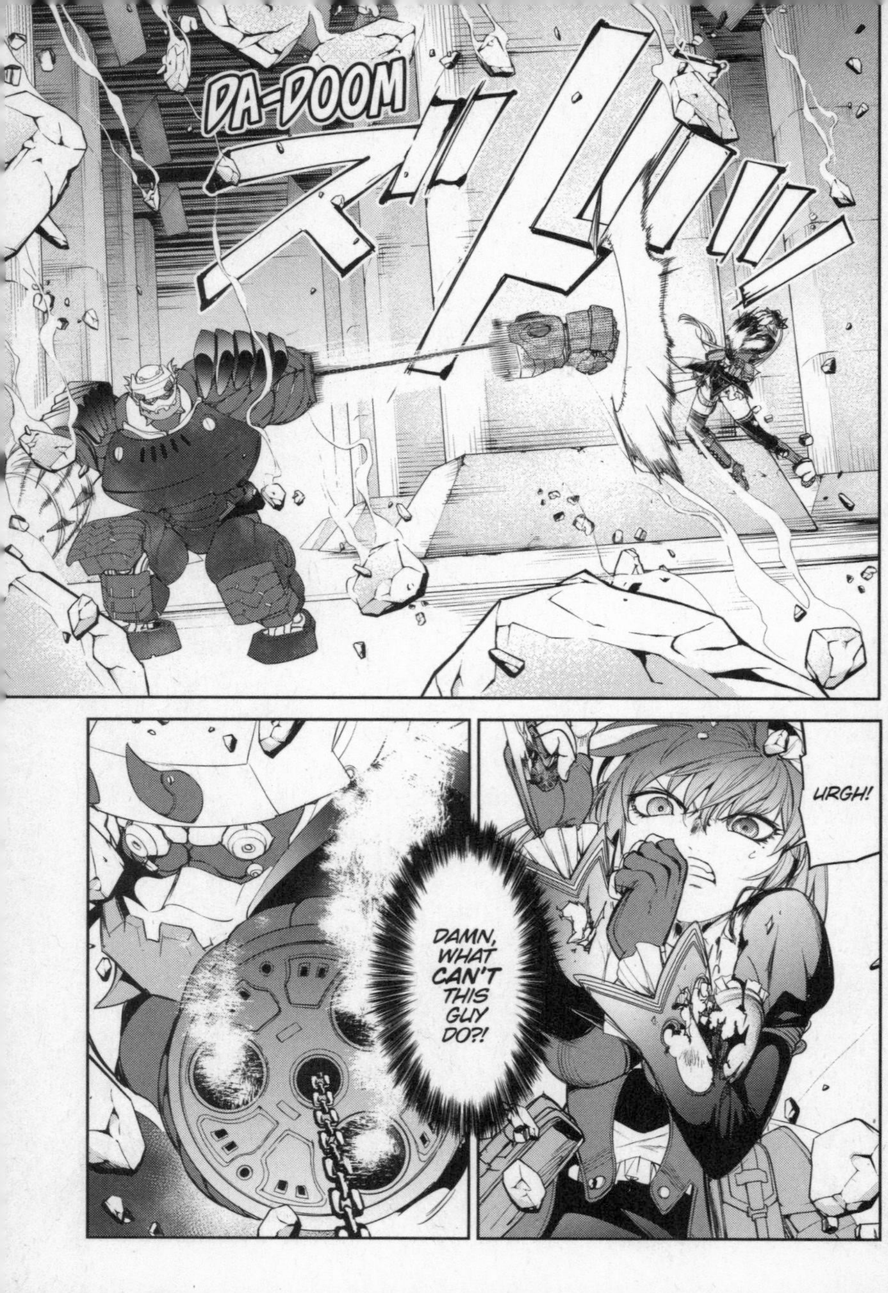
DA-DOOM
URGH!
DAMN, WHAT CAN'T THIS GUY DO?!

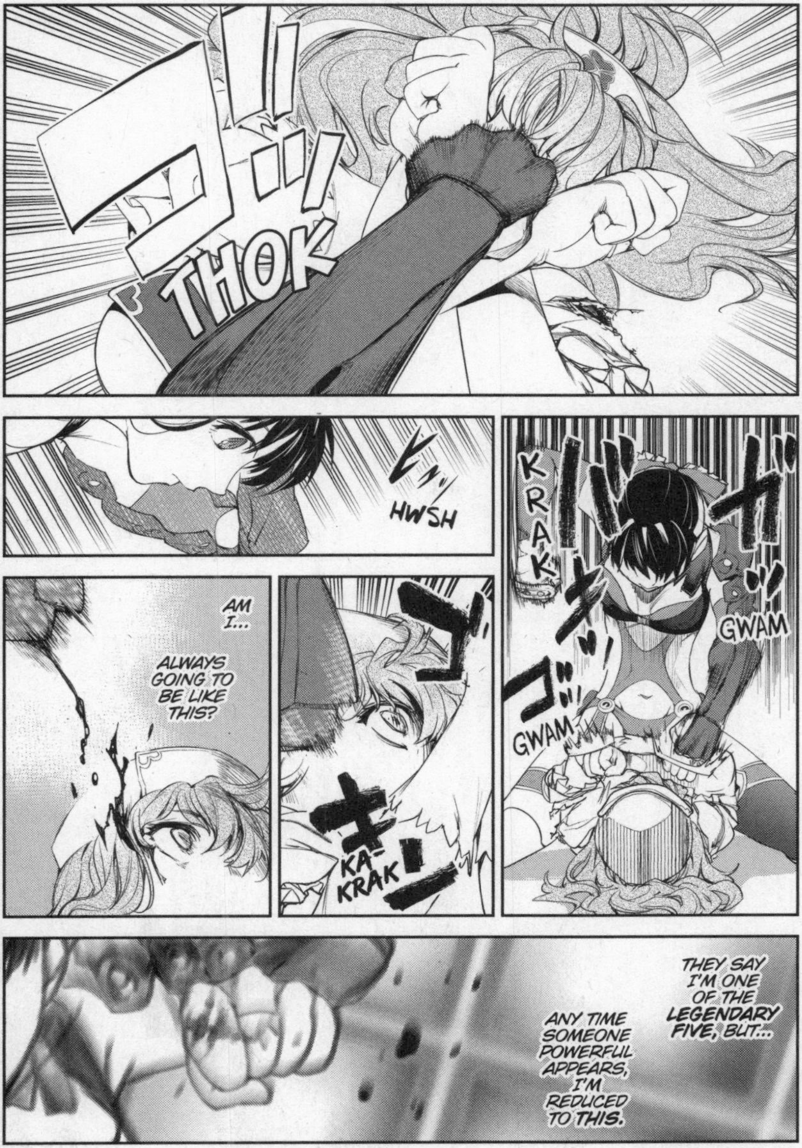
THOK
KRAK
GWAM
GWAM
HWSH
KA-KRAK
AM I...
ALWAYS GOING TO BE LIKE THIS?
THEY SAY I'M ONE OF THE LEGENDARY FIVE, BUT...
ANY TIME SOMEONE POWERFUL APPEARS, I'M REDUCED TO THIS.

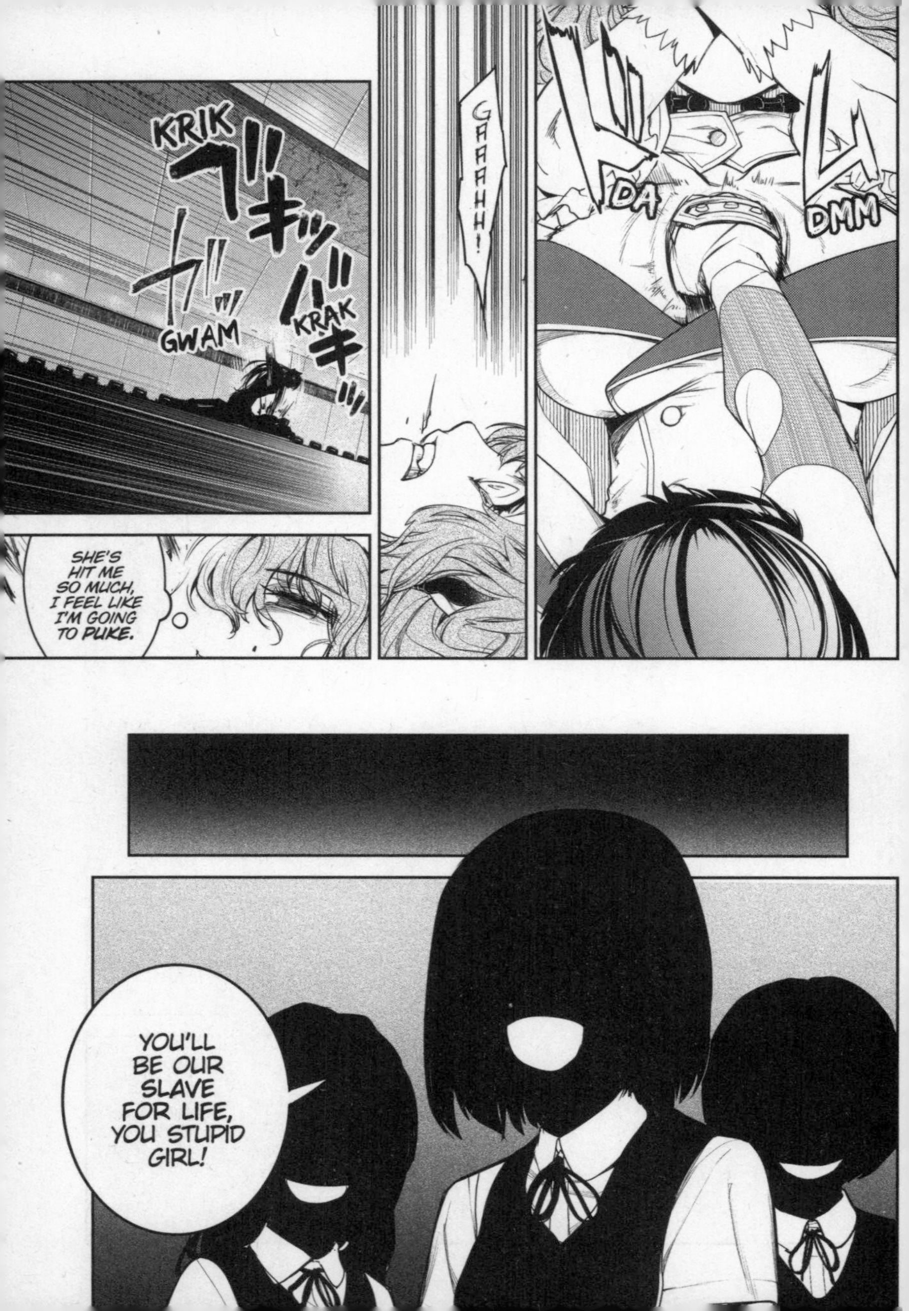
DA
DMM
GAAAHHH!
KRIK
GWAM
KRAK
SHE'S HIT ME SO MUCH, I FEEL LIKE I'M GOING TO PUKE.
YOU'LL BE OUR SLAVE FOR LIFE, YOU STUPID GIRL!

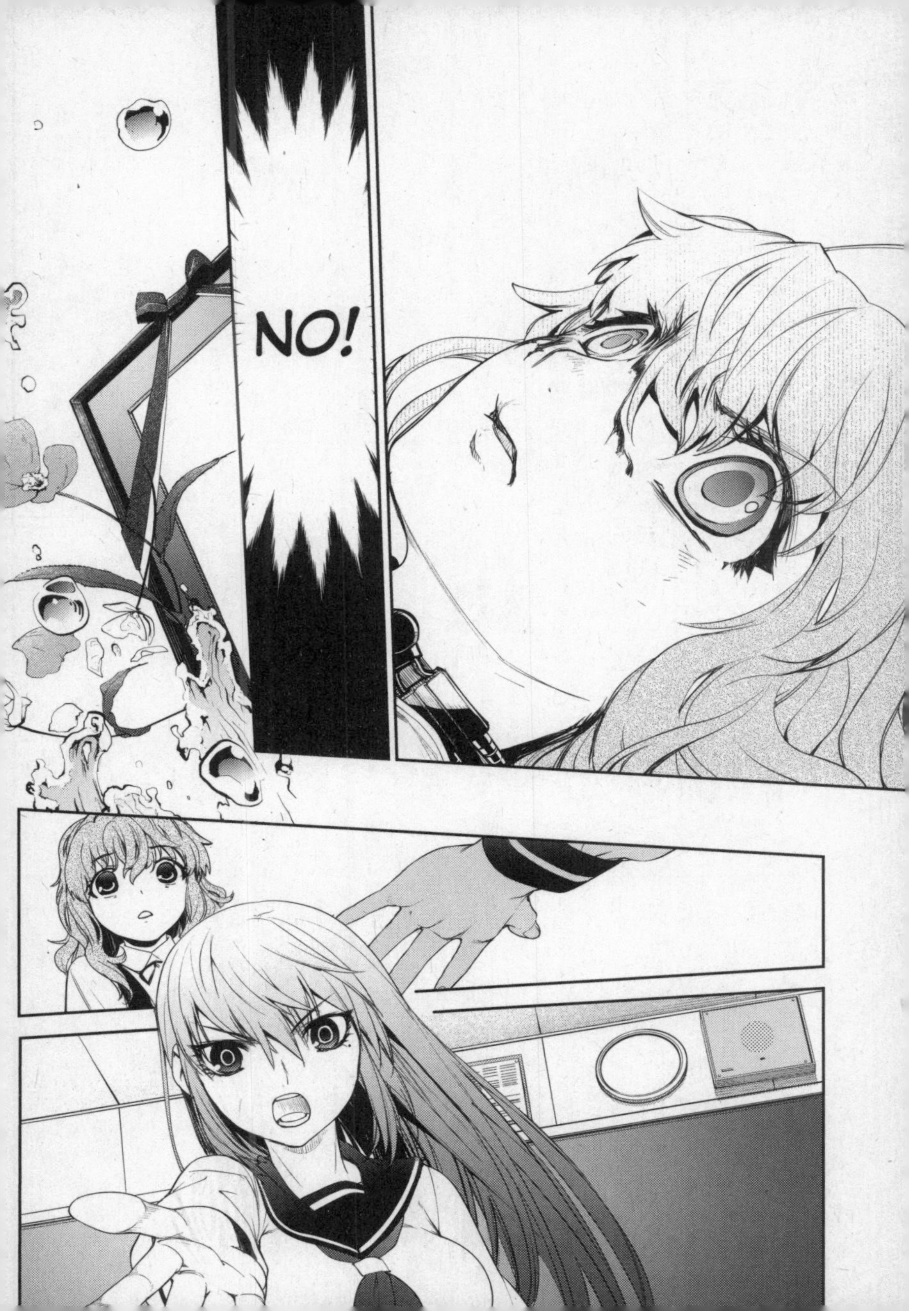
NO!

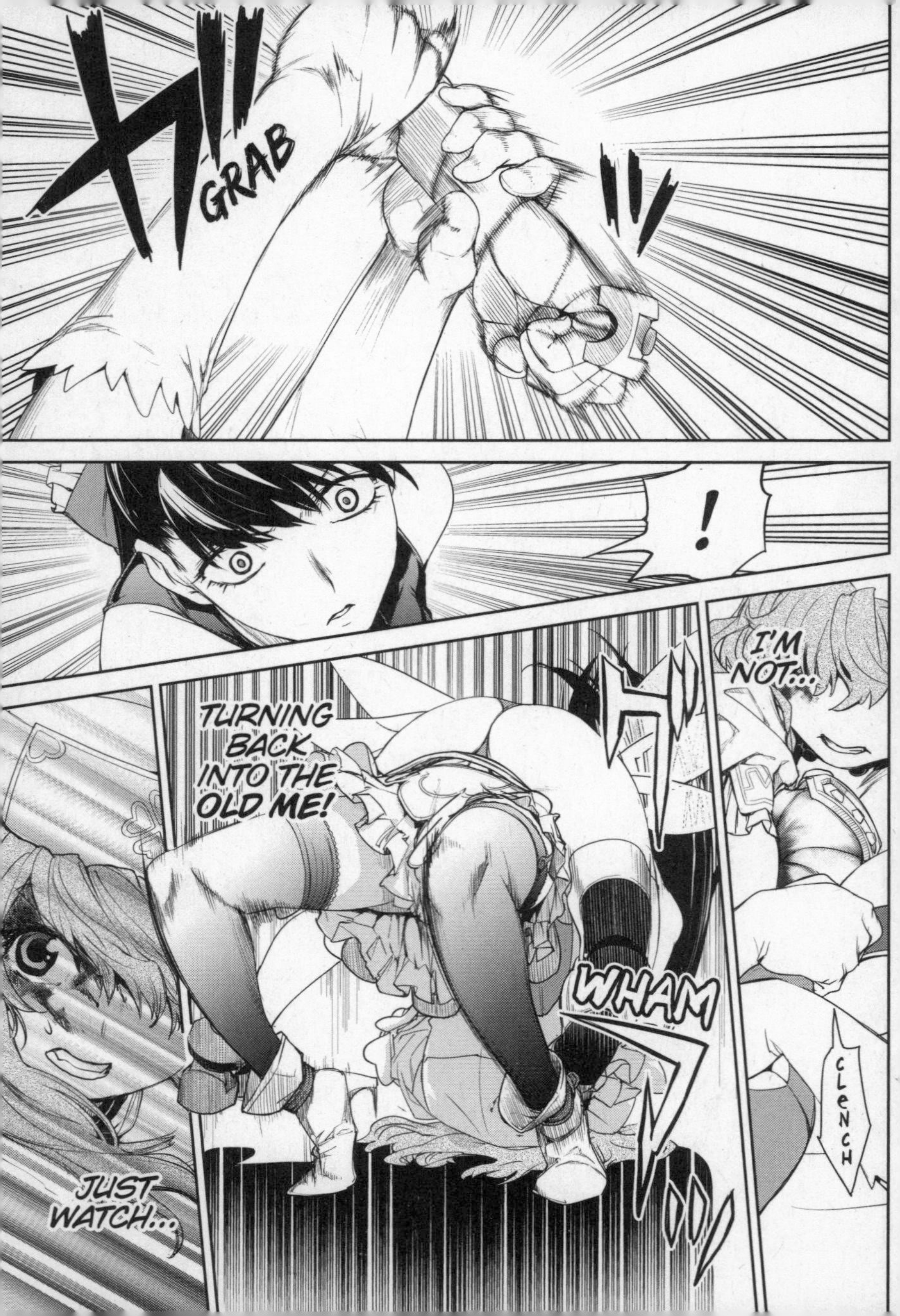
GRAB
!
I'M NOT...
CLENCH
TURNING BACK INTO THE OLD ME!
WHAM
JUST WATCH...

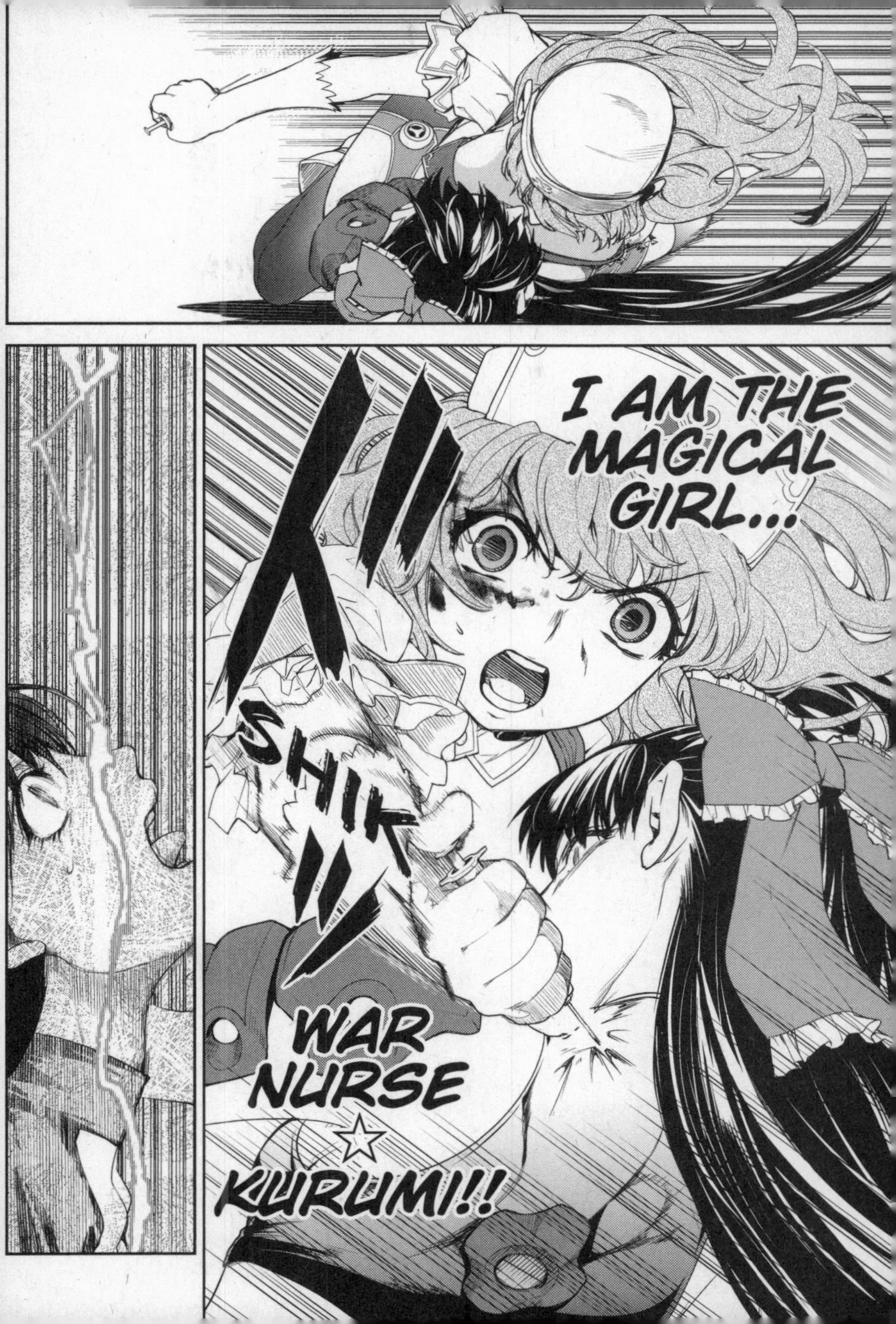
I AM THE MAGICAL GIRL...
SHIK!!
WAR NURSE ☆ KURUMI!!

MAGICAL GIRL
SPEC·OPS
ASUKA

魔法少女特殊戦

あすか

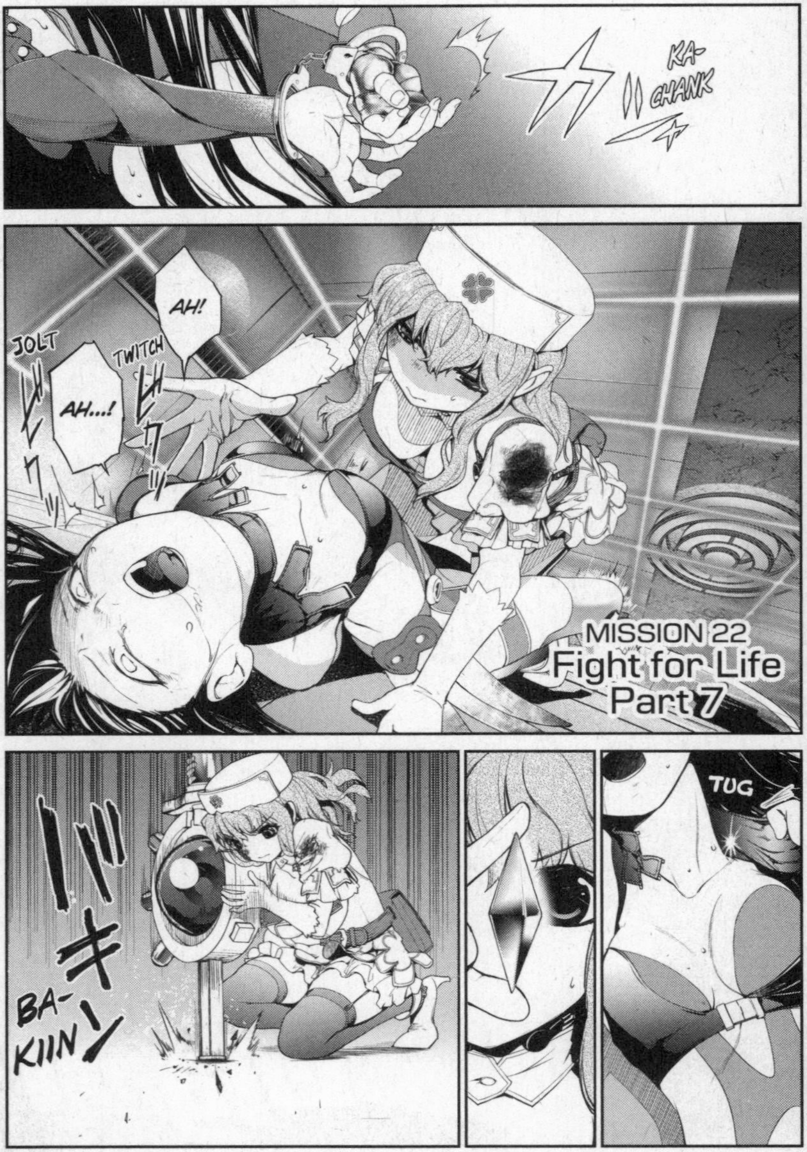
KA-CHANK
AH!
TWITCH
JOLT
AH...!
MISSION 22
Fight for Life
Part 7
TUG
BA-KIIN

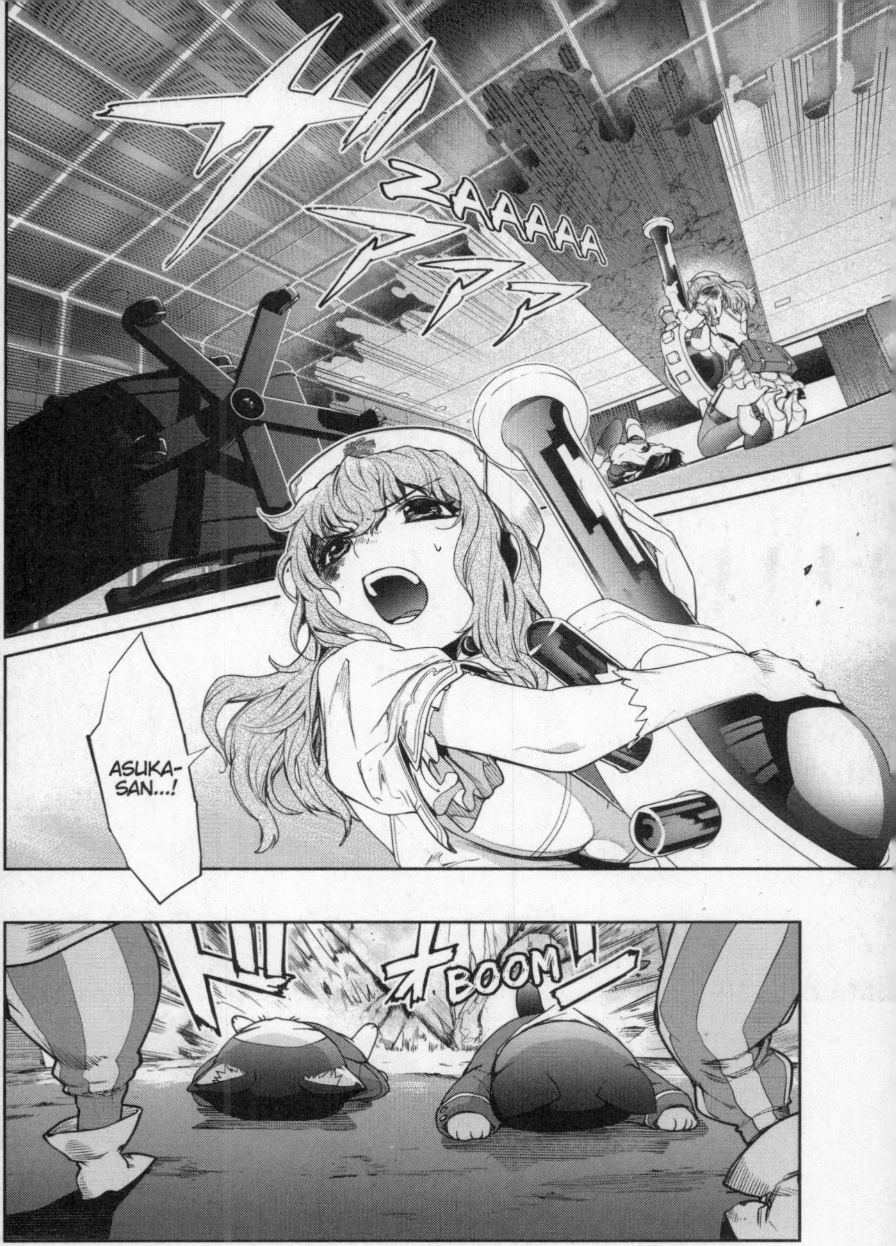
ZAAAAAA
ASUKA-SAN...!
BOOM

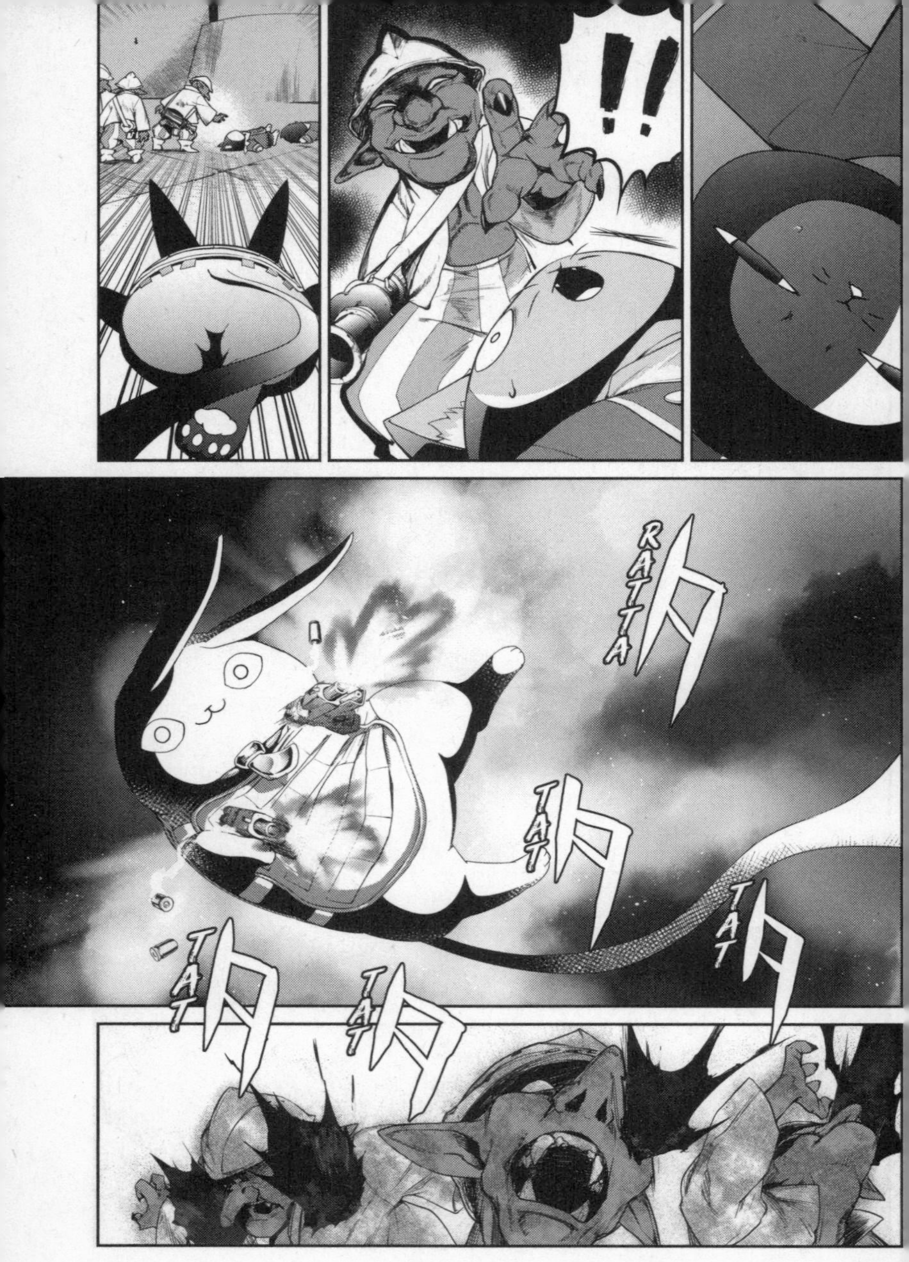
!!
RATTA
TAT
TAT
TAT
TAT

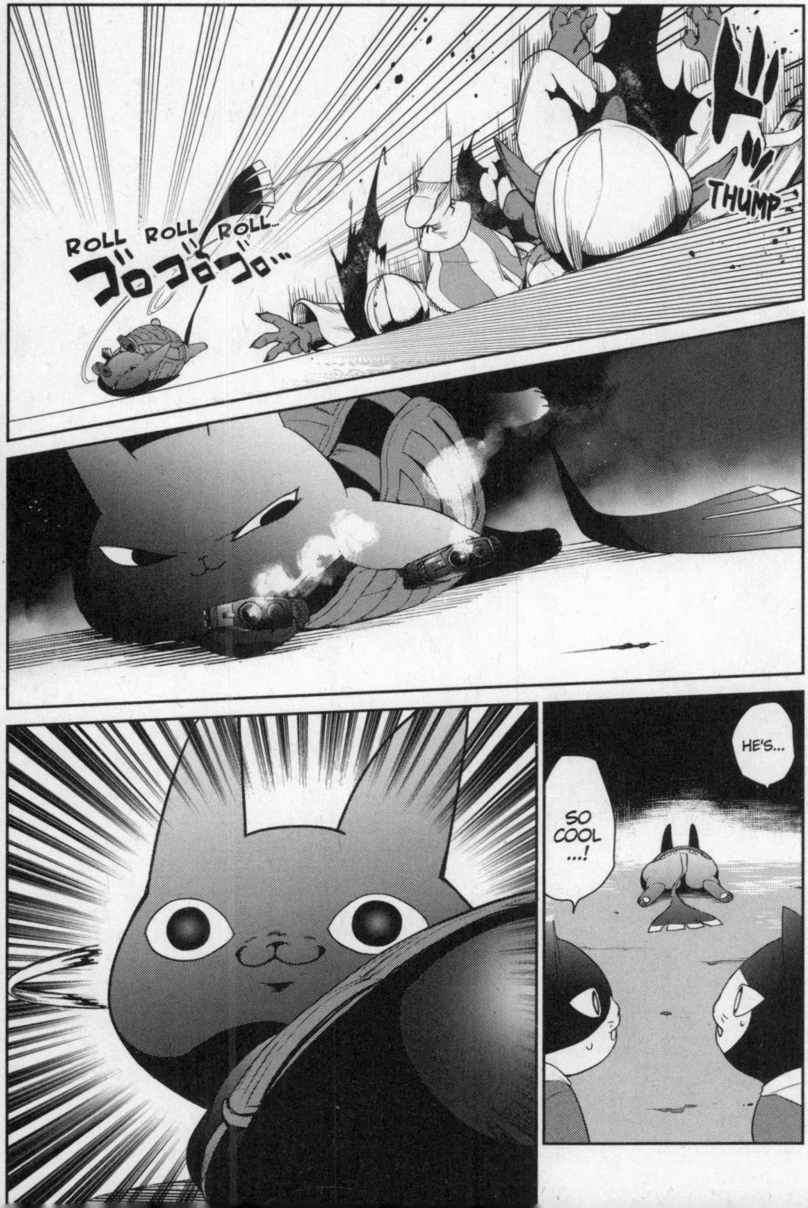
ドッ
THUMP
ROLL ROLL ROLL...
ゴロゴロゴロ...
HE'S...
SO COOL...!

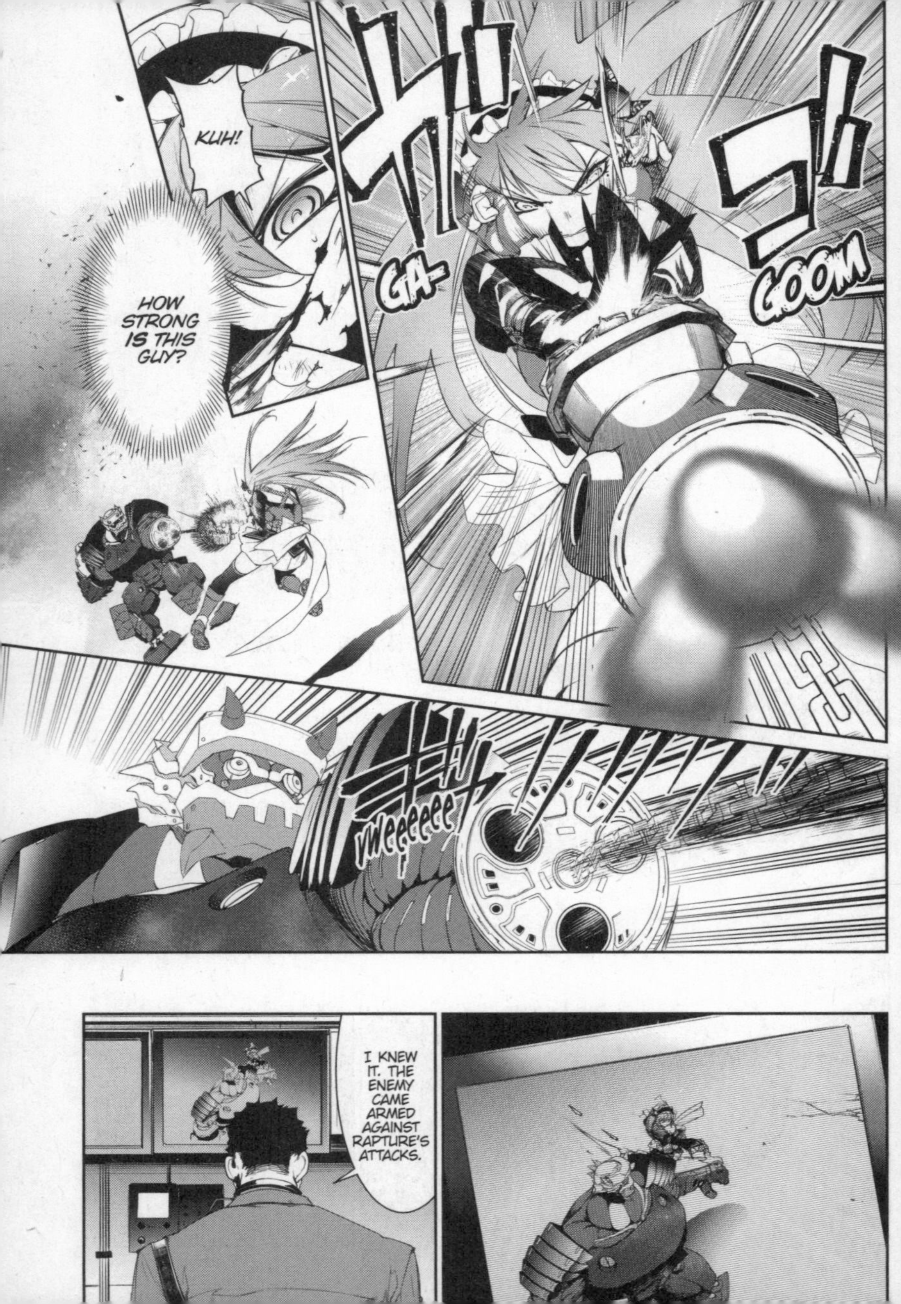
GA
GOOM
KUH!
HOW STRONG IS THIS GUY?
vweeeeee
I KNEW IT. THE ENEMY CAME ARMED AGAINST RAPTURE'S ATTACKS.

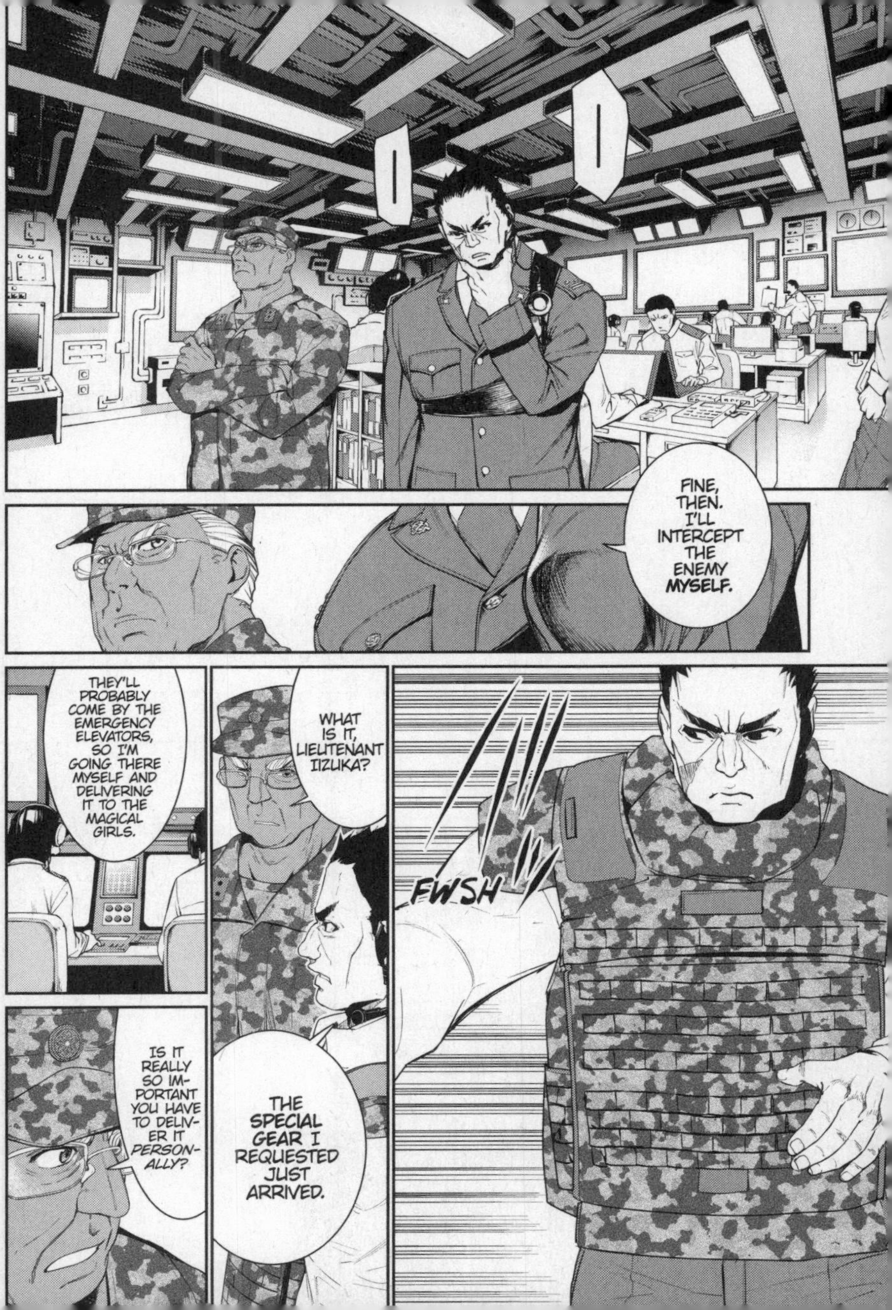
FINE, THEN. I'LL INTERCEPT THE ENEMY MYSELF.
FWSH
WHAT IS IT, LIEUTENANT IIZUKA?
THEY'LL PROBABLY COME BY THE EMERGENCY ELEVATORS, SO I'M GOING THERE MYSELF AND DELIVERING IT TO THE MAGICAL GIRLS.
THE SPECIAL GEAR I REQUESTED JUST ARRIVED.
IS IT REALLY SO IM-PORTANT YOU HAVE TO DELIV-ER IT PERSON-ALLY?

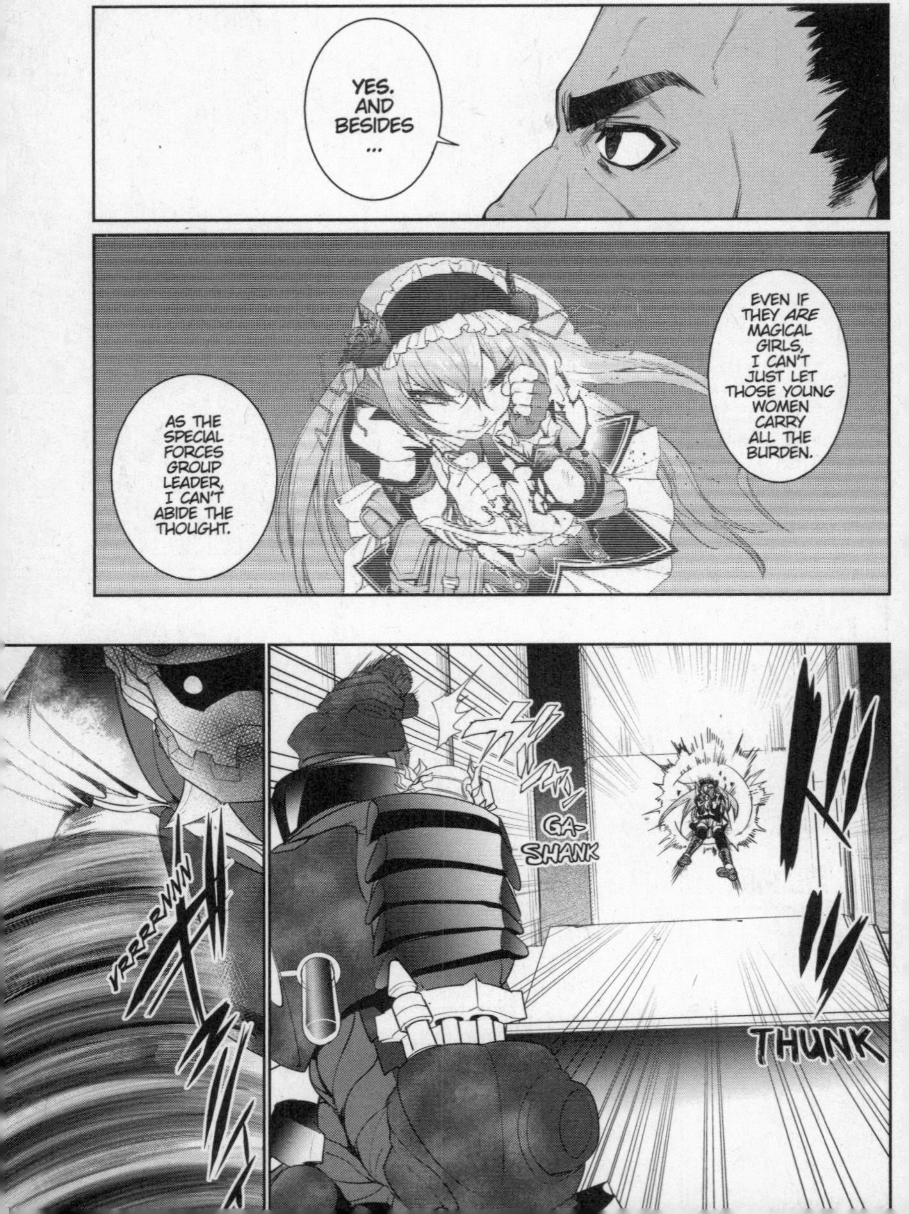
YES. AND BESIDES ...
EVEN IF THEY *ARE* MAGICAL GIRLS, I CAN'T JUST LET THOSE YOUNG WOMEN CARRY ALL THE BURDEN.
AS THE SPECIAL FORCES GROUP LEADER, I CAN'T ABIDE THE THOUGHT.
GA-SHANK
THUNK
VRRRRNNN

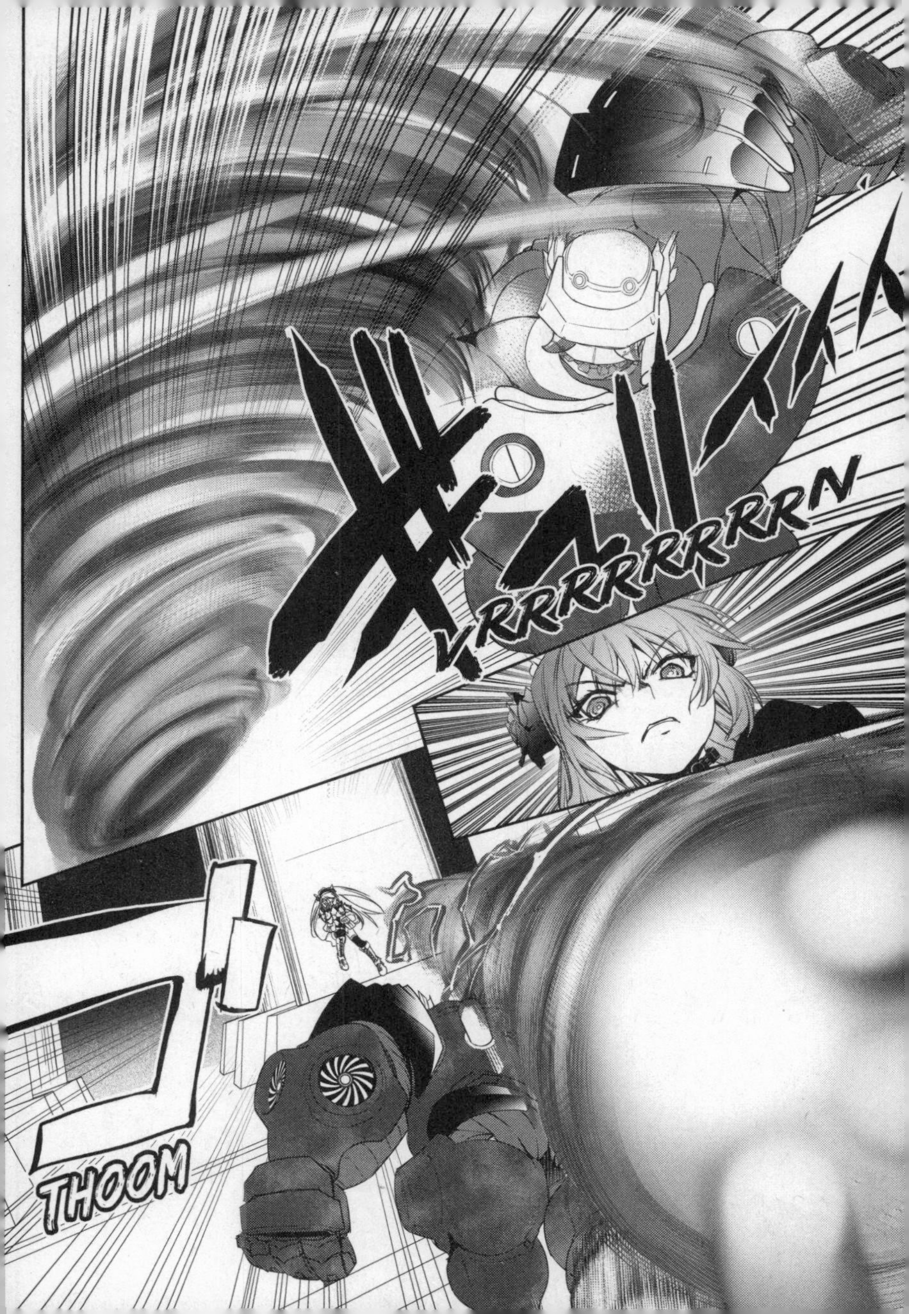
VRRRRRRRRRN
THOOM

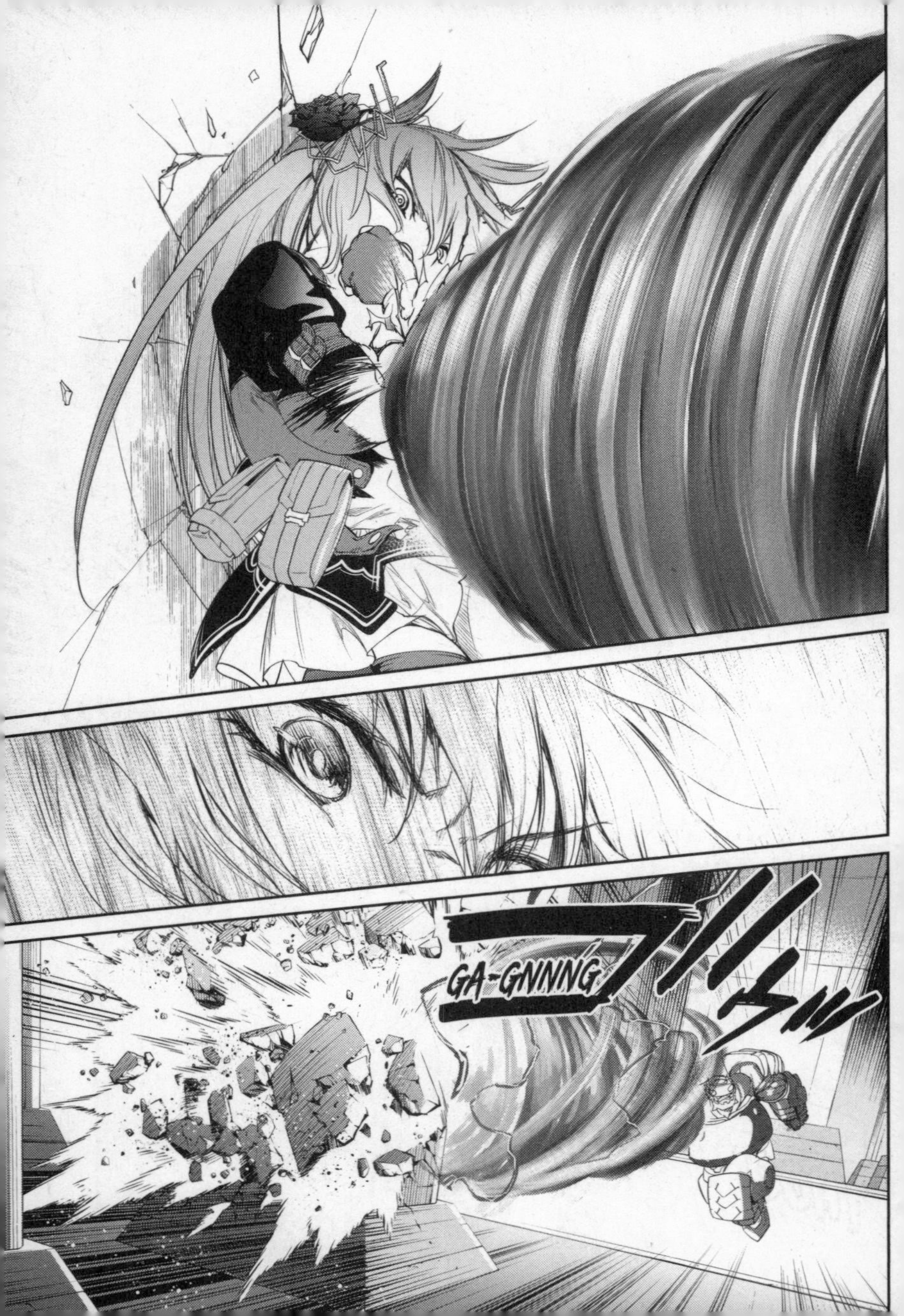
GA-GNNNG

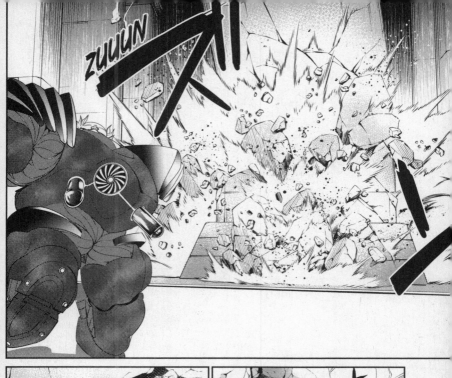

ZUUUN

FSHHHHHH

WELL THEN...

I HOPE CHISATO'S OKAY.

GA-SHANK

GA-SHUNK

ASUKA....?

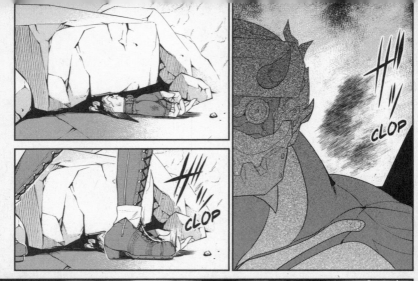

CLOP

CLOP

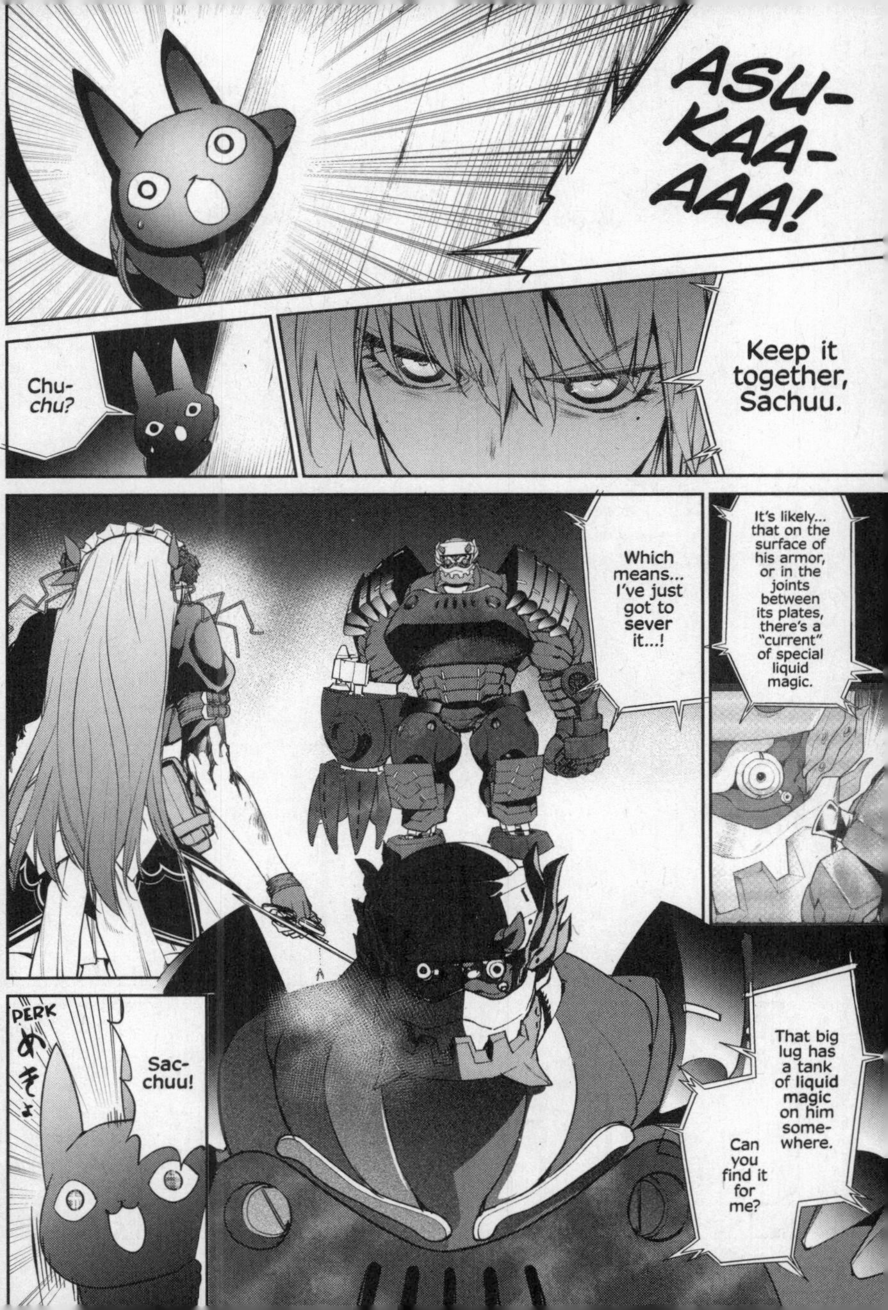
ASU-KAA-AAA!
Keep it together, Sachuu.
Chu-chu?
It's likely... that on the surface of his armor, or in the joints between its plates, there's a "current" of special liquid magic.
Which means... I've just got to sever it...!
That big lug has a tank of liquid magic on him somewhere.
Can you find it for me?
PERK
めきょ
Sac-chuu!

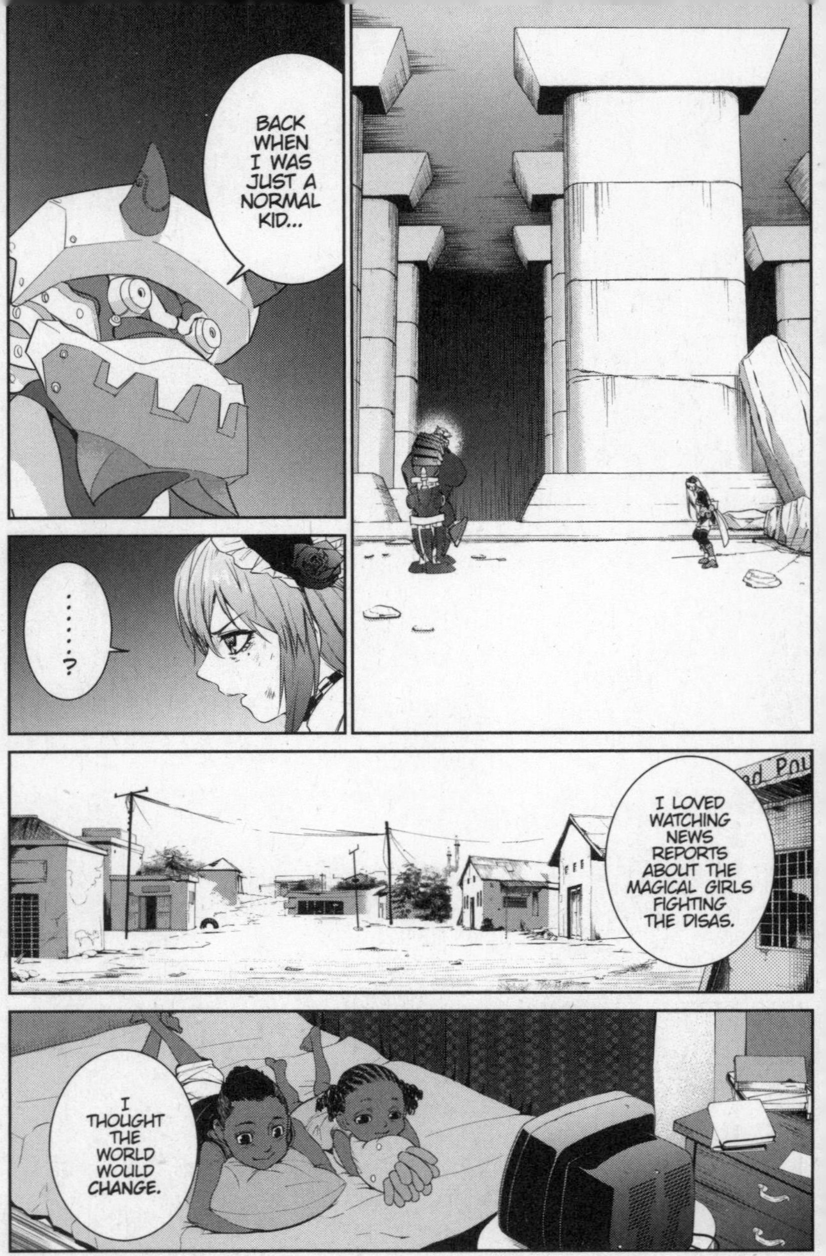
BACK WHEN I WAS JUST A NORMAL KID...
......?
I LOVED WATCHING NEWS REPORTS ABOUT THE MAGICAL GIRLS FIGHTING THE DISAS.
I THOUGHT THE WORLD WOULD CHANGE.

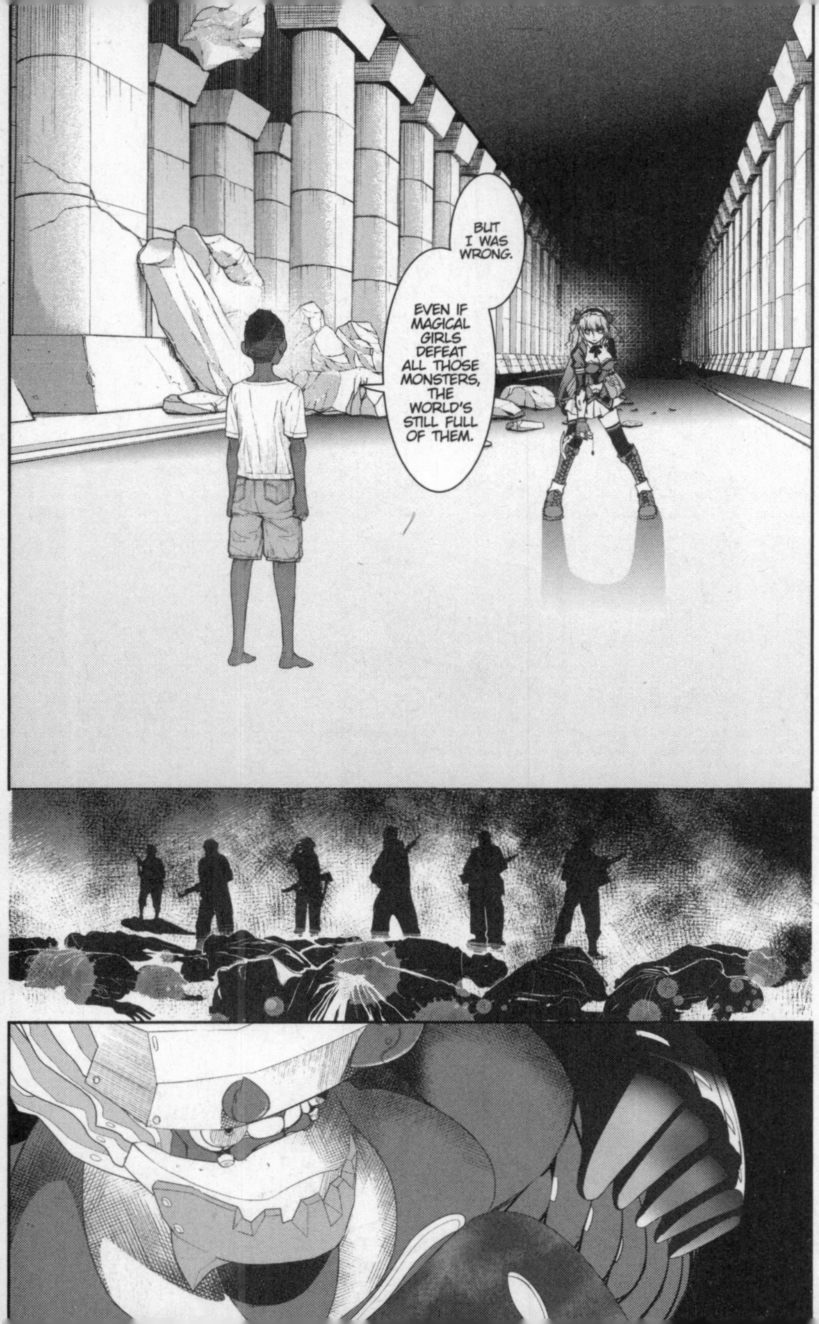
BUT I WAS WRONG.
EVEN IF MAGICAL GIRLS DEFEAT ALL THOSE MONSTERS, THE WORLD'S STILL FULL OF THEM.

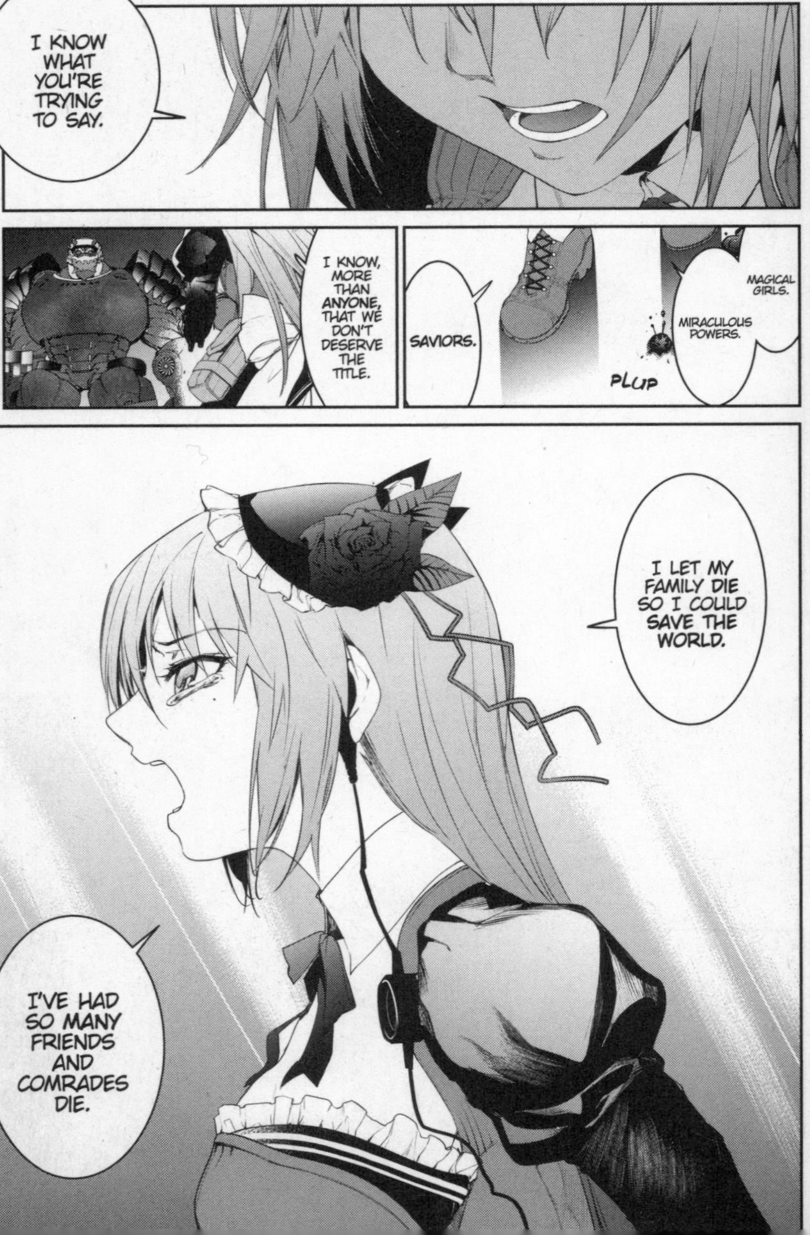
I KNOW WHAT YOU'RE TRYING TO SAY.
MAGICAL GIRLS.
MIRACULOUS POWERS.
PLUP
SAVIORS.
I KNOW, MORE THAN ANYONE, THAT WE DON'T DESERVE THE TITLE.
I LET MY FAMILY DIE SO I COULD SAVE THE WORLD.
I'VE HAD SO MANY FRIENDS AND COMRADES DIE.

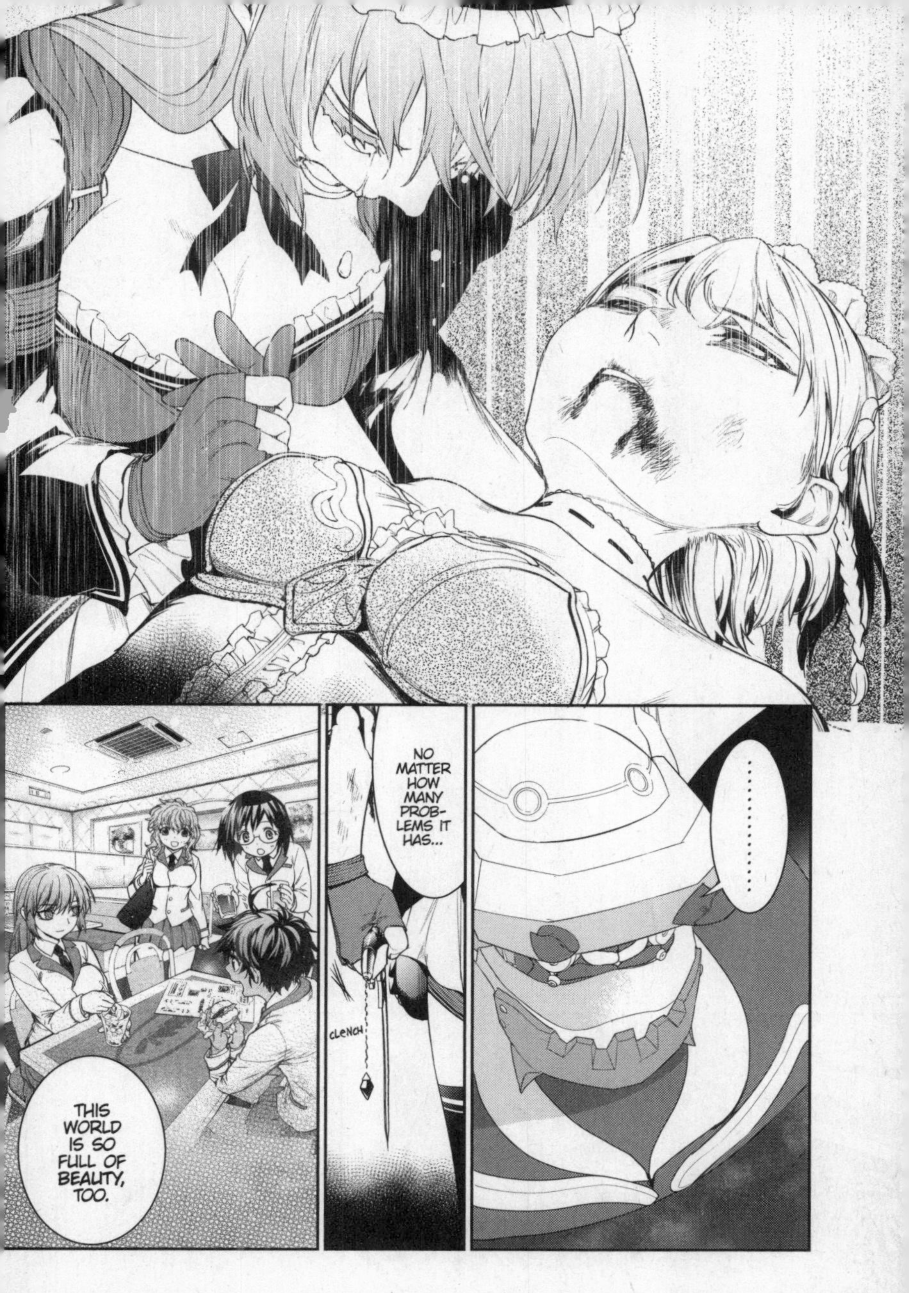
......
NO MATTER HOW MANY PROB-LEMS IT HAS...
CLENCH
THIS WORLD IS SO FULL OF BEAUTY, TOO.

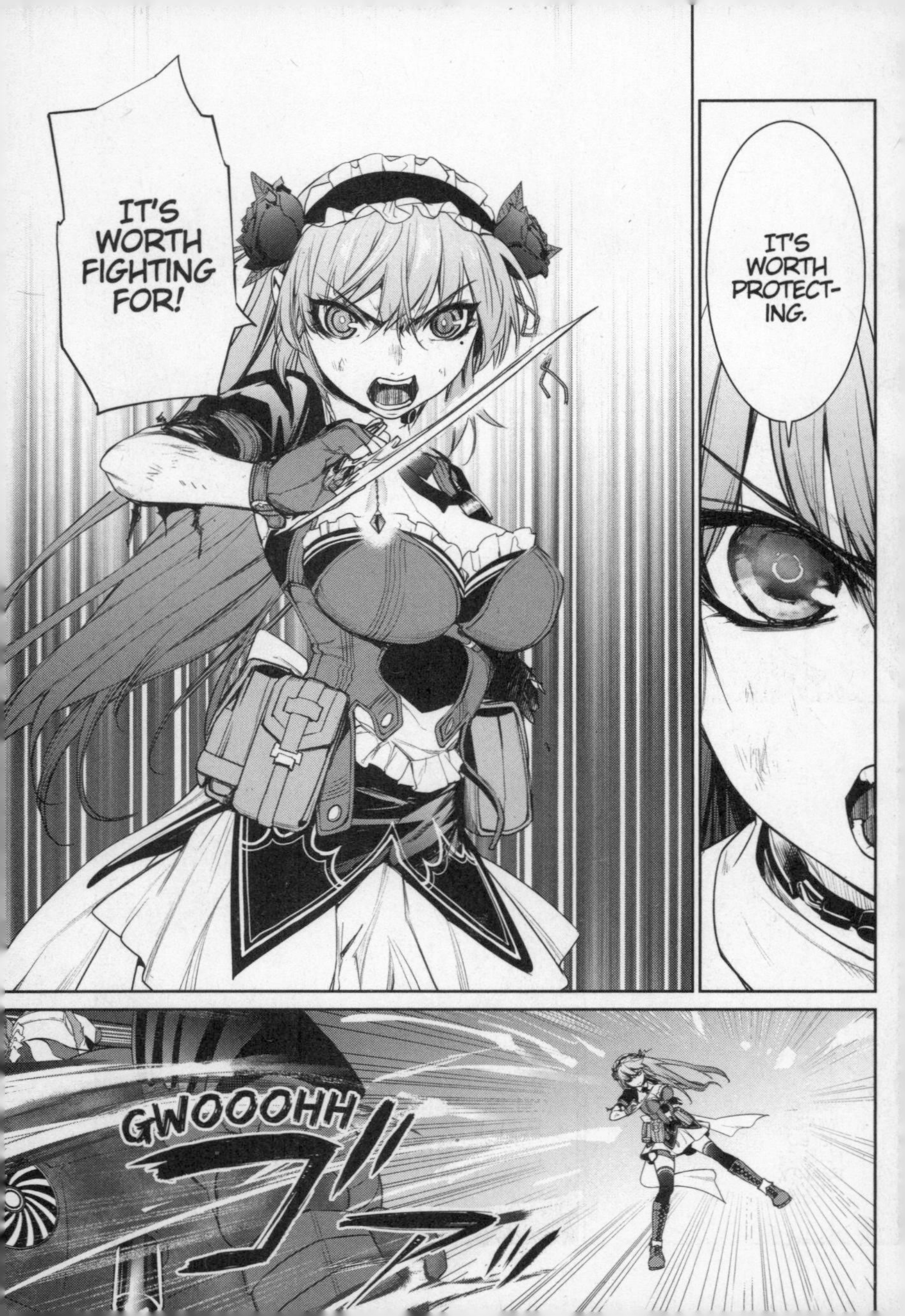
IT'S WORTH PROTECTING.
IT'S WORTH FIGHTING FOR!
GWOOOHH

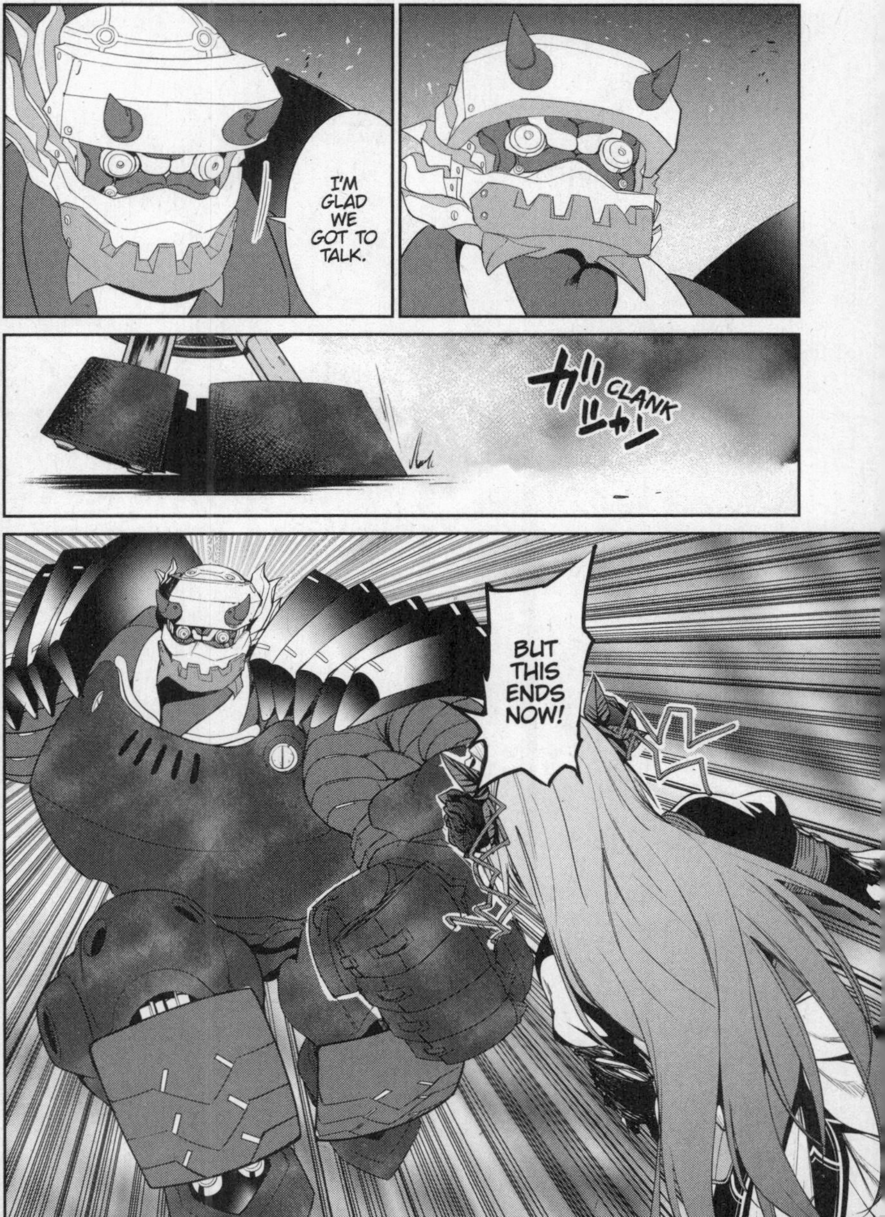
I'M GLAD WE GOT TO TALK.
CLANK
BUT THIS ENDS NOW!

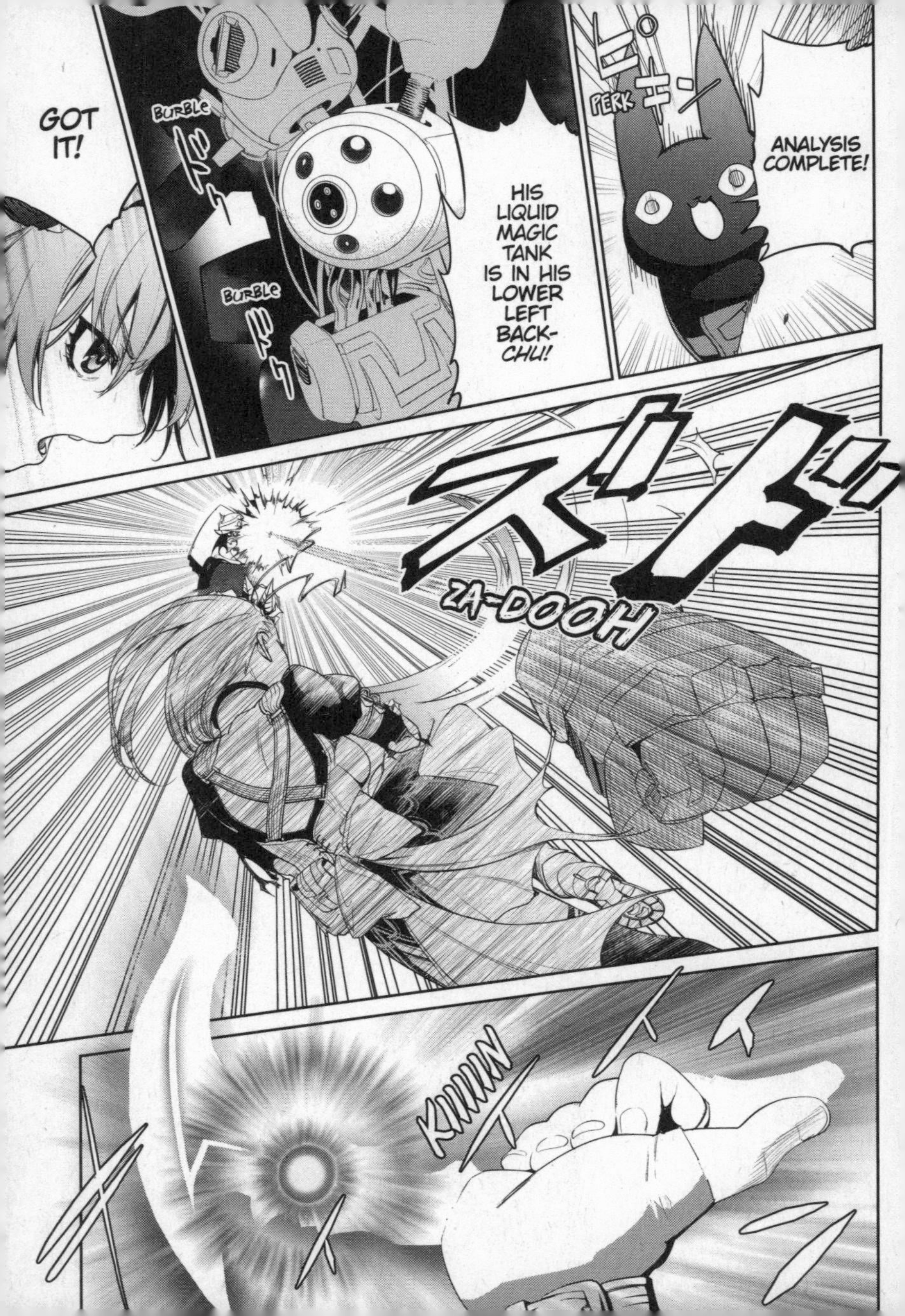
PERK
ANALYSIS COMPLETE!
BURBLE
HIS LIQUID MAGIC TANK IS IN HIS LOWER LEFT BACK-CHU!
BURBLE
GOT IT!
ZA-DOOOH
KIIIIIN

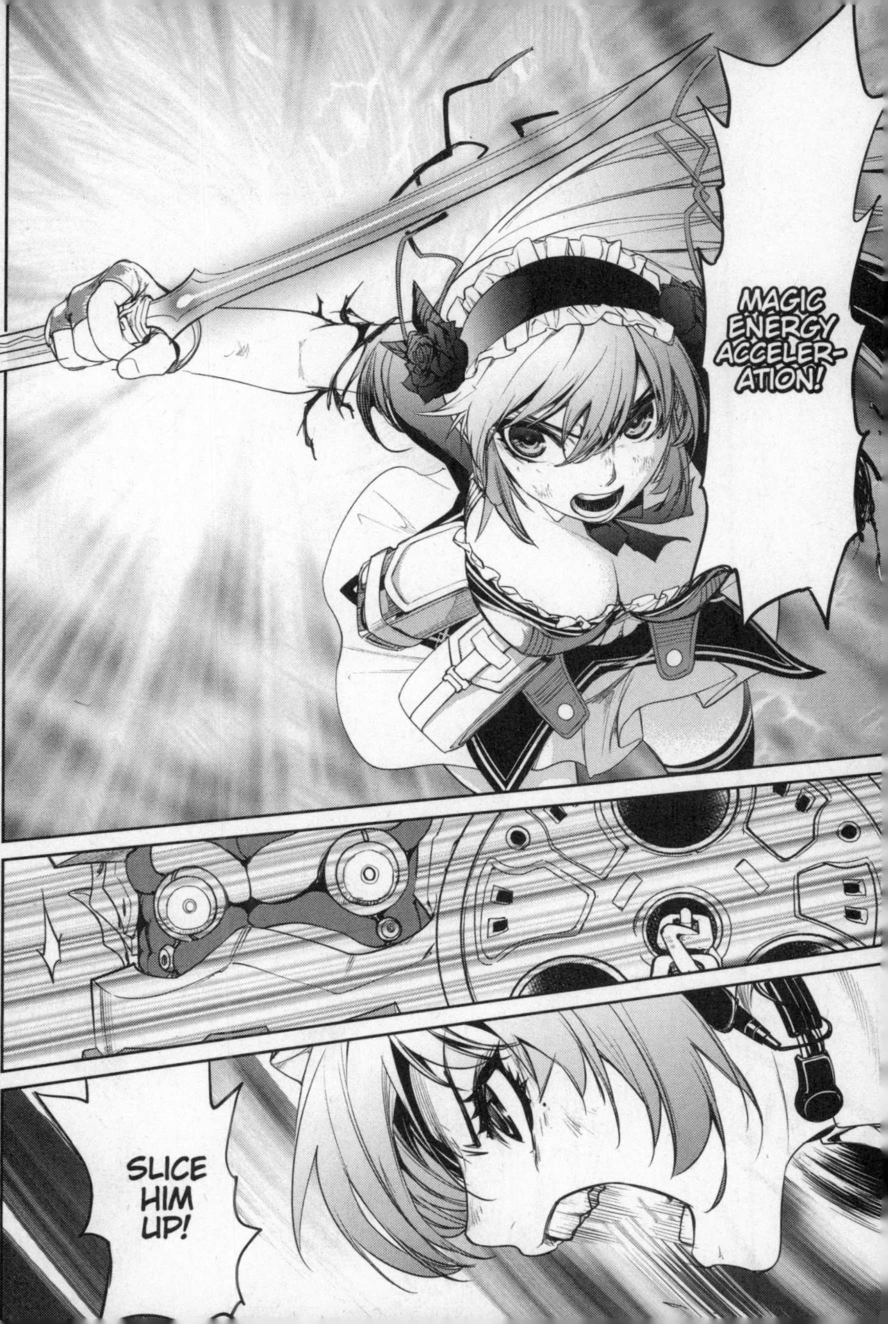
MAGIC ENERGY ACCELER-ATION!
SLICE HIM UP!

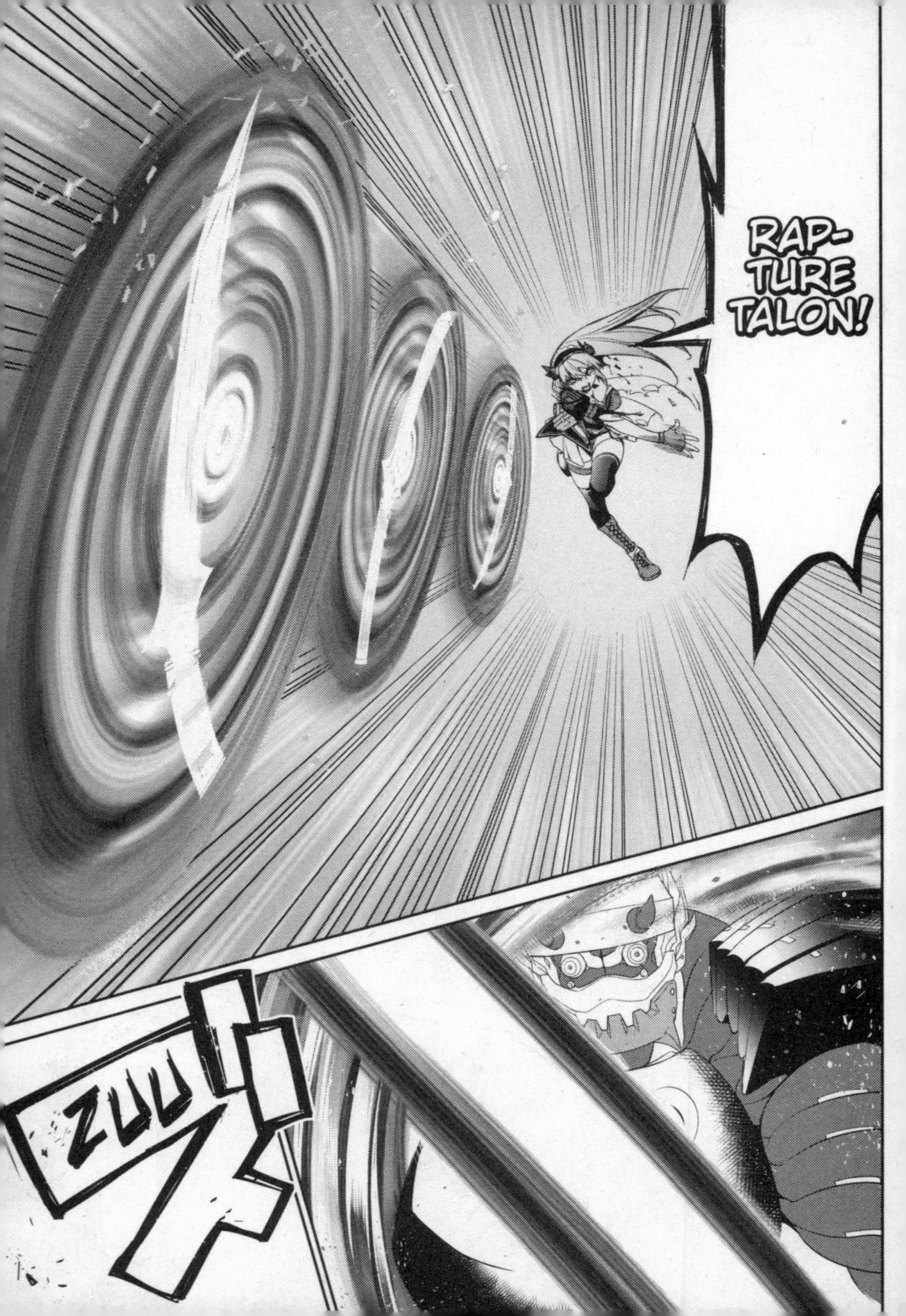
RAP-
TURE
TALON!
ZUUN

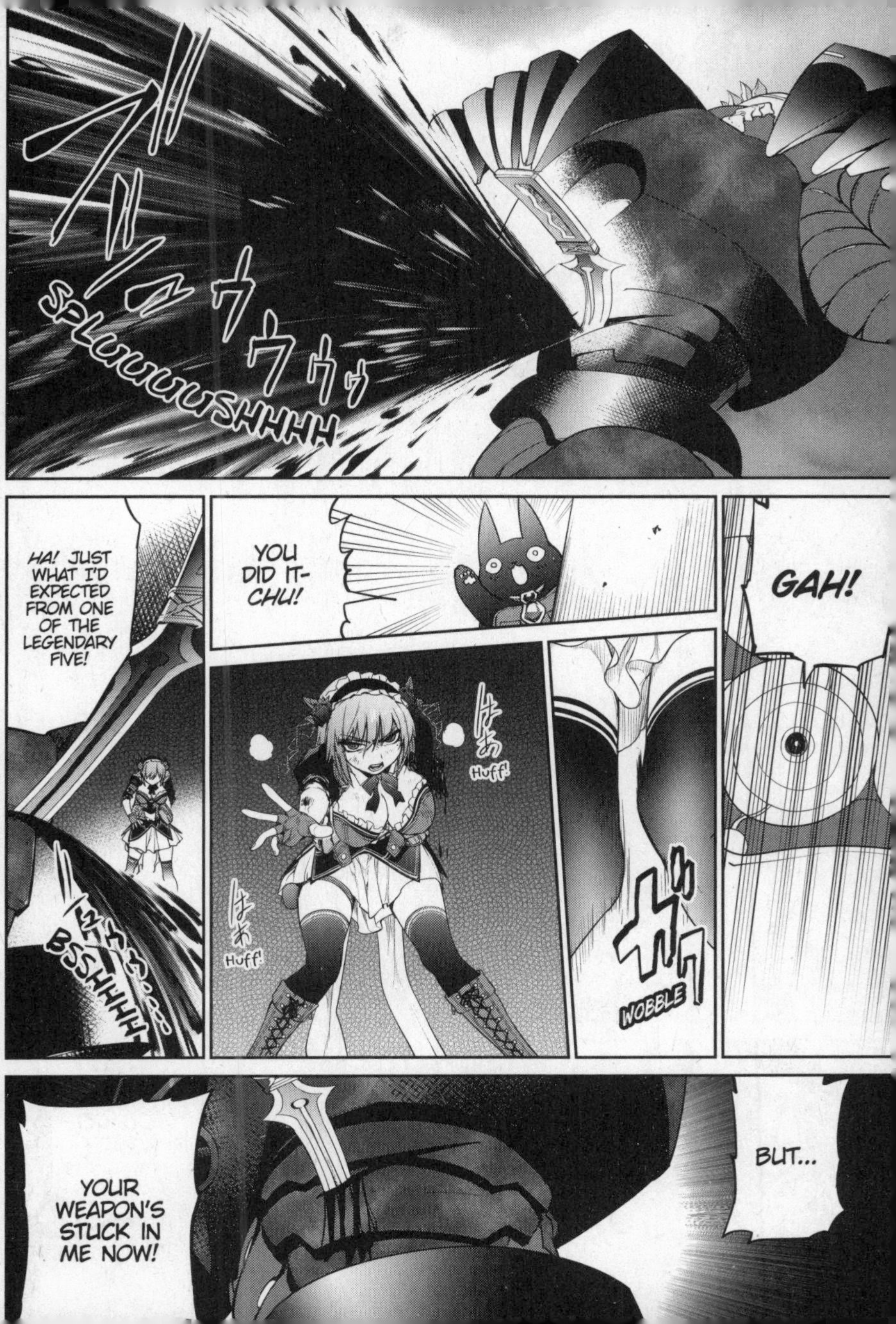
SPLUUUUSHHHH
GAH!
YOU DID IT-CHU!
WOBBLE
Huff!
Huff!
HA! JUST WHAT I'D EXPECTED FROM ONE OF THE LEGENDARY FIVE!
BSSHHHH
BUT...
YOUR WEAPON'S STUCK IN ME NOW!

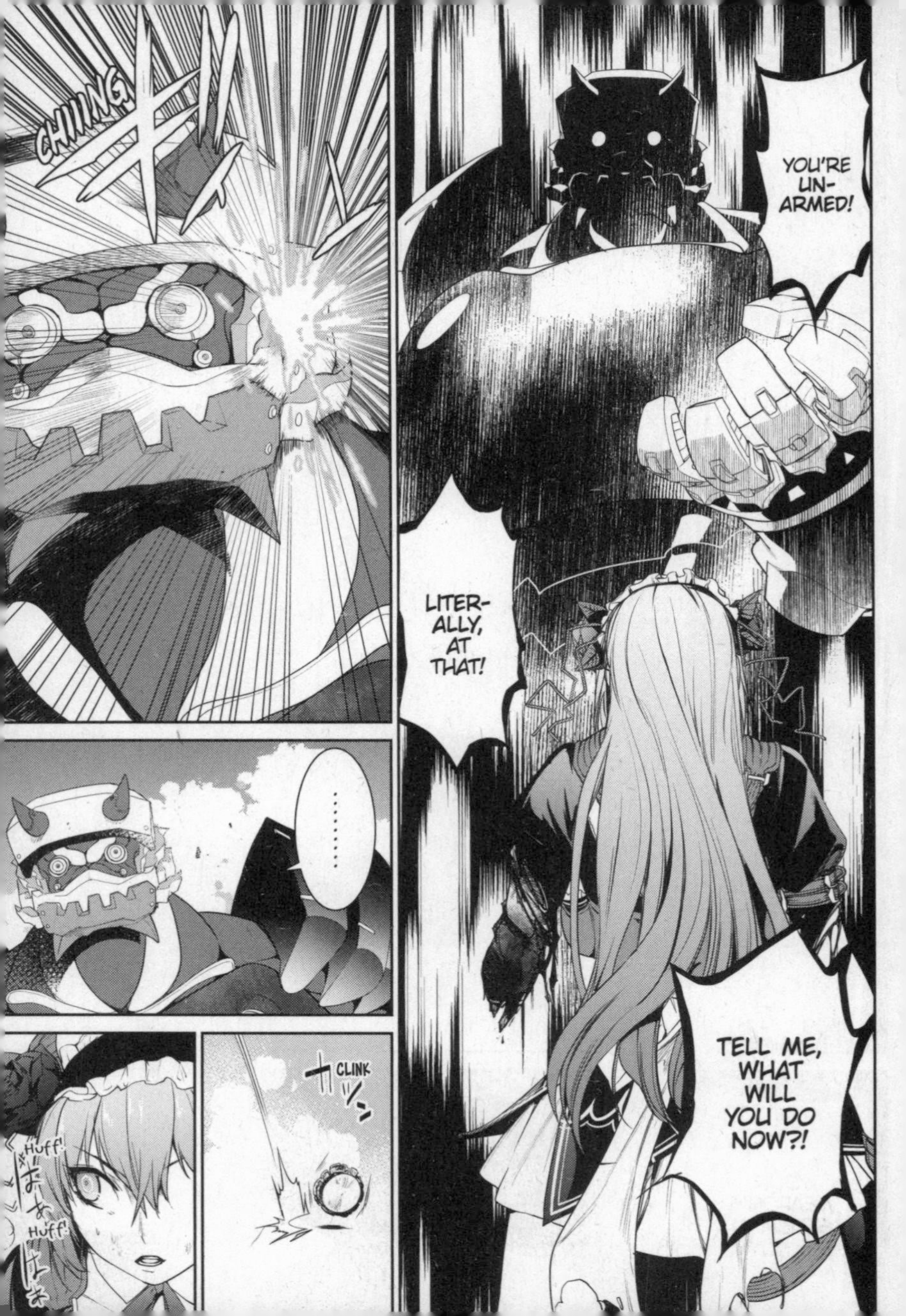
YOU'RE UN-ARMED!
LITER-ALLY, AT THAT!
TELL ME, WHAT WILL YOU DO NOW?!
CHIIING
......
CLINK
Huff!
Huff!

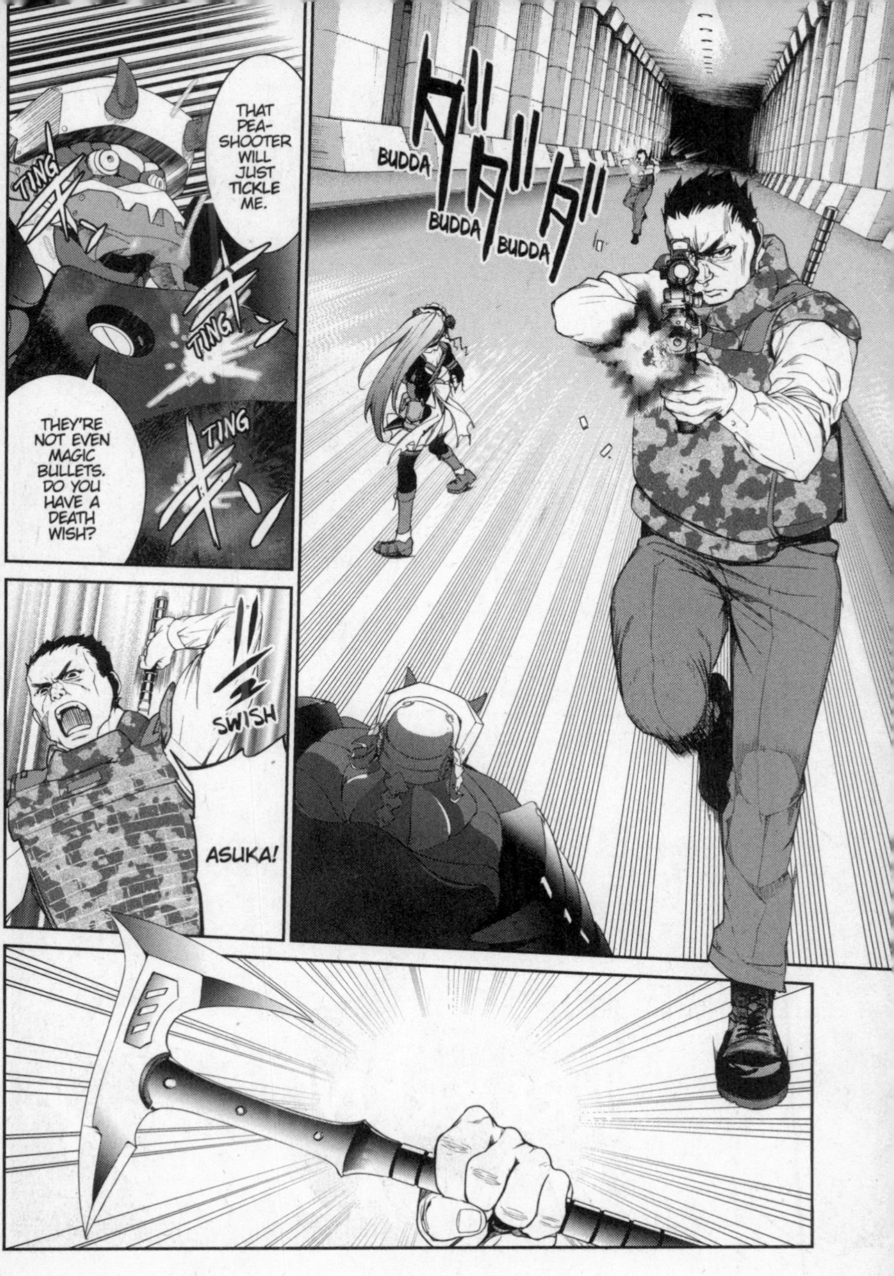
BUDDA
BUDDA
BUDDA
THAT PEA-SHOOTER WILL JUST TICKLE ME.
TING
TING
TING
THEY'RE NOT EVEN MAGIC BULLETS. DO YOU HAVE A DEATH WISH?
SWISH
ASUKA!

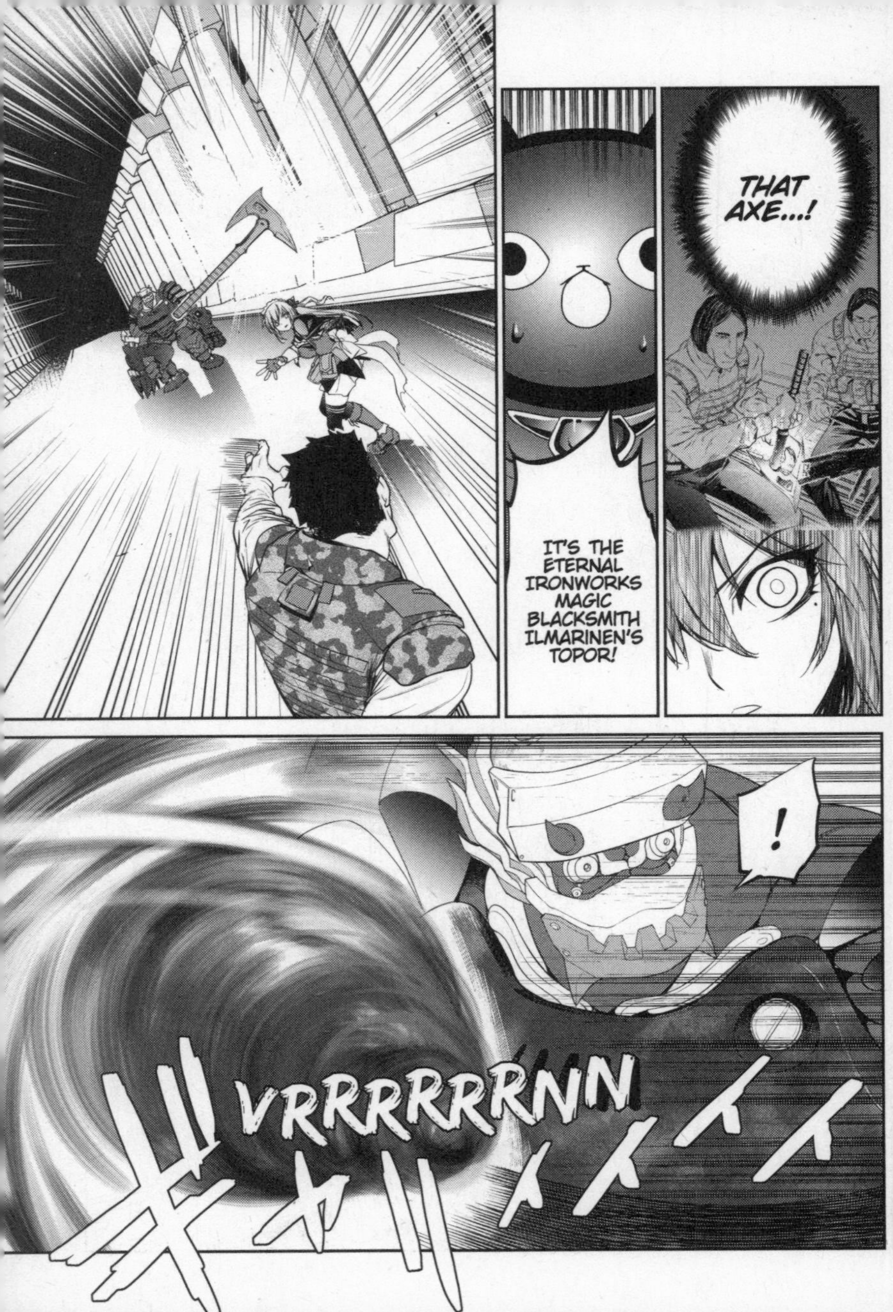
THAT AXE...!
IT'S THE ETERNAL IRONWORKS MAGIC BLACKSMITH ILMARINEN'S TOPOR!
!
VRRRRRRNN

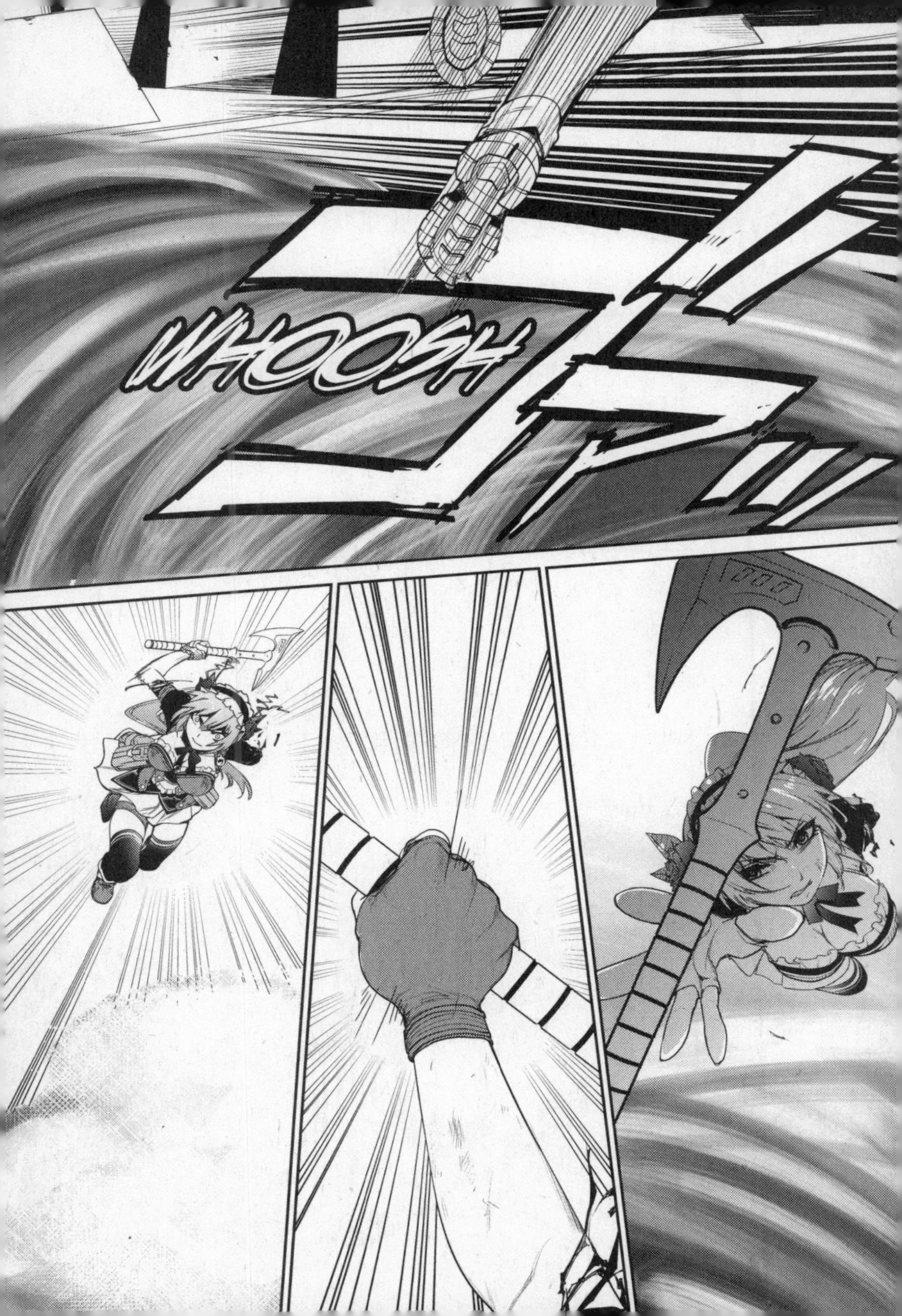
WHOOSH

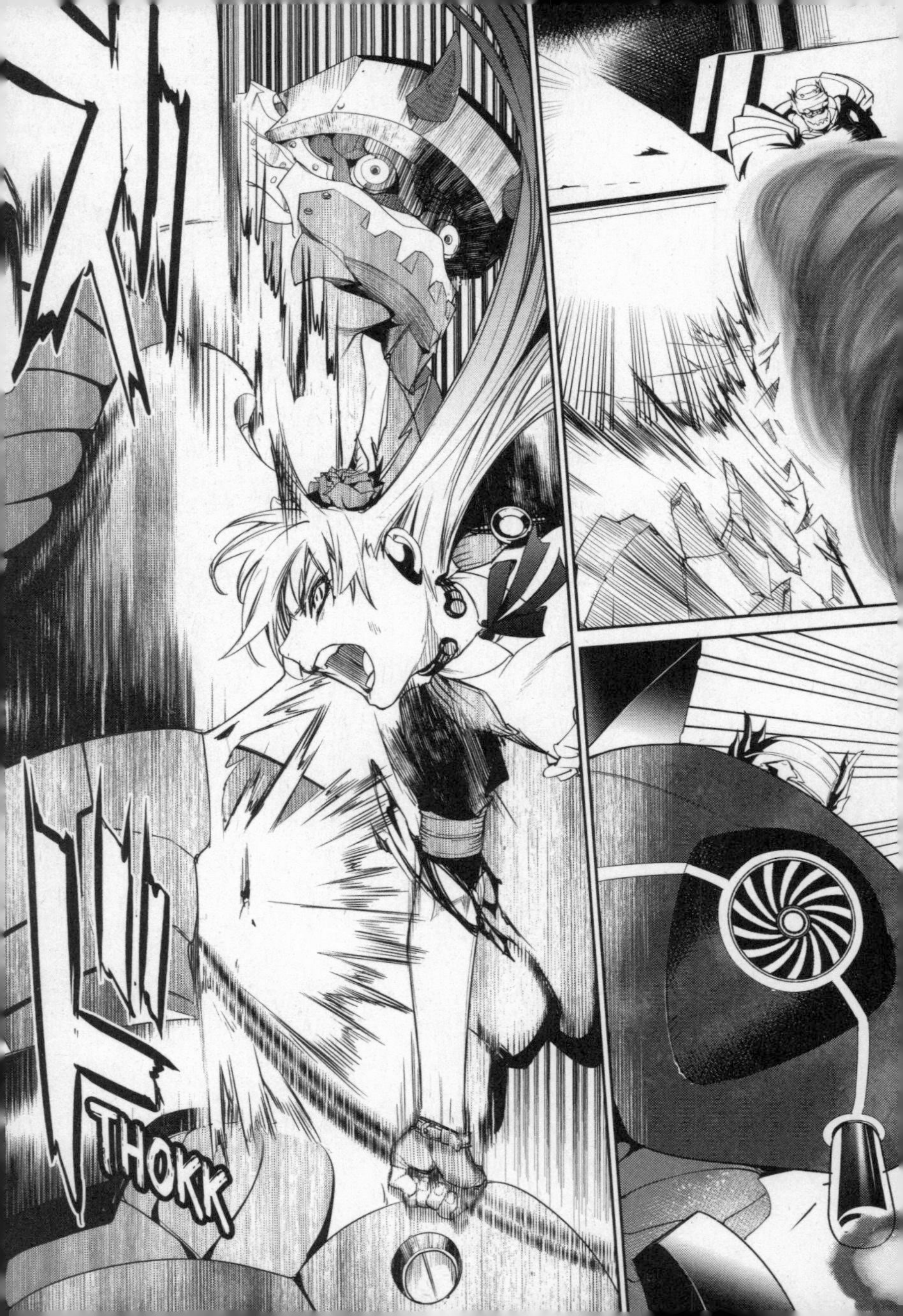
THOKK

魔法少女特殊戦
あすか

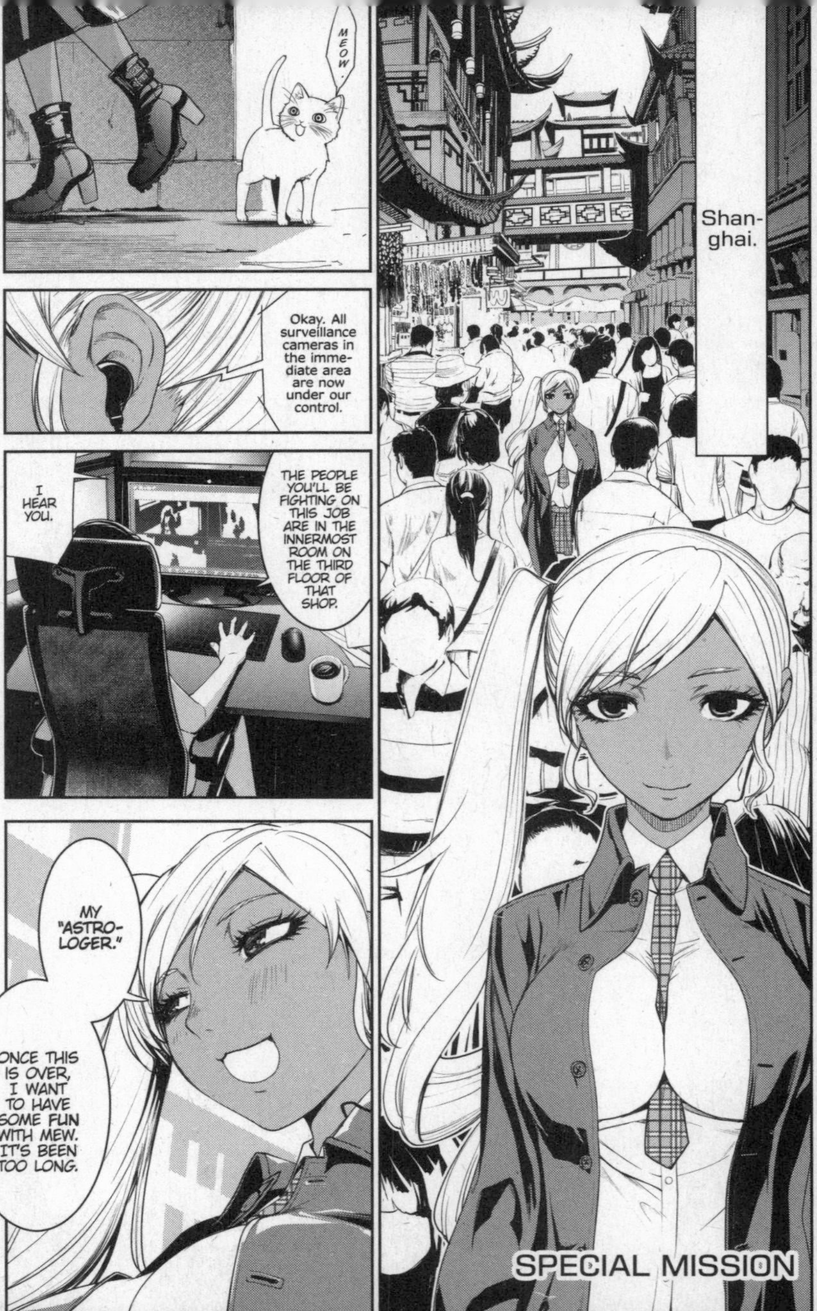
Shanghai.
SPECIAL MISSION
MEOW.
Okay. All surveillance cameras in the immediate area are now under our control.
THE PEOPLE YOU'LL BE FIGHTING ON THIS JOB ARE IN THE INNERMOST ROOM ON THE THIRD FLOOR OF THAT SHOP.
I HEAR YOU.
MY "ASTROLOGER."
ONCE THIS IS OVER, I WANT TO HAVE SOME FUN WITH MEW. IT'S BEEN TOO LONG.

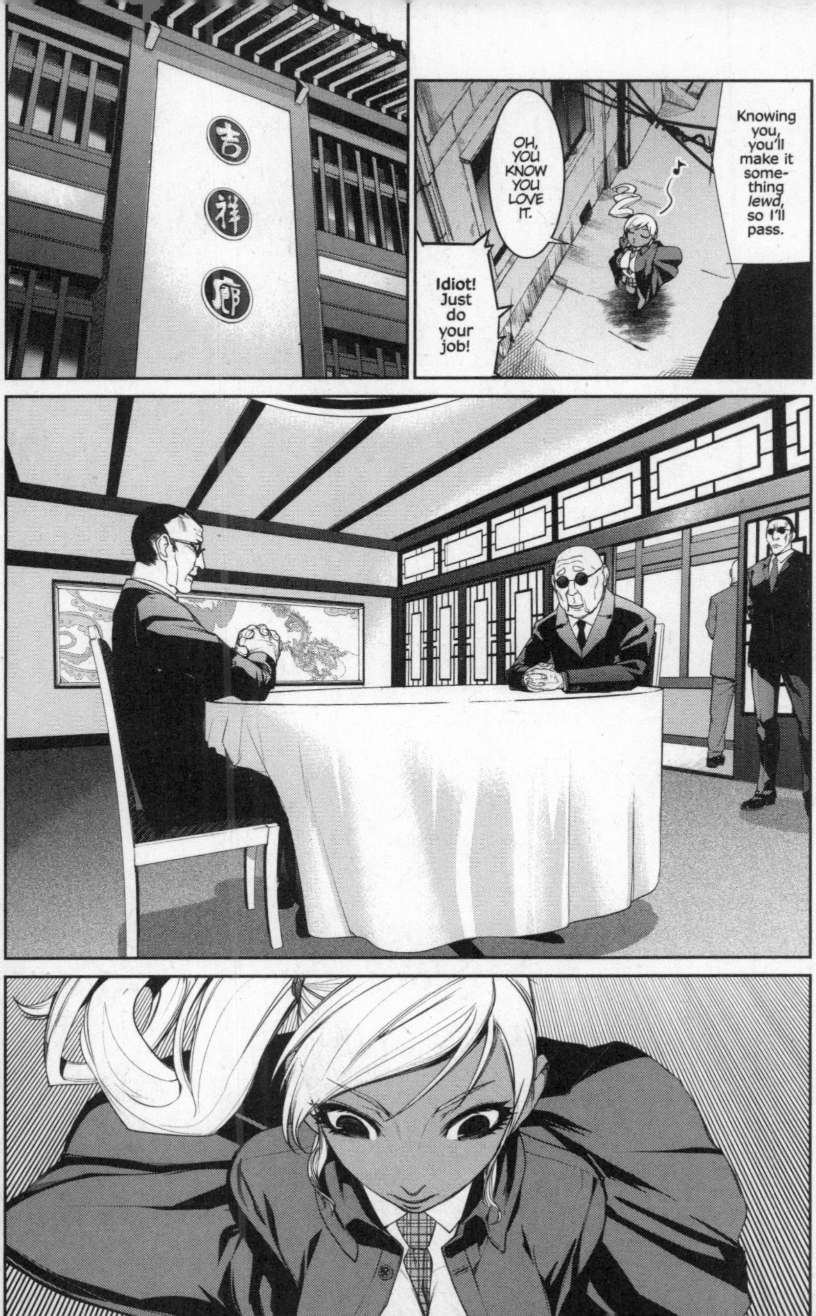
Knowing you, you'll make it something *lewd*, so I'll pass.
OH, YOU KNOW YOU LOVE IT.
Idiot! Just do your job!

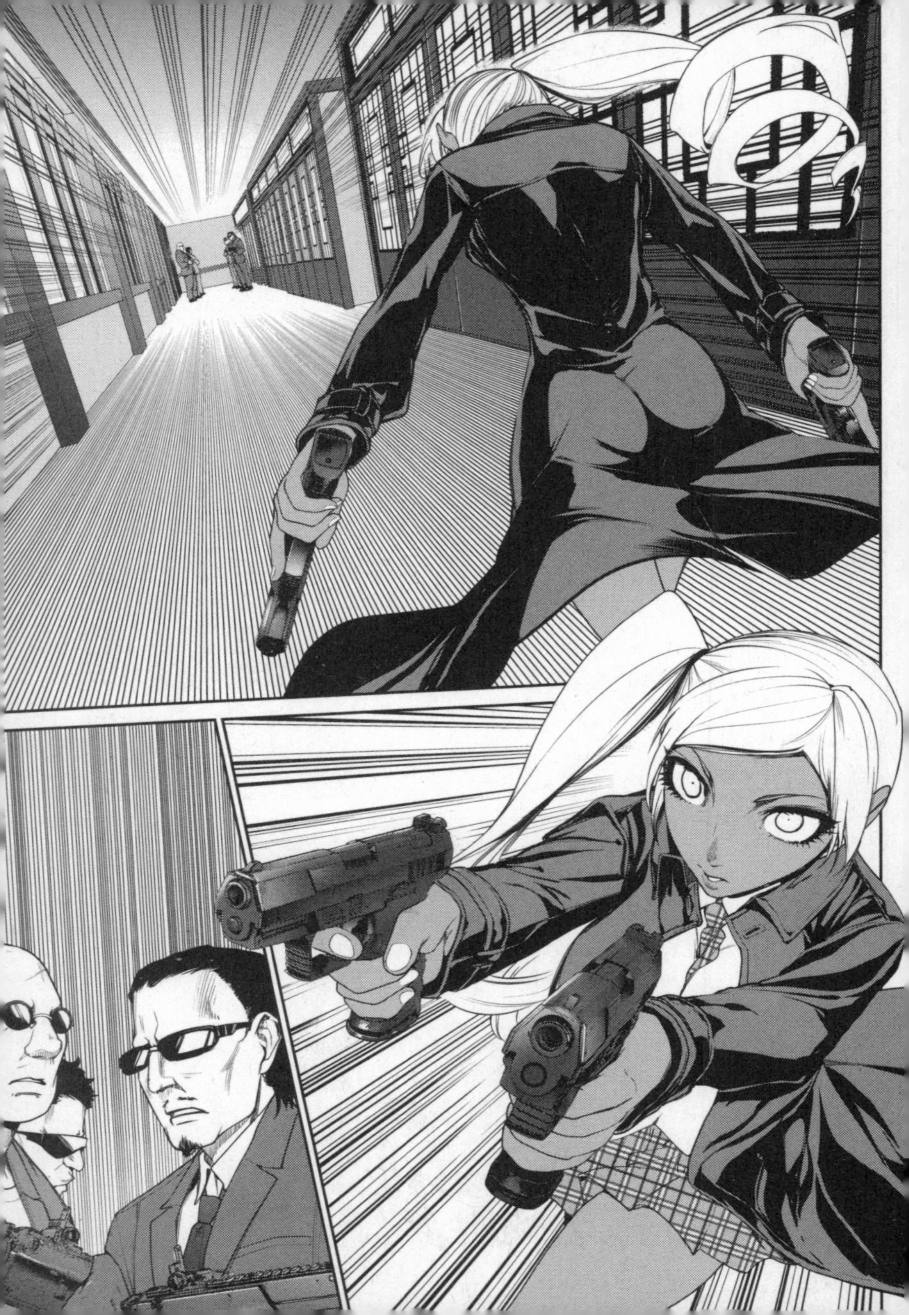

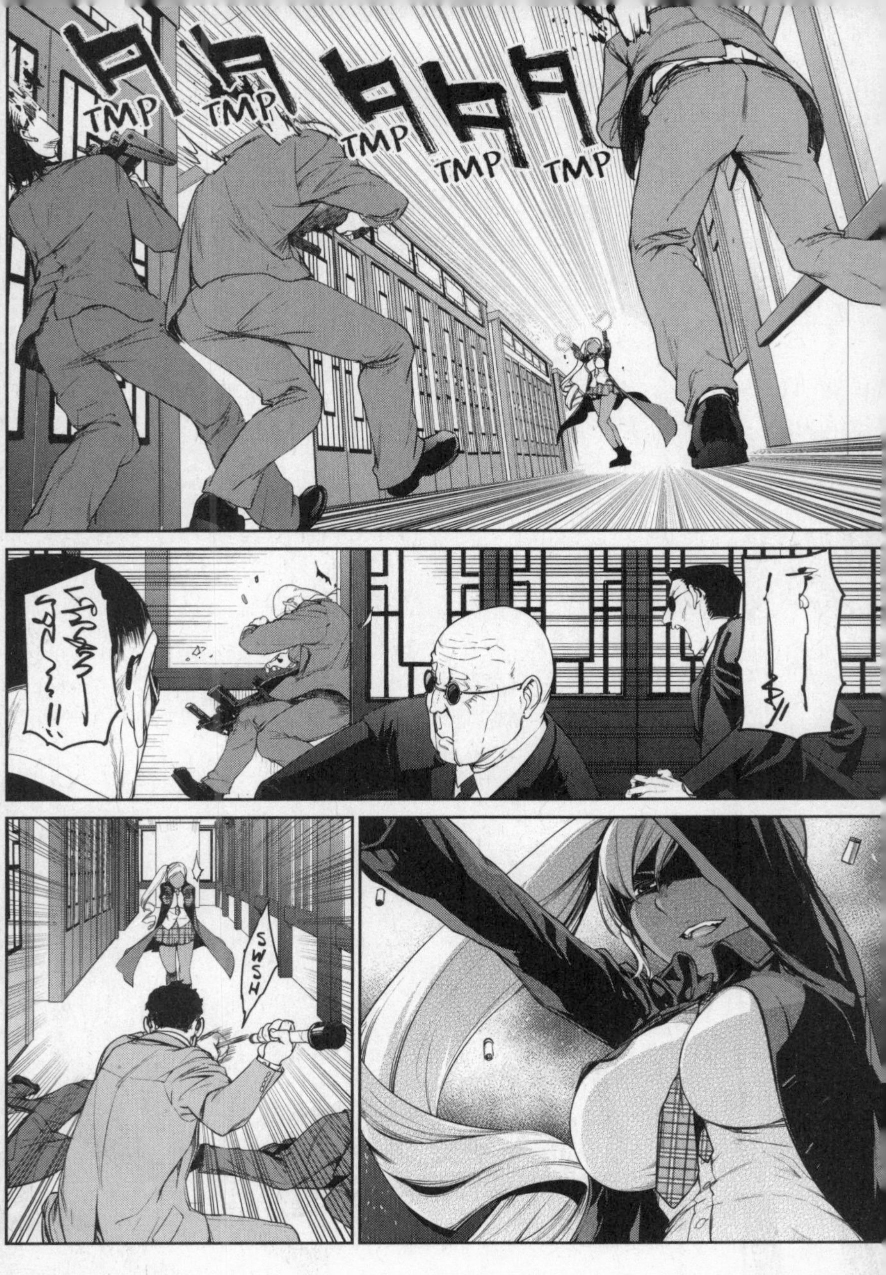
TMP
TMP
TMP
TMP
TMP
SWSH

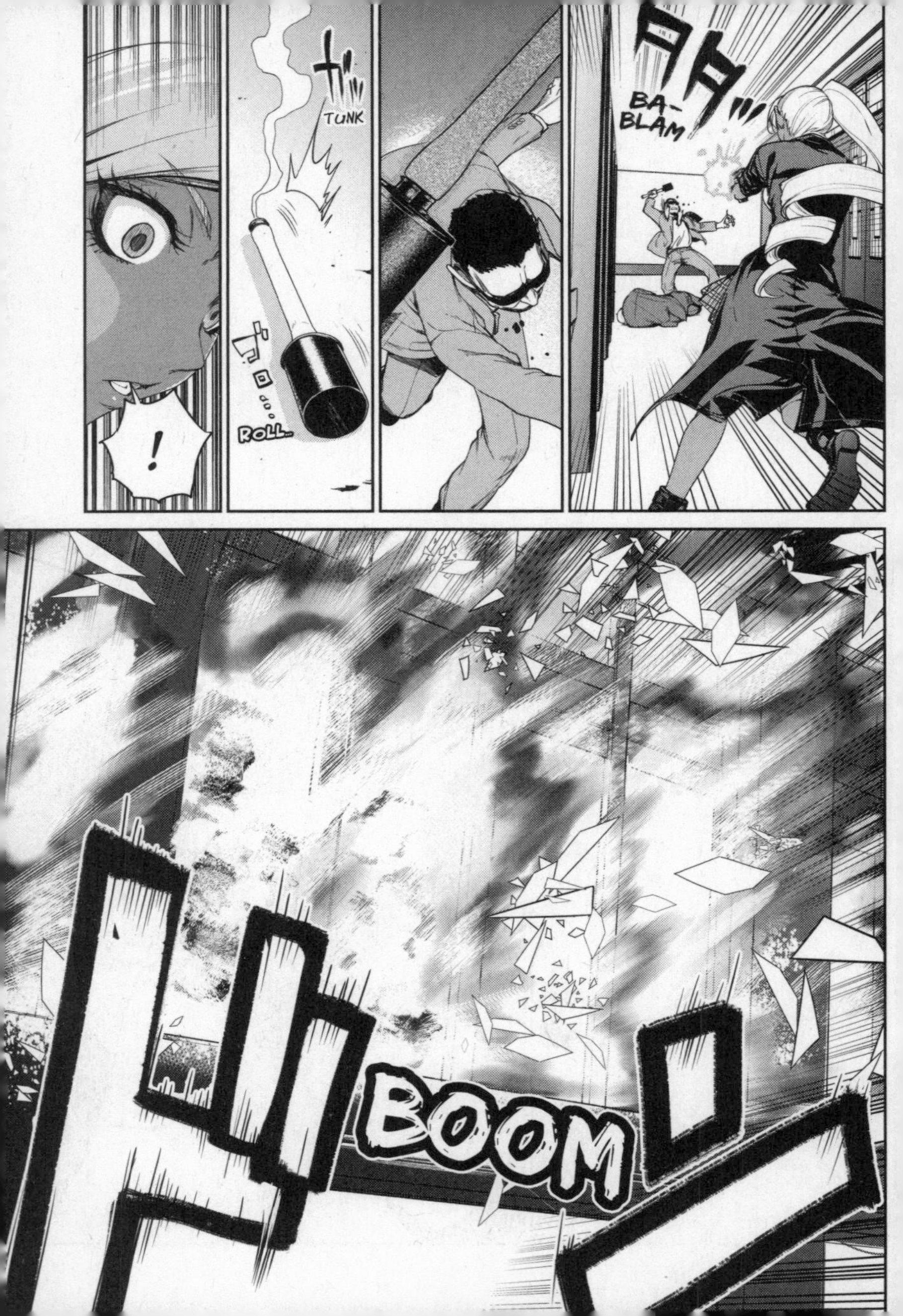
BA-BLAM
TUNK
ROLL...
!
BOOM

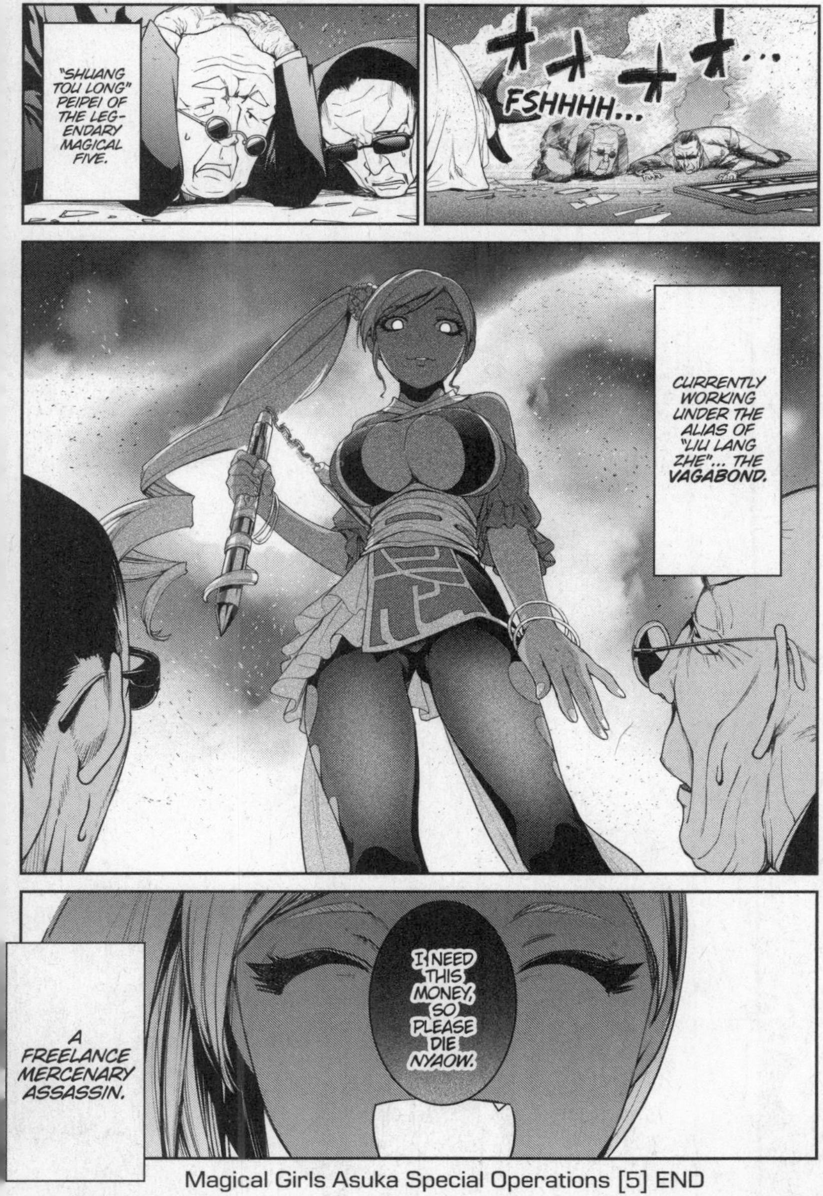
オオオオ…
FSHHHH...
"SHUANG TOU LONG" PEIPEI OF THE LEG-ENDARY MAGICAL FIVE.
CURRENTLY WORKING UNDER THE ALIAS OF "LIU LANG ZHE"... THE VAGABOND.
I NEED THIS MONEY, SO PLEASE DIE NYAOW.
A FREELANCE MERCENARY ASSASSIN.

Magical Girls Asuka Special Operations [5] END

MAGICAL GIRL
SPEC-OPS
ASUKA

A new story arc begins!!!

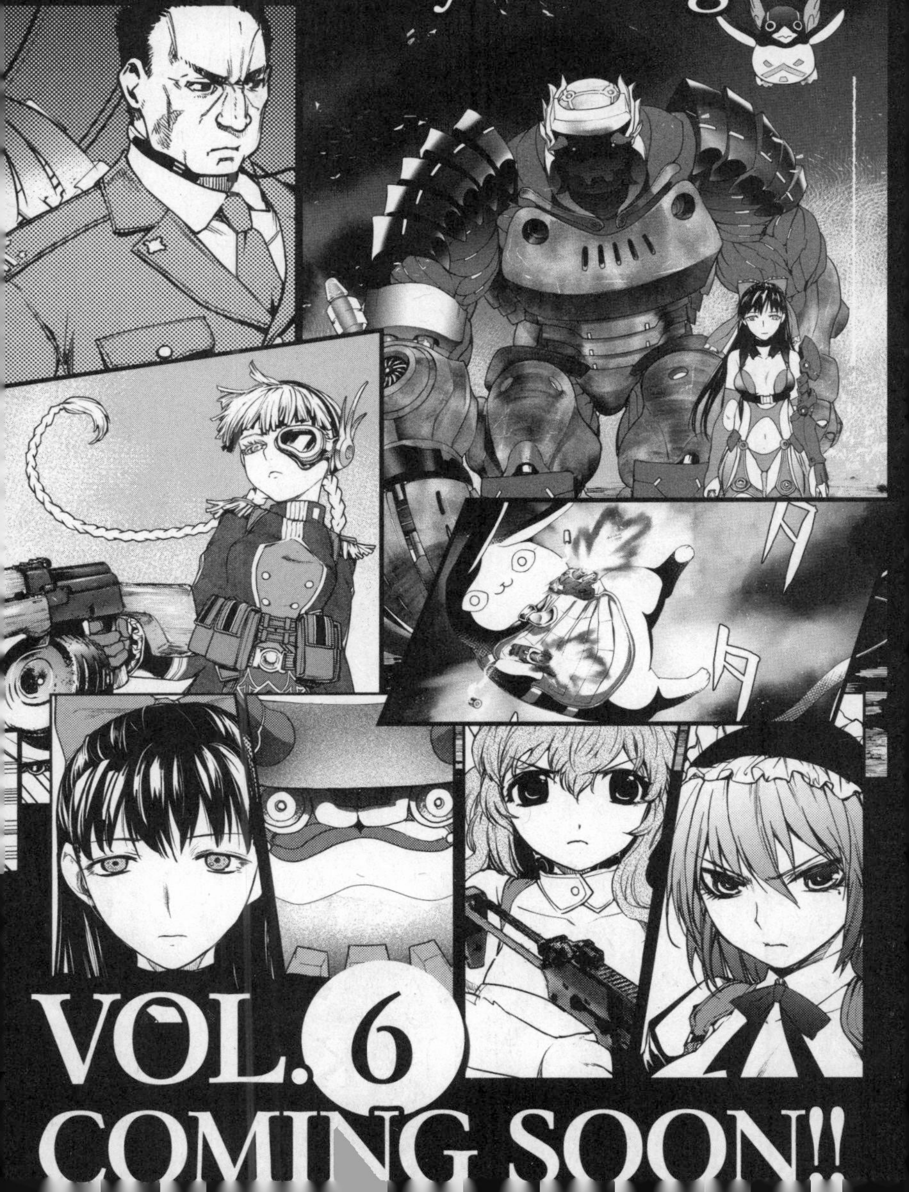

VOL. 6 COMING SOON!!

The Okinawa Arc comes to an explosive end!

MAGICAL GIRL SPEC-OPS

ASUKA

story by
MAKOTO FUKAMI

art by
SEIGO TOKIYA

military advisor:
NAOYA TAMURA

It Does Match Him

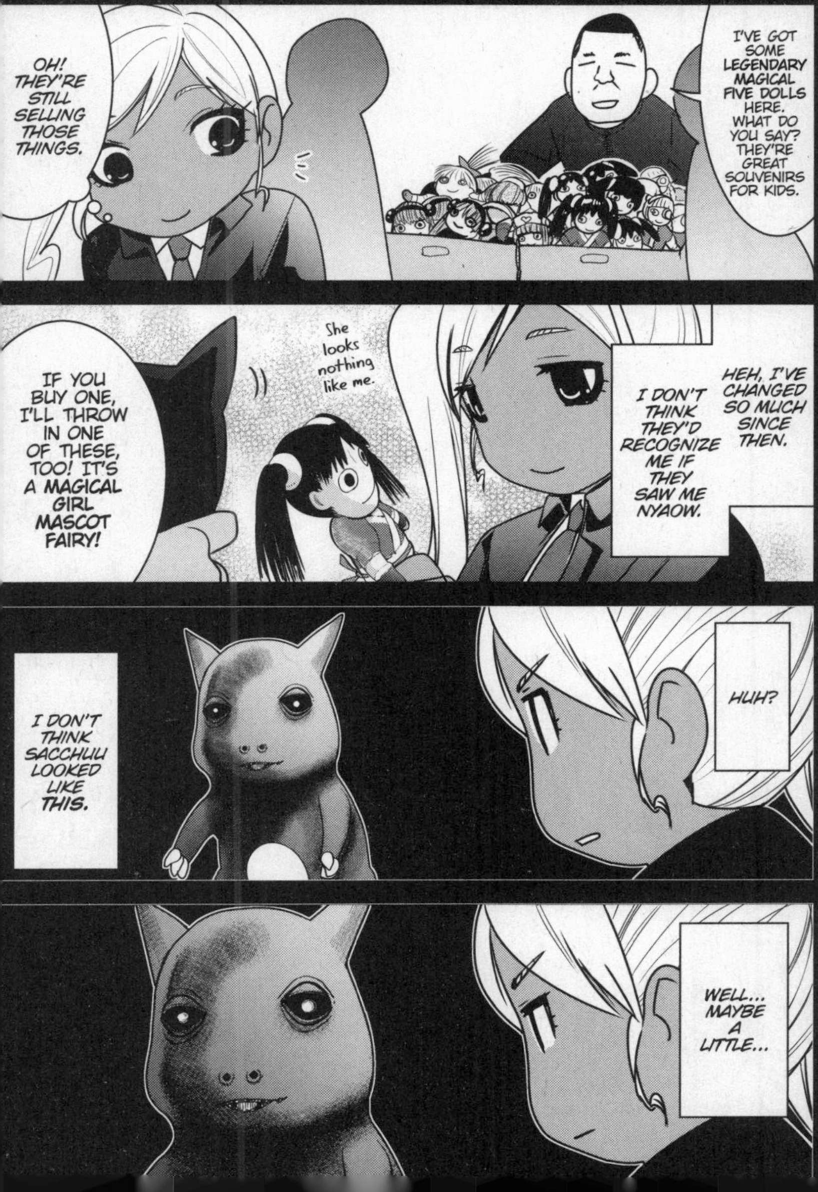

I'VE GOT SOME LEGENDARY MAGICAL FIVE DOLLS HERE. WHAT DO YOU SAY? THEY'RE GREAT SOUVENIRS FOR KIDS.
OH! THEY'RE STILL SELLING THOSE THINGS.
HEH, I'VE CHANGED SO MUCH SINCE THEN.
I DON'T THINK THEY'D RECOGNIZE ME IF THEY SAW ME NYAOW.
She looks nothing like me.
IF YOU BUY ONE, I'LL THROW IN ONE OF THESE, TOO! IT'S A MAGICAL GIRL MASCOT FAIRY!
HUH?
I DON'T THINK SACCHUU LOOKED LIKE THIS.
WELL... MAYBE A LITTLE...

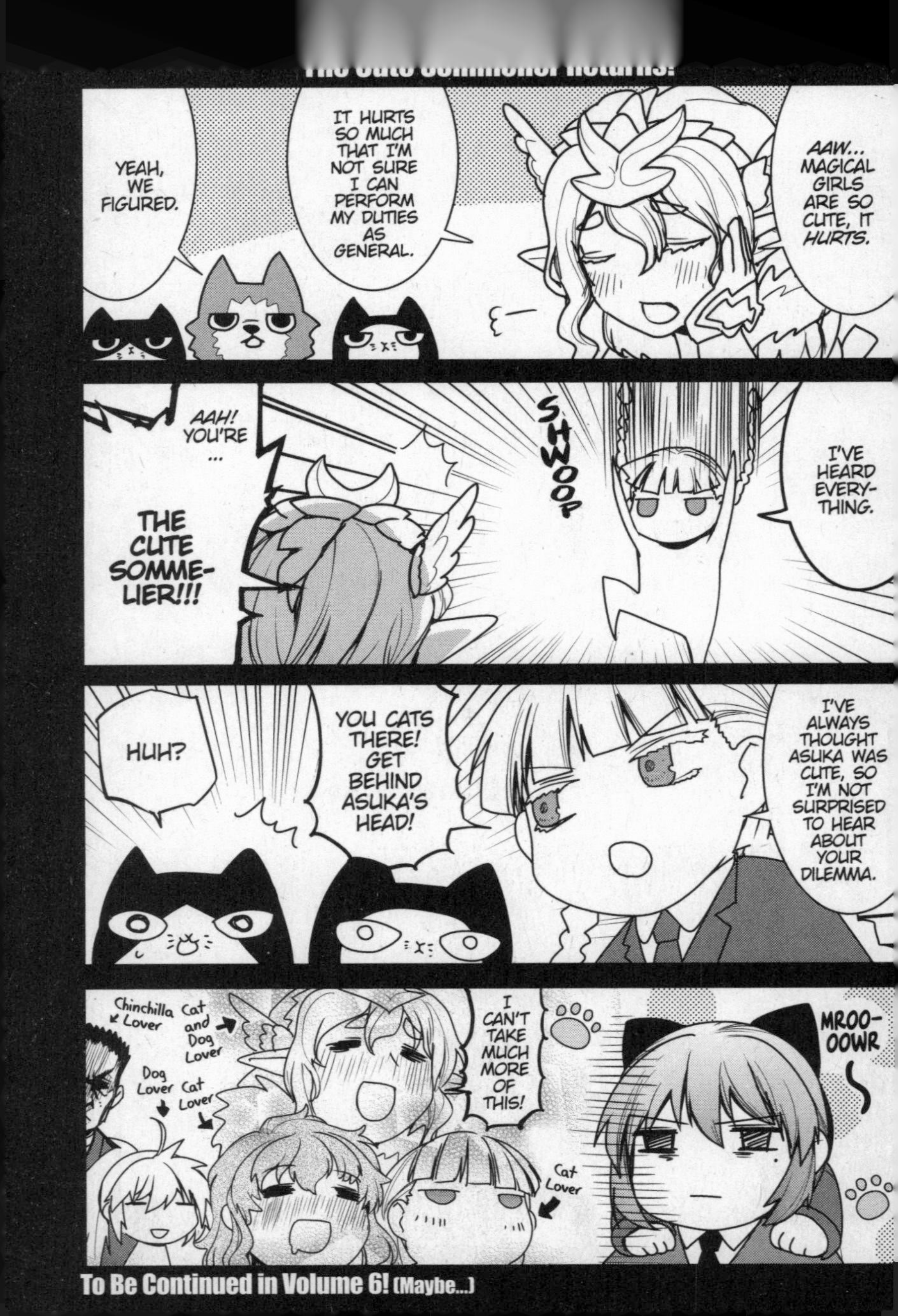
AAW... MAGICAL GIRLS ARE SO CUTE, IT HURTS.
IT HURTS SO MUCH THAT I'M NOT SURE I CAN PERFORM MY DUTIES AS GENERAL.
YEAH, WE FIGURED.
I'VE HEARD EVERYTHING.
SHWOOP
AAH! YOU'RE ...
THE CUTE SOMMELIER!!!
I'VE ALWAYS THOUGHT ASUKA WAS CUTE, SO I'M NOT SURPRISED TO HEAR ABOUT YOUR DILEMMA.
YOU CATS THERE! GET BEHIND ASUKA'S HEAD!
HUH?
MROO-OOWR
I CAN'T TAKE MUCH MORE OF THIS!
Cat and Dog Lover
Chinchilla Lover
Cat Lover
Dog Lover
Cat Lover

To Be Continued in Volume 6! (Maybe...)

MAKOTO FUKAMI

In volume 5, the Okinawa arc approaches its end.
It sure was a short time between volumes 4 and 5!
And there's going to be a lot of unbelievable action!
Thank you for all your hard work, Tokiya-sensei.

SEIGO TOKIYA

At long last, all of the Legendary Magical Five have made it
onto the covers! I was shocked at how much Peipei had
changed. Now we can clearly see how the Legendary Magical
Five excel in the bosom department, with Tamara the most
lacking. You can look forward to the kind of love triangles that
tend to happen in an odd-numbered group!

NAOYA TAMURA

Before we knew it, it's volume 5 already! When I was first asked
to help with this project, I never would've imagined it'd be so
much fun helping out with a manga. Thank you once again to
Fukami-sensei and everyone else involved for granting me this
opportunity! And I appreciate the support of all the readers who
keep it fun!

[COVER DESIGN]
Nartis: Masataka Hamasaki

MAGICAL GIRL
SPEC-OPS
A S U K A

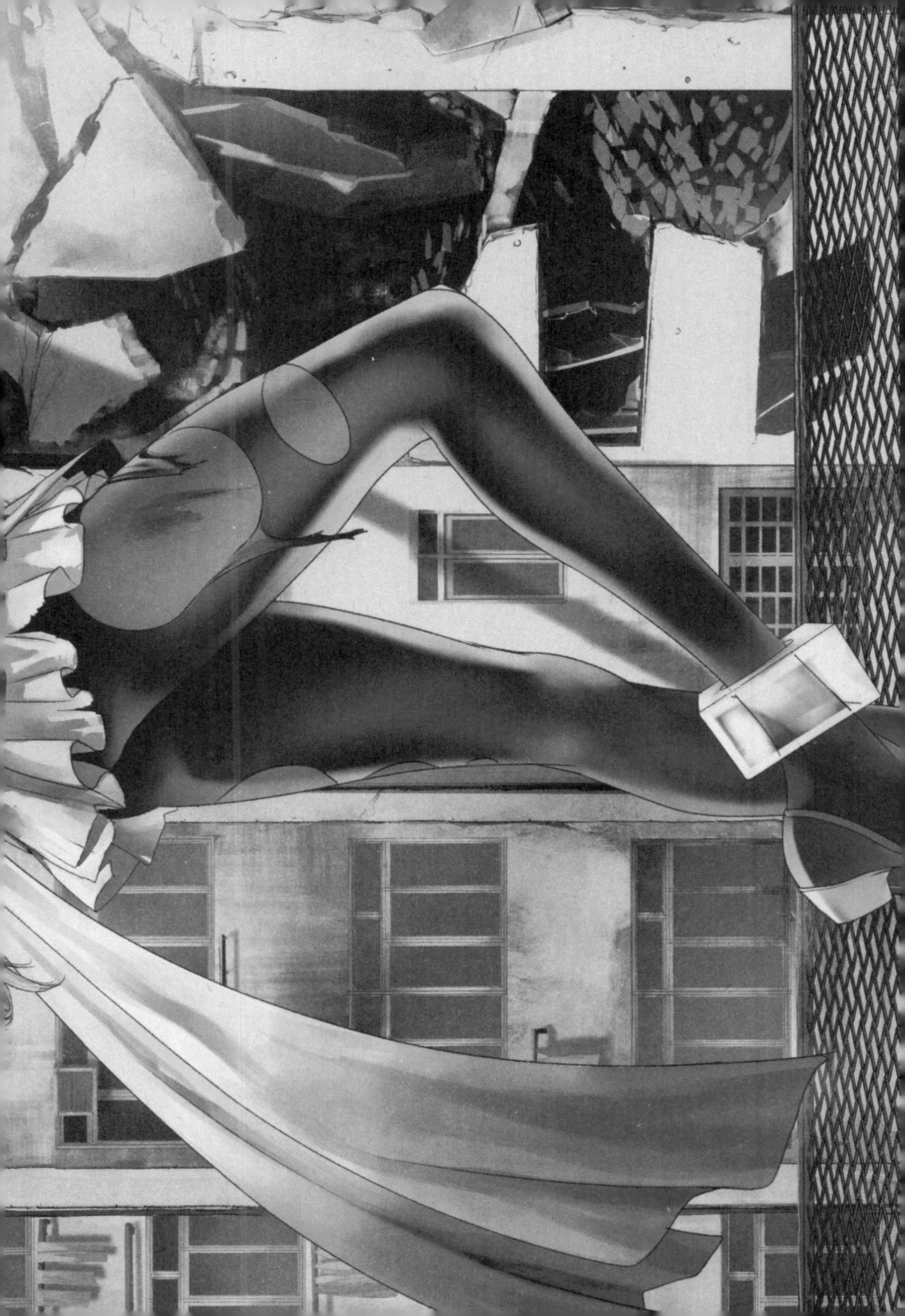

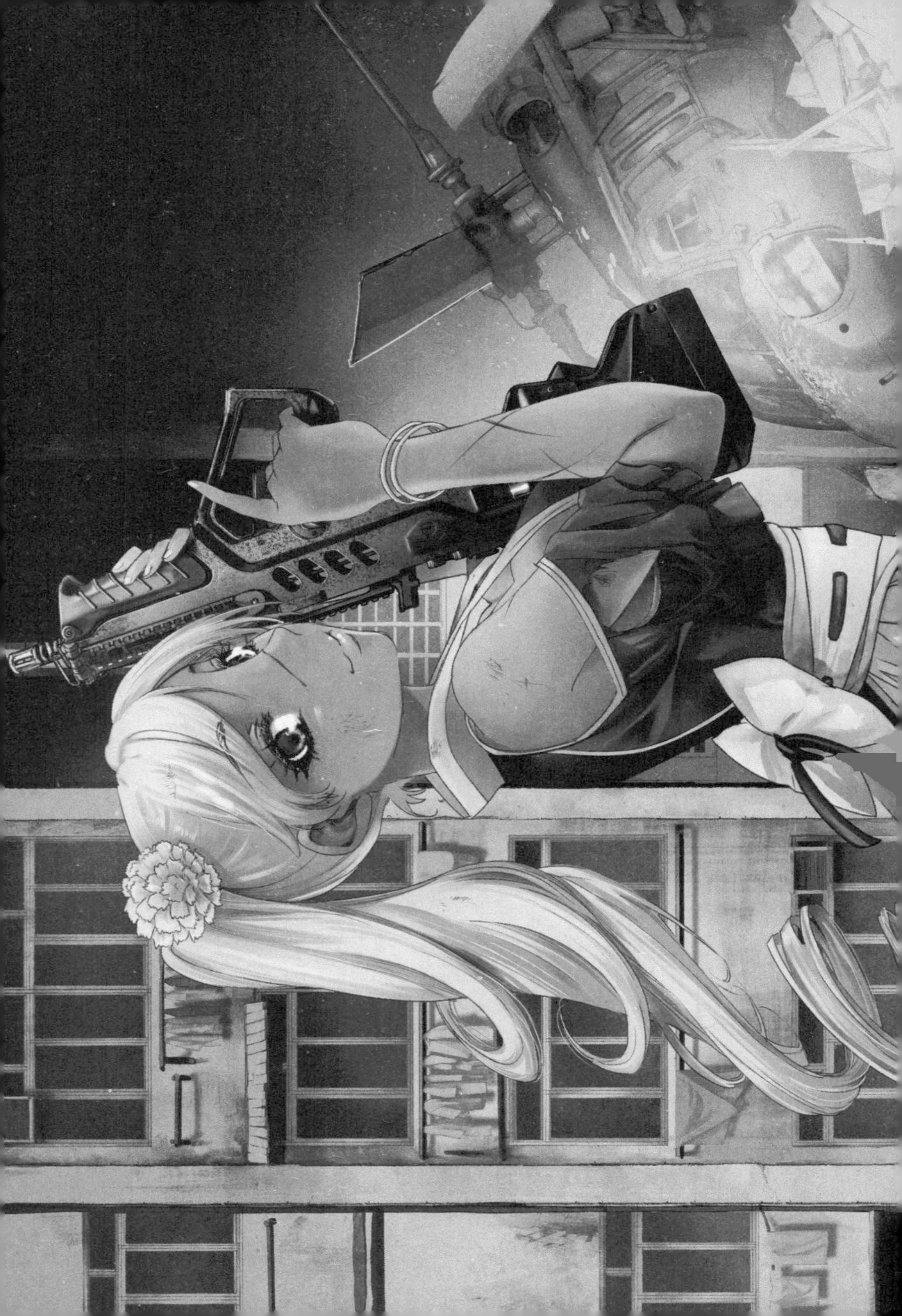

魔法少女特殊戦
あすか